The Insider's Guide to
Mental Health Resources Online

THE CLINICIAN'S TOOLBOX™

A Guilford Series

EDWARD L. ZUCKERMAN, Series Editor

BREAKING FREE OF MANAGED CARE
A Step-by-Step Guide to Regaining Control of Your Practice
DANA C. ACKLEY

THE PAPER OFFICE, 2nd Edition
Forms, Guidelines, and Resources
EDWARD L. ZUCKERMAN

THE ESSENTIAL GUIDE TO GROUP PRACTICE IN MENTAL HEALTH
Clinical, Legal, and Financial Fundamentals
SIMON H. BUDMAN AND BRETT N. STEENBARGER

OUTCOMES AND INCOMES
How to Evaluate, Improve, and Market Your Psychotherapy Practice
by Measuring Outcomes
PAUL W. CLEMENT

THE INSIDER'S GUIDE TO MENTAL HEALTH RESOURCES ONLINE
2000/2001 Edition
JOHN M. GROHOL

TREATMENT PLANS AND INTERVENTIONS FOR
DEPRESSION AND ANXIETY DISORDERS
ROBERT L. LEAHY AND STEPHEN J. HOLLAND

CLINICIAN'S THESAURUS, 5th Edition
The Guidebook for Writing Psychological Reports
EDWARD L. ZUCKERMAN

CLINICIAN'S THESAURUS
Electronic Edition
EDWARD L. ZUCKERMAN

The Insider's Guide to Mental Health Resources Online, 2000/2001 Edition

JOHN M. GROHOL

THE GUILFORD PRESS
New York   London

© 2000 The Guilford Press
A Division of Guilford Publications, Inc.
72 Spring Street, New York, NY 10012
www.guilford.com

Printed in the United States of America

This book is printed on acid-free paper.

Last digit is print number: 9 8 7 6 5 4 3 2

Library of Congress Cataloging-in-Publication Data
is available from the publisher

ISBN 1-57230-549-5 (pbk.)

In memory of Rob & Anne

About the Author

John M. Grohol, PsyD, is an Austin, Texas, online psychologist, author, and cofounder of Mental Health Net. He developed and built drkoop.com's mental health center in 1999, then left to become the vice president of research and development for an Internet startup company whose goal is to empower people with self-help and professional tools and services. Trained and educated as a clinical psychologist at Nova Southeastern University, he now acts as a patient advocate, mental health educator, and online services innovator. While he was involved in online services as early as 1981, he began on the Internet in 1991 as a regular contributor to the Internet's discussion forums, Usenet newsgroups. He has founded and moderated a number of newsgroups since then, including sci.psychology.research and sci.psychology.announce.

As one of the pioneering leaders in psychology online, Dr. Grohol was the editor-in-chief and founder of *Perspectives: A Mental Health Magazine* (`http://mentalhelp.net/perspectives/`) and an associate editor of *Behavior OnLine* (`http://www.behavior.net/`) and the bimonthly newsletter *PsychNews International* (`http://mentalhelp.net/pni/`). Dr. Grohol is also an associate editor of the print journal *Journal of Technology in Human Services* (`http://www.uta.edu/cussn/wwwrevgu.htm`).

Dr. Grohol is a visiting instructor with the Department of Epidemiology and Social Medicine (`http://desm.aecom.yu.edu/`), Albert Einstein College of Medicine. He has chaired and presented at a number of symposia about online mental health, online psychotherapy, and psychology at American Psychological Association conventions, for the Cape Cod Institute, and for Behavioral Informatics Tomorrow (where he also is an advisory board member). Dr. Grohol is on the editorial boards of the *Journal of Online Behavior* and *CyberPsychology & Behavior* and is the past president of the International Society for Mental Health Online (ISMHO; `http://www.ismho.org/`). Dr. Grohol maintains his own Web site at Psych Central (`http://psychcentral.com/`) and hosts two, free weekly mental chats online.

Acknowledgments

A book of this undertaking could not have been accomplished without the help of many people, to whom I owe a great deal. Thanks to The Guilford Press, Ed Zuckerman, and Barbara Watkins for recognizing the potential of this book and skillfully guiding it through the publishing process. Thanks to Tom Ferguson and Ed Madara for providing me with the model, motivation, and words of encouragement to take on this project. I am grateful to CMHC Systems, John Paton, and David Chrestay for providing me with the time and resources necessary to disseminate my knowledge in writing and expand my work online. Thanks to my parents, Lillian and Paul, for their encouragement, support, and love, imbuing within me the ability to achieve my simple goal in life: helping others.

stay on top of what's on the net...on the net

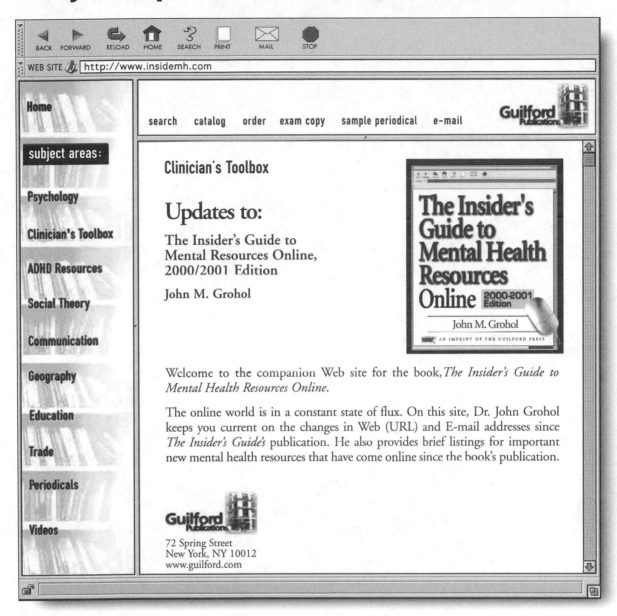

Foreword

One cannot escape hearing about the Internet and today it is relatively easy to get "on the net." But what will mental health professionals find there that enables them to do their work better? When I first got online, I spent several dozen hours "surfing the net." It was exciting and entertaining but did not make me a better psychologist. Then I found Dr. Grohol's site, and he pointed me to the treasures. (You can find his site now at `http://grohol.com`.)

If anyone is an expert on the online world, surely it is Dr. Grohol. I e-mailed my appreciation for his helpful advice and out of that initial contact has developed this superb guide to the net's riches.

There are hundreds of books on the Internet and several that deal in some way with the mental health area. But, as you would expect from an Internet expert who is also a psychologist, this book is a treasure house of professional riches. He is not content simply to offer us lists of the many fine materials on the net. He goes on to share with us how he, as a clinician, really uses the net. He shows us all the searching techniques he uses to find resources to enrich his professional activities. With his expert guidance, you will learn to use the many "search engines" effectively, to join mailing lists of colleagues who share your specific interests, to find online jounals with the most up-to-date information, and where to post your questions on electronic "bulletin boards" to tap into the collective wisdom of the mental health community.

He shows us how to find answers to the kinds of everyday clinical and research questions we have. Best of all, as we accompany him on his search and learn the actual methods he uses, he tells us which are the sites most worth our professional time.

This book is indeed the "Insider's Guide" we need to the world of the net. It gently and clearly guides our exploring, making the trip both productive and pleasant. It takes us to destinations local and all over the globe. It introduces us to colleagues who share our interests and invites productive dialogues. Like the best of guidebooks, it excites with its promises, touches us with it personal relevance, and educates us as travellers.

EDWARD L. ZUCKERMAN, PH.D.

Contents

The Insider's Guide to
Mental Health Resources Online

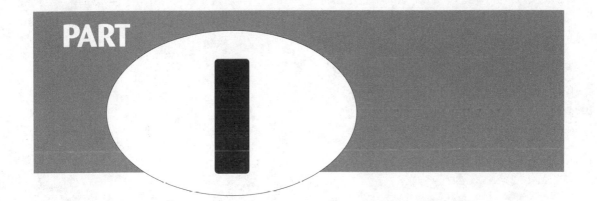

PART I

Basic Map and Tools for Finding Mental Health Information Online

1

Why and How to Look Online

As a professional, you no doubt find the demands on your time are increasing. Managed care is loudly knocking on clinicians' doors. Universities are demanding more of faculty but offering less. Grant funding through federal government agencies is drying up. You have probably never worked harder and longer for less money. So it's no surprise that a majority of professionals within the mental health field, and psychology especially, are not making use of online resources. There's no time to become familiar with this new landscape and use it effectively in your day-to-day job. Furthermore, you've probably heard many different things about getting online, including: "I hear of people getting online and simply getting lost!"; "Why should I waste my time?"; "I've heard it can be frustrating and expensive."

It *is* easy to get lost online if you don't know where to look for information. In this book, I show you where to go to find what you need professionally. It takes an immense amount of time to discover what's available and where to find it online. I have already done that—with you, the professional, in mind. Out of the myriad resources available online, how do you know what is good and worth your professional time? In this book, I give you my assessments of quality and rate each online resource. With these tools in hand, you can *choose* your best bet, rather than having to stumble upon it.

WHAT'S AVAILABLE ONLINE FOR YOU?

How can online resources help you, the mental health professional? Communication and convenience are two significant assets. Communication with other professionals—not just across the nation, but across the world—is quick, easy, and cheap online. E-mail (electronic mail) allows this, providing greater collaborative possibilities for research and clinical case consultation. For example, clinicians or researchers working alone or in remote or rural areas can now present difficult or challenging cases to their international colleagues to get useful feedback on treatment approaches. Questions about new medications coming on the market can be answered by experts within the psychopharmacology field who maintain Internet mailing lists. E-mail and mailing lists are described in greater depth later in this chapter.

While communication is the key to many professionals' choosing to get online, increased convenience in accessing information resources is often the reason professionals stay. Most academics and clinicians cannot access databases such as MEDLINE or PsycLIT without making a trip to the university library. But such databases are easily accessible online and, in some cases, free. Not everyone has a copy of the *Physicians' Desk Reference* (PDR) ready to hand. Resources similar to the PDR are available online. In-depth clinical and research articles and references, which summarize the major treatment approaches and latest research developments for any given disorder, can be browsed online. The *Diagnostic and Statistical Manual of Mental Disorders* (DSM) diagnostic codes and *International Classification of Diseases* (ICD) definitions of mental disorders are available at your fingertips online. Going online gives you access to all kinds of information easily and conveniently. How many libraries are open 24 hours a day, 365 days a year?

As a clinician online, you will be able to consult on difficult cases; learn about new theories, therapies, methods, and assessment measures; and talk to colleagues with similar therapeutic interests around the world (see Chapters 4, 6, and 7). As a researcher, you can collaborate with other researchers on the same study much easier than in the past, with the use of e-mail and the World Wide Web. New information can often be obtained more easily online, through news resources, current tables of contents for relevant journals, and databases (see Chapters 3, 7, and 9). The Web offers connections to such information, research and medical databases, and many similar resources. And because the entire Web is searchable, finding all of this information is much easier than you might think. Journal articles will sometimes be available by subscription, as well as news updates through a professional organization's Web site. Continuing education calendars are available online, and some online continuing education courses allow you to take courses at your leisure, and at greatly reduced costs (Chapter 5). You can find professional employment opportunities online (Chapter 4), discover the wealth of psychological software available (Chapter 10), and obtain patient education resources and materials (Chapters 12, 13, and 14).

WHAT'S NOT AVAILABLE ONLINE (YET)

When I first wrote this book in 1996, a great deal of information was not yet available online. Much has changed since then, with some journal publishers embracing the Internet and allowing subscribers online access to articles. Although it is not clear that the vast majority of older journal articles will ever make it online, those published in the past few years and those published from now on often have electronic versions available. Some journals provide online access to their articles as a part of their base subscription fee, and others charge extra for such access. Author self-archiving, through initiatives such as the National Institutes of Health's PubMed Central, will "archive, organize and distribute peer-reviewed reports from journals, as well as reports that have been screened but not formally peer-reviewed (see http://www.nih.gov/welcome/director/pubmedcentral/pmc.htm). Such archives have the potential to provide a rich array of readily available, free scientific articles to consume.

One of the world's largest medical databases is freely available online (MEDLINE). What many mental health professionals don't realize is that it includes most of the larger and better-known social science and psychological journal abstracts. So although proprietary, commercial databases such as the American Psychological Association's PsycINFO(r) are also available online for the right cost (if you cannot obtain access through a local university's library), many times the free MEDLINE database will suffice for quick literature searches.

ABOUT THIS BOOK

Throughout this book I highlight not only the key resources but also some of the lesser-known corners of the online world, to give you the insider's perspective to what is available online. The book is arranged into three major parts. This first part orients you to the online world and shows you how to make it work for you. It gives advice on formulating questions that get useful results, and where best to look for the answers. I also offer a step-by-step search strategy. The second part addresses the specific topics professionals are likely to want more information about. These topics range from how to find a job to where to look for cognitive therapy resources. If what you are looking for is not specifically covered in Part II, the tools and resources described in Part I and throughout the book should enable you to find it. The third part helps clinicians help their clients find online resources for patient education and self-help.

Appendix A offers a glossary of terms used throughout this book. There are many books about the Internet that devote entire chapters to the basics of getting online and the differences between online commercial service providers. I believe these are useful things to know, but I do not spend a lot of time covering them. For more information, I refer the reader to the publications in Appendix B. See Appendix C for a brief guide to getting online. Appendix D discusses how to create a simple World Wide Web page of your own. A list of grant resources available to researchers today makes up Appendix E.

If you're new to the whole online world, I suggest you read Appendix C first, get online successfully, and then continue with the rest of this book. Specific information about the minimal computer requirements for making the most out of online resources is discussed in the accompanying box as well as in Appendix C. The key to accessing online resources is not the computer you use, but the speed of your connection to the online world. While I try to be as non–computer specific and unbiased as possible throughout

MINIMAL COMPUTER REQUIREMENTS FOR MAKING THE MOST OF YOUR ONLINE EXPERIENCE

While you can use almost any computer to access many online resources, your online experience will be best if your computer setup meets the following minimal technical requirements. See Appendix C for a more thorough description and discussion of these requirements.

Your Computer:

- An IBM-PC compatible computer with an Intel or Pentium-class processor running at 133 MHz minimum or

- a Macintosh II, Quadra, Performa, PowerPC of any kind, G3, G4, or iMac.

- Memory: 32 MB of RAM for Windows 95/98
                   64 MB of RAM for Windows NT 3.51/4.x/2000
                   32 MB of RAM for Macintosh System 7.x/8.x/9.x

- Hard disk space: 40 MB available (free)

Your Modem:

- An internal or external modem running at 14.4 Kbps minimum, although 28.8 Kbps, 33.6 Kbps, or 56 Kbps is strongly recommended

Online Access:

- An Internet service provider (local or national) or online commercial service provider (such as America OnLine or CompuServe)

the book, I conduct all of my work online with an IBM-PC compatible computer. Where appropriate, I make reference to software that is computer specific. One of the nicest advantages to the online world, though, is that *it really doesn't matter* what kind of computer or operating system you use to access it. The online resources will generally work and look the same. The next part of this chapter gives a basic orientation to the important areas in the online world: e-mail, newsgroups, the World Wide Web, and search engines. If you already know about each of these, you might want to skip ahead.

While I have gone to great pains to ensure the timeliness and accuracy of all the resources listed througout the book, electronic addresses do change from time to time. Please check out the book's Web site (`http://www.insidemh.com/`) for updates.

THE MAJOR RESOURCES IN THE ONLINE WORLD

The online world is made up of millions of computers in thousands of locations throughout the world. It consists not only of the popular World Wide Web, but of many other older and less glamorous resources, including simple e-mail, newsgroups, mailing lists, interactive real-time chat rooms, and much more. I highlight the resources most actively used by professionals online today, outlining them briefly below.

About E-Mail

The easiest and most widely-used aspect of being online is called "electronic mail," or "e-mail" for short. As the name implies, this is an electronic version of regular mail, though it is not as secure (see cautions below). E-mail comes to your own electronic mail box, usually supplied as a service of your online access provider. At the cost of a local phone call, it allows a rapid, convenient method of corresponding and communicating with others around the world.

E-mail is also a gateway to online discussion areas called "mailing lists." Mailing lists (also known as "listservs" for the software that runs them) are where e-mail messages on specific areas of interest are publicly distributed. Many professionals-only mailing lists exist online to discuss specific mental health and behavioral health care topics. Each mailing list focuses on a specific topic. These can range from addictions and affective disorders to traumatic stress, psychotherapy treatment and research, and more. See Chapter 6 for a more detailed discussion of specific professional mailing lists together with a step-by-step guide on how to join—or "subscribe"—to them.

Once subscribed, you automatically receive a copy in your e-mail box of any message other members send to the list. You may simply read the messages then delete them, or you and other subscribers may choose to respond. These responses are also sent to every subscriber. In this manner, an interactive discussion can take place among the participants of the mailing list.

Cautions

E-mail is not as secure a method of correspondence as regular mail. The latter carries with it criminal charges for tampering. While online etiquette ("netiquette") dictates that e-mail is not to be shared publicly unless both parties first agree, the reality is that e-mail may be made public with little recourse if one party decides to do so. E-mail is adequate for most communications with your colleagues, but I'd never send credit card or other confidential information through it, unless encryption, a way of sending secure information online, is used.

About Newsgroups

"Newsgroups" (also known as "Usenet" or "Usenet newsgroups," their proper name) are also public discussion forums on the Internet. Unlike mailing lists, you access them through special software called a "news reader." Most online service providers give users a choice of software from which to read newsgroups. Some popular Web browsers also include this software. Newsgroups' advantages over mailing lists is that the format naturally supports "threading." A threaded discussion is one where you can read all of the messages on a particular topic more easily because they follow one another in order under that topic's title. Mailing lists, on the other hand, rely on your e-mail software to support threading. Users can also choose to delete entire threads in which they have no interest.

Newsgroups' advantage is disappearing because of new advances in e-mail software. As well, newsgroups also have their pitfalls. They are more public and easily accessible to everyone, and so everyone uses them. That makes some of them very busy. In addition to the high volume of messages, most newsgroups do not have any supervision or ownership (unlike mailing lists). This lack of supervision can result in a great deal of irrelevant and off-topic discussions. "Moderated" newsgroups help offset this problem, because messages must first be reviewed for appropriateness to the newsgroup's specific topic area before being published.

Newsgroups are categorized hierarchically by broad topic areas (e.g., recreational, science, computers, miscellaneous), which are then broken down into more specific subjects (e.g., psychology, medicine, physics), which are further broken down into still more discrete categories. For example, one newsgroup is named

```
sci.psychology.research
```

Each period, or "dot," denotes hierarchical level. "Sci" tells us this newsgroup is in the "science" hierarchy, under the subcategory of "psychology." This specific newsgroup, then, appears to be related to research topics in psychology. Newsgroups are generally much broader in scope and content than mailing lists are. They are also readily accessible through the Web at Deja.com (`http://deja.com`).

About the World Wide Web

E-mail and newsgroups are good for exchanging words but not images. The Web does both. The World Wide Web (also known simply as "the Web") is easily the most popular yet least interactive of online resources. Its popularity springs from the ease with which people can access it and the information found there. The Web was the first freely available Internet resource that allowed for the reproduction of graphics. Before the Web, the display of graphics online was generally a rare and tedious process. Graphics can still take a long time to be displayed because of their size and your connection speed to the online world. In the chapters that follow, I try to note when graphics may present a problem. The Web made it easy for anyone not only to access text and graphics, but also to create their own Web presence for others to access. (I will discuss how to create *your* own Web presence in Appendix D.)

The Web is made up of places called "Web sites" or "home pages." Some people use these terms interchangably, though I prefer to use the term "home page" to refer specifically to the first screen that is displayed when you access a Web site. A Web site is a person's or organization's entire Web offering, which may be made up of no more than one screen (called a "page" in Web lingo) of text information. More elaborate and larger Web sites might contain hundreds or thousands of individual Web pages, each with dozens of graphics. The most successful Web sites online today find a balance between judicious use of graphics and a great deal of original and useful content.

Web Site and E-Mail Addresses

Web sites have addresses, just like homes and businesses do in the real world. Web site addresses are called "URLs" (uniform resource locators) and always start with `http://` on the Web. An example of a Web URL might be:

`http://www.nimh.nih.gov/`

Typing this address takes you to the National Institute of Mental Health's Web site.

All Web addresses are case sensitive, meaning that you must type in the address in upper- and lowercase letters exactly as it is shown. So while `http://mentalhelp.net/prof.htm` takes you to the Professional Resources room of Mental Health Net, `http://mentalhelp.net/PROF.HTM` will take you to an error message. Most e-mail addresses, however, are not case sensitive; that is, it does not matter whether you type the address in upper- or lowercase letters. For example, `webmaster@cmhc.com` and `WEBMASTER@CMHC.COM` would both be properly delivered. Newsgroup addresses are also not case sensitive.

Web Browsers

Your computer accesses the Web through a piece of software called a "Web browser." Web addresses (URLs) are typed into your Web browser and it, in turn, will find and display Web sites, including graphics and text. Browsers are available for any computer and operating system: One of the two most popular is published by Netscape, a division of America Online and is called "Netscape." Microsoft Corporation's "Internet Explorer" is the other most popular. Both are available online and at your local computer store. The Microsoft browser is included with their operating system, Windows , so you may already have it. Web browsers allow you to mark Web sites you like. Called "bookmarks" or "favorite places," this feature allows you to save and subsequently easily access the address of a site. Some Web browsing software also have news readers and e-mail software built into them to enhance usability.

Once you are at any Web site, you navigate it by clicking on highlighted text or graphics called "links." When links are text, the word or phrase is often underlined or in a color different from the rest of the text on the screen.

Whether text or graphics, you can recognize a link because your cursor will change into something other than an arrow (for instance, to a hand) when passed over it. For example, if you're reading about depression on a Web site, the terms "serotonin," "bipolar," and "suicide" may be highlighted as links. Clicking on any one link takes you to a new page—or even a new site— with more information on that topic. In this manner you can spend hours clicking on links, going from Web site to Web site, in search of additional information on a topic. This is what is meant by "surfing" the Web. The person responsible for maintaining a Web site is called a "Webmaster."

Web sites come in two major flavors—"framed" and "normal" (or unframed). A framed Web site is one in which your Web browser's screen is divided up into smaller screens (called "frames"), each of which contains different information. Some Web site designers do this to place a menu selection at the bottom or on the side of your Web browser's screen to help you navigate through the Web site more easily. Most Web browsers today can display frames. The drawback is that you generally need a larger screen to make the most use of them. On a too-small computer screen, you will be unable to see some of the information contained in one or more of the frames. Most Web sites in this book are of the normal, or unframed variety. When a framed version is offered or available, I will usually note that in the site's review. Even when a framed version of the Web site is offered, you can typically choose whether you want a framed or unframed version. The choice you make will probably depend on the opinion you form after trying out this feature on a few sites.

About Search Engines

One of the keys to making the Internet work *for* you is knowing how to use a search engine or guide. The online world is large and growing at an extraordinary rate. The amount of information to be searched, therefore, is also immense. While it is useful to know specific URLs and go directly to specific Web sites (or use your bookmarks), what else are you missing? Using a search engine, you can obtain a listing of possibly relevant sites and go directly to the site from the list. There are many different kinds of search engines, some better than others.

To use a search engine, type in a few words or topics you're interested in. Click on the "Search" button and the search engine will return some results. Results typically include the Web page's name or title, a summary or short description of the Web page, and a link directly to that page. You need only click on a result to go to that Web page.

The closest matches—that is, the most relevant documents found—will be listed first. The list is typically organized by declining relevancy—at least ideally. But different search engines have different algorithms for determining relevancy. The relevancy of the results to your initial query may vary greatly. For example, a story about a young woman who happened to read Freud's *Interpretation of Dreams*, may be indexed under "Freud." The hapless researcher types in "Freud" looking for biographical information, and the search engine returns this story about the young woman's reading material. If our researcher checks it out, she will have wasted time following an irrelevant path. Searching for information can often be a frustrating back-and-forth trudge from the search engine's list of results to the results themselves, most of which can turn out to be largely irrelevant to your intended purpose. But don't give up searching online. There are many useful and easy strategies to greatly enhance your search skills. See Chapter 2 for the different kinds of search engines available.

The Host of Other Internet Resources

There are many other resources I may mention throughout this book and you may hear about in your online travels. Some of these are covered in the glossary, found in Appendix A. The online world is so vast and expansive, it would be impossible for me to cover all the online resources that may have some relevance to professionals. For example, there are interactive, live chat rooms online in which people congregate 24 hours a day, 365 days a year. Most of these are for nonprofessionals, but there are a handful of areas like this where professionals occasionally meet. I expect that as more professionals discover the benefits of getting online, such live, interactive areas for professionals will increase in number.

FORMULATING QUESTIONS THAT GET RESULTS

Anyone who has done any type of research knows that formulating the right question is essential to getting useful answers. If the question is too vague or general, you may get little useful information. If the question is too narrowly defined, it may be impossible to generalize from your research findings. The same is true of searching for information online. If your search query is too broad, you will receive thousands of generally irrelevant results; if too narrow, you may not find anything at all. Either way, you'll probably become frustrated and give up. This section covers the tricks of the trade for searching for useful and relevant information online.

Most searching online is done *through* as well as *on* the World Wide Web. The results will be limited to information that has been published on the Web. (Some search engines can also search newsgroups—see Chapter 2.) There is a lag between the time a site is published on the Web and the time it is indexed. The Web has a tremendous size and growth rate—the indexing software simply cannot keep up. For example, if I publish a copy of my research on eating disorders on my Web site tomorrow, it may not be indexed by the Web indexing software for weeks or even months. While there are ways for authors and developers of Web sites to decrease this time lag, most do not actively do so. This means that while searching the Web is a potentially powerful tool, it should be just one of many such tools you use while online. I have sometimes discovered information in other online recesses, such as mailing lists, that don't exist on the Web (and therefore can't be found by a Web search engine).

Search Tools and Tips

Forming a Search Concept and Using Synonyms

Start a search by choosing a thorough and well-defined search concept. This concept should not only include your initial idea and its initial terms, but also include all terms related to that idea. Suppose we want to search for "teenage depression." That's our concept. If we just typed those two words into most search engines, we would be assaulted with thousands of relevant but also irrelevant results. For example, some search engines will automatically assume you're searching for the individual terms teenage *or* depression, but others will use teenage *and* depression. To get the most relevant results, you'll want to type in and between those two keywords.

Next we want to think of popular synonyms for these words, to ensure we gather *all* possibly relevant data. We will want the search engine to look for all these synonyms as well. For the search term "teenage," we may also want to include:

teenager
teenagers
adolescent
adolescents
youth

For "depression," we may also want to include:

suicide
depressed
loneliness
dysthymia
mood

We will want to search for each of the individual synonyms for `teenage` and `depression`. Therefore, you will want to type in `or` between the synonyms for each word. The term `and` goes between the two sets of synonyms. Our search query is now expanded from "teenage and depression" to "(teenage or teenager or teenagers or adolescent or adolescents or youth) and (depression or suicide or depressed or loneliness or dysthymia or mood)." By using synonyms in this way, you can probably expand any search that is retrieving too few records (or too few *relevant* records). Notice the quotation marks and parentheses. They matter. The next section explains why.

By including all of the above choices, we can ensure that the search is the most thorough possible. This is no different from how most of us were taught to think about our queries before conducting a thorough literature search. For some reason, when professionals get online, they often forget these important lessons.

Tools for Precision Searching: Booleans, Phrases, and Other Operators

Ideally, we would like to search with greater precision and have fewer, but more relevant records returned. Search engines have been developed and equipped with tools to help increase the precision of a search. Some search engines' tools, however, are more powerful than others. It is these tools, *not the size of a search engine's database*, that make one search engine better than another. After all, what's the point of searching the largest library in the world if it has a poorly indexed card catalog? Unfortunately for you, each search engine has slightly different ways of implementing these tools, also known as "operators" in computer lingo.

Booleans   Most search engines allow you to insert the words "and," "or," and "not" to connect words or logical groupings of words. This is called "Boolean" searching and is the most basic search method. We've already used "and" and "or" in this way in our search for teenage depression. All search engines available today offer some means like this of limiting and broadening your searches. For instance, `mice and men` will retrieve items containing both terms, limiting the search, while `mice or men` will retrieve all items that have either term, broadening the search. `England not New` will provide you with items about England, but not about New England, thereby narrowing a search.

Phrases   A second method for helping you limit your search is through the use of "phrases." Search engines will recognize that words go together if you bracket them, for example, with quotation marks. The search engine will retrieve items that only match the specific phrase within the quotes. Typing quotes around `"teenage depression"` should be quite useful in retrieving results that discuss teenage depression. It should limit retrieval of documents that may use the words separately throughout that document, which can happen when using the Boolean operator `and`. The two main ways to indicate a phrase in a search engine is through the use of quotation marks or parentheses. Some search engines use one method and not the other, while some let you use both at the same time. Each search engine's help section offers additional information about which operators and punctuation they recognize (see Table 1.1). In our last search query for teenage depression, we created phrases with both quotation marks and parentheses. The quotations bracket the total concept with all the synonyms, while the

TABLE 1.1   Quick Reference of Search Operators and Examples

Operator	Description	Example
and	Used between two or more search terms or expressions, **all** of which must appear in each result	`teenage and depression` will return only results with both the word "teenage" and the word "depression" in them
or	Used between two or more search terms or expressions, **any** of which may appear in each result	`teenage or depression` will return results with either of these two words in them
not	Used between two or more search terms or expressions; acts to exclude the search term or expression following it	`depression not teenage` will exclude any depression-related results that have the word "teenage" in them
"..."	Used around a group of words to denote a phrase	`"teenage depression"` will find those documents with these two words appearing together as a phrase
near	Used between two or more search terms or expressions; acts to exclude results based upon proximity	`teenage near depression` will find those documents with these two words appearing close to one another, which is a broader form of phrase searching
+	Used in front of a word or phrase to denote the word or phrase that must appear in all results	`Freud +Anna` would return only those results that include "Anna"
−	Used in front of a word or phrase to denote the word or phrase that must not appear in any result	`Freud −Anna` would return only those results that did not have "Anna"
Fields	Used to specify where to locate your search within each document, in order to increase relevancy of results	`title:depression` will return only those results that have the word "depression" in the document's title

parentheses contain the two sets of synonyms (much like a complex math equation!).

Other Operators   Additional tools (or "operators") are helpful in limiting or broadening our search. Like the Boolean terms, a word suggesting proximity to each of our search items tends to provide us with results of higher relevance. The most common such operator is near. For example, "`teenage` <u>`near`</u> `depression`" will provide us with perhaps more relevant results than just using the Boolean operator `and`.

Another operator, an asterisk `*`, acts as a "wildcard symbol." Using it, you can easily find variants to a root term. For "teenage," "teenager," and "teenagers," we can instead specify "`teenag*`." This will find all three variants and cut down on the number of synonyms we need to search under. The wildcard symbol can be combined with any of these other tools to provide greater flexibility.

Other helpful tools are "require" and "exclusion" operators. These are plus and minus signs, respectively: `+  −`, and are similar to the Boolean operators `and` and `not`. While not all search engines support this function, you will find it useful with those that do. By placing a plus sign (`+`) in front of a word (without any spaces between), you can direct the search engine to return only results that include that word. This can be helpful in limiting searches. For example, we may be interested in learning more about Jung's work in psychoanalysis, but not anyone else's. We could, therefore, use a search term such as, `psychoanalysis +Jung`. This would guarantee that Jung's name will appear in the results, increasing the relevance of our search. In the same way, the minus sign (`−`) can help you get rid of results which keep showing up which are of no relevance to you. Wanting to learn more about Sigmund Freud via a biography online, for instance, I might want to exclude his daughter, Anna, from the search. Our search term might look like, `Freud −Anna`. Note that there is no space between the operator and the search term. Some search engines require you use these operators rather than Boolean operators.

The last search tool that will be of use to you is the ability to search only within specific fields. Users of PsycLIT and other commercial databases are undoubtedly accustomed to providing instructions on which field to search in the database. Web search engines, however, tend to be more rudimentary and limit the fields that you can search on. Some of these fields will be of little help to most professionals looking to obtain more relevant results. There is one field, though, which you should become familiar with using. Named the "title:" field, it specifies the title of the Web document and can therefore be useful in trying to find relevant documents. *But beware!* The inclusion of a useful title is solely up to the authors of the document being sought. Many times authors leave specific document titles out (because of space limitations) or have to truncate it severely. So while this may be a good method to try initially, it may restrict your results to too great an extent and will miss many pertinent documents. Fields available for searching are limited to those fields supported by the search engines. A date field, for example, is not available.

Distinguishing Search Engines, Subject Guides, and Meta-Search Engines

There are important differences between a *search engine*, a *subject guide* (or search guide), and a *meta-search engine*. Understanding these differences can make navigating the Web much easier and hassle-free. Search engines are the most popular and widely used ways of searching the Internet for many reasons. First, they are very good at collecting *all* of the data online and indexing it. Second, most provide search tools that allow for relatively easy extraction of that data. Third, there is a wide variety of search engines to choose from, ensuring that individuals are likely to find one that they like the most.

Sometimes search engines, for all of their power and potential, simply don't work well enough. They can still return too many irrelevant results. Also, if you don't know the name of something or the correct term for a subject, a search engine isn't going to help you much. It requires a specific search concept made up of specific keywords.

For these reasons, subject guides (also known as search guides) were developed. They are much like compiled bibliographies or indexes, but they don't rely on software to compile their databases. Instead, they rely on a staff of human editors to search for relevant content online, review it, and place it in their database. This means more of the content will be directly relevant to what you're looking for. It also allows you to find information on a specific topic when you're not sure where to start. You may be able to search *inside* one of these guides. Both search engines and subject guides typically display the results of a search in rank ordering; that is, the most relevant results to your search are displayed first, at the top of the list. As you go further down the list, the relevancy decreases. The downside to guides is that, by definition, they cannot be as comprehensive as a search engine. So you may not be seeing *every* resource listed under a particular subject heading.

Meta-search engines offer you the ability to search across multiple search engines *at the same time.* These meta-search engines also usually offer the ability to intelligently collate the corresponding results, remove duplicate links, check for and remove outdated links or links to online resources that are no longer valid (often referred to as a "bad link"), and then present the results in a rank ordering, with the most relevant results being near the top of the listing.

Other search engines that don't fall neatly into any of the above categories are also becoming available online. One such engine is a piece of software that you download and run from your computer. Much like a meta-search engine, it will send out your search query to a specified set of search engines, collect and collate the results on your desktop. Some of this software may be further specialized to search only certain kinds of databases online, such as those containing only health information. Another search engine that doesn't fall neatly into any category is one that indexes only a few, specialized sites. For example, the American Psychological Association developed PsycCrawler, a search engine that only indexes four or five psychology-oriented Web sites. This was designed to limit the number of irrelevant results returned on a search of the index.

PUTTING THE TOOLS TO USE: DEFINING A SUCCESSFUL SEARCH STRATEGY

How can you successfully and sensibly implement all these search tools? I suggest you think in terms of a *search strategy.* First, you determine whether the type of search you are conducting is one for commonly-available material (e.g., professional resources for the treatment of alcoholism) or more obscure material. If it is a topic that is general and popular, you will have much less difficulty finding it. Beginning in a *subject guide* (also referred to as a *search guide*) is usually the easiest method for this type of search. If you would like to conduct a much more thorough search online, or the material you're seeking is more obscure or specific, you would instead begin with a search engine.

Begin your search by typing in a keyword or two to see how many results you receive. You will probably get quite a few! Then type in the same search phrase using some of the tools listed earlier in the chapter. For example, we could have started off typing in the two words `teenage` and `depression` into the query field. Then we could try placing quotation marks around the terms, such as `"teenage depression"`, or using a Boolean operator such as, `"teenage and depression."` We could also try including all variants of each word and synonyms.

Unfortunately, there is no one or single "correct" way of conducting this search. Why not? Because the type of strategy you will use is determined by the type of search you are conducting. For example, if you'd like to conduct an exhaustive search of all references to Aaron T. Beck online, you may want to use a multitude of keywords, such as `cognitive-behavioral therapy`, `cognitive-behavioral theory`, `RET`, and `Ellis`. An advanced query on a search engine such as AltaVista might look like

```
Beck and "cognitive behavioral" near (theory or
therapy) and not (RET or Ellis)
```

That is, we want references to Beck, the phrase "cognitive behavioral" near either of the words "theory" or "therapy" and no results returned on either RET (Rational Emotive Therapy) or Ellis (Albert). This isn't really a complete comprehensive search on Beck references online, but it is one of the easiest ways of conducting something close to it (and would be considered a "detailed" search; see Figure 1.1, next page). As you can see, a good query can net you good results. If you take a moment to thoughtfully compose your query using the operators described above, your results will be more rewarding *every time you use a search engine*. This is one of the most important pieces of information you can take away from this book—learn to fully use the power of the search engine you like the best. If you take 5 minutes to read that search engine's help section now, it will save countless hours later of slogging through irrelevant results. As the old computer programming saying goes, "garbage in, garbage out."

What if You Get No Results?

What if your search comes up empty-handed? Usually you will always get *something* in the way of a result when you type in a query. But it's possible, as I've already mentioned, that the information you're seeking simply isn't yet available online. Don't forget: As vast as the Internet is, it still can't com-

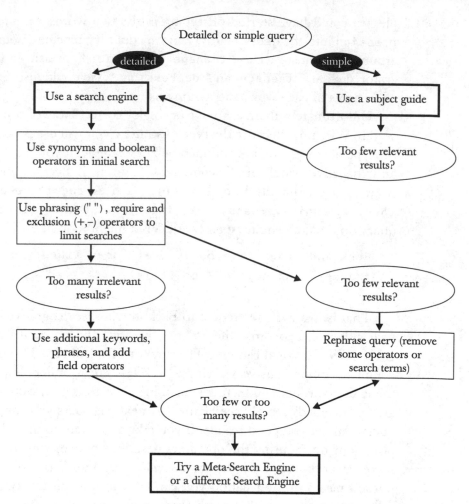

FIGURE 1.1   A simple, general search strategy

pare to the information found in a university's library. Your best strategy when you come up empty-handed is to try rearranging the search terms and use a different combination of operators with different synonyms. If that continues to bring you no relevant results, move on to another search engine. See Chapter 2 for a list of search engines.

A word of caution, however. The Web is still only as good as its current content. Obscure and detailed research topics or highly-specialized and specific subject searches aren't likely to turn up many results no matter what

TABLE 1.2   Search Engines and the Search Tools They Support

	AND	OR	NOT	Proximity	Phrase	Inclusion/ Exclusion	Wildcard	Field[1]
AltaVista Basic	N/A[2]	default[3]	N/A	N/A	"..."	+ / −	*	host: image: link: text: title: url:
AltaVista Advanced	and/&	or	not	near	"..."	N/A	*	Same
Excite	and	or	and not	N/A	"..."	+ / −	N/A	N/A
FAST Search	default	N/A	N/A	N/A	"..."	+ / −	N/A	N/A
Google	default	N/A	N/A	N/A	"..."	+ / −	N/A	link: flink:
Hotbot	Form-based[4]			N/A	Advanced search			domain: title:
Infoseek	and	or	N/A	N/A	"..."	+ / −	N/A	link: site: url: title:
Lycos	Form-based[4]			N/A	"..."	+ / −	$	N/A
Northern Light	default	or	not	N/A	"..."	+ / −	*	url: title: pub: company: ticker: text;
Webcrawler	and	default	not	adj or near	"..."	+ / −	N/A	N/A

Notes:
Different search engines use different combinations of terms to get the same result. For example, Alta-Vista uses just plain not, while Excite requires the words and not to be used instead. Within individual search engines, they may also allow different operators to get the same result (e.g., AltaVista allows you to use either and or the ampersand symbol (&) to specify the Boolean term and).

[1]Field—Search engines may allow searching on technical fields such as anchor, applet, or host, which are not relevant for most readers.

[2]N/A—Not applicable. This operator is not supported by this search engine.

[3]Default—This is the default operator used when you type in two words together. For example, "teenage depression" will be searched for as "teenage or depression" in AltaVista, but Open Text will interpret the query as "teenage and depression."

[4]Form based—Lycos uses a specialized form you fill out on their Web site in order to specify these options.

search methodology you use. If you use two or three of the search engines mentioned in the next chapter and keep turning up few results, it's likely that the material you're seeking simply is not available yet online. If your professional area happens to *be* that topic, you could always consider adding to the international knowledge base by putting up your own Web site (which I talk about in Appendix D). Sometimes the library will still be the first and last place to look for information on those kinds of highly-specific topics. By using these search tools, combined with synonyms and an effective search strategy, you will probably be able to find documents on the World Wide Web in a much more time-efficient manner. A summary of the search tools discussed in this chapter is given in Table 1.2.

2

Knowing Where to Look Online

Now that you've got the tools and the search strategy down, where do you go to employ them online? You can use these tools at many of the Web sites listed in Part II of this book. But every day new materials and sites come online. How can you be sure to stay current? This chapter tells you how. But first, let me mention where *not* to start looking online.

A lot of people start their searches online with the tools made available to them within their Web-browsing software. For instance, in Netscape's browsing software, there is a button in the program labeled "Net Search." By clicking on this button, the user is taken to a choice of one of the five major search engines or guides online. This is a bad way to start for—two reasons: (1) It is a mistake to believe that those five search engines listed are somehow better than all of the others online, just because they are found on Netscape. The fact is, the developers of these tools paid Netscape large sums of money to appear there. Some of the best search engines won't be found by pressing the "Net Search" button at all! (2) It's a drawback that Netscape browser software is so popular (accounting for roughly 70% of the Web-browsing public of around 30 to 40 million users worldwide). Every one of those users has that same "Net Search" button and may be pressing it. That means Netscape's Web site, which serves up those five search engine choices, can get *very, very busy*. This, in turn, means the Web site can become *very, very slow*. It is just as easy and usually faster to access these search engine Web sites directly (from the listings below), and I strongly suggest you do so.

This chapter presents a list of search engines, search guides, or meta-search engines. I don't pretend the list is comprehensive. What I have provided is a wide selection of some of the more popular search software available online, along with brief descriptions and reviews of their abilities. Those listed tend to have a record of stability and are therefore likely to be around for a long time. I'll also discuss other methods for finding information that go beyond simple Web searches (such as utilizing newsgroups and mailing lists). I will discuss the pros and cons of each method for searching and tell you what kind of searches are best for each method. Before going on to this list, you should take a look at the box explaining the list's format and the rating system I have used for each resource.

UNDERSTANDING WEB RESOURCE HEADINGS AND THE RATING SYSTEM

In most sections of this book, World Wide Web resources are listed in alphabetical order by their respective names or what I refer to as "titles." The "owner" of the resource is then noted. The owner is the person or organization responsible for the Web site, its ongoing maintenance and most importantly, its content. Listed next is the Web resource's address online, also known as its *uniform resource locator* or URL. Additional URLs, which point to a specific resource described within the narrative or if two services reside on the same site, may be listed. A rating and narrative review of each site summarizes the highlights and downsides of the site.

The system I use throughout this book to rate Web sites is based on those commonly used by other online rating services. Ratings take into consideration four central quality categories:

■ *Content*–Does the site add *new and unique* material to the online world, or does it simply list or link to existing material well covered by other sites already? Does it offer new insights or offer information not found elsewhere? Does it offer refreshing perspectives, and/or regularly updated new content in the form of news articles, opinions, or other forms of communication? Does it include interactive features? Is it just an advertisement for an organization or company? Is it objective and fair? Does it present misinformation or common popular fallacies?

■ *Presentation*—Is the information laid out in a logical and well-organized manner? Are graphics designed appropriately for the site and do they appear on your computer quickly? Do the graphics overwhelm the user and the content? Is it arranged so the best material the site has to offer is clearly delineated from other, less-important material?

■ *Ease-of-use*—Can you find your way to particular content quickly using the navigation aids provided, and then get back to where you entered the Web site just as easily? Is the *user interface* (the means by which the Web site interacts with you) well designed? Are a search engine or other tools provided to help a person find information more quickly (when appropriate)? Can you easily find an e-mail address on the page to provide feedback about broken links or the like?

■ *Overall experience*—What kind of feelings did I have when I came away from the site? Was it enjoyable or painful to read? Was I expecting more and became disappointed by the content or presentation or difficulty in navigating through the site? Would I *bookmark* (add it to my "bookmark" or "favorite places" list in my Web browser) the site myself or find myself wanting to return on a regular basis?

A four-star system is used to denote the result of ratings in these categories:

■ ★★★★—*Excellent.* One of the best sites on the Web for this topic due to its outstanding design and content.

■ ★★★—*Very good.* Worth your time to visit. Well designed with robust and useful content.

■ ★★—*Average.* A solid online resource filled with basic but generally uninteresting information.

■ ★—*Poor.* Lacking important content or difficult to use.

Please note that a site may obtain different ratings throughout the book depending on the category under which it is being rated. The American Psychological Association's PsychNET Web site, for example, is an excellent professional association site (rating four stars), but a less-interesting consumer resources site (rating only three stars).

THE FIRST CHOICE FOR DETAILED QUESTIONS: SEARCH ENGINES

All search engines use automated software (referred to as Web "crawlers," "spiders," or "robots") to compile their databases. This software is generally very good at finding information on the Internet and storing it within an index. The numbers bandied about to claim each is the "largest and most comprehensive" database online are largely meaningless. All such databases are pretty much similar in size. Size, here anyway, doesn't really matter. What is important is the flexibility and power of the retrieval software. If a search engine has a large database, but the tools for extracting information from it are rudimentary, it's not going to be all that useful. On the other hand, a large database combined with excellent tools make for a winning combination. The key to those tools, though, is knowing that they exist, learning how to use them effectively, and having them work as they were intended to work.

None of the currently available search engines remove duplicate results. Most also have difficulty in discriminating among results that point to the slightly different pages of the same Web site. This means that you could view a search engine's results of four or five pages, all of which lead to the same Web site! This may not be a bad thing if all the pages are relevant to your search topic, but more often than not, that is not the case.

The Most Popular, Useful, and Widely Used Search Engines

There are dozens of search engines available for searching the Web. Only a handful of them, however, are widely used because of their ability to provide reliable access to their large databases. Search engines are the most-often visited Web sites online, so being able to reach them is an important factor to consider. All of the engines listed below are stable online resources with similarly large databases, which are updated daily. They differ mainly in their ability to provide relevant results. They are listed alphabetically.

Title (or descriptor):	AltaVista
Owner:	AltaVista
URL (Web address):	http://www.altavista.com/
Rating:	★★★★

AltaVista is the most powerful and widely used search engine today, for good reason. Not only does it offer a large database, but it has the most powerful and flexible retrieval tools available. AltaVista offers one of two types of searching: "Basic" and "Advanced." Basic searching is the default and is often adequate. One of AltaVista's quirks is that when using "Basic" searching, you cannot use Boolean operators (such as `and`, `or`, and `not`) or the `near` operator. To use these options, you must choose "Advanced" searching. Use the advanced option to conduct a serious AltaVista search on the Internet.

AltaVista offers several features not found on most other search engines. One is the choice of searching the Web or Usenet newsgroups (discussed in-depth later in the chapter). Another is the ability to search the Web by specific fields within each Web document. Every document on the Web, much like every page in a book, is displayed in a visual format defined by hidden formatting codes. By searching within these specific codes, or fields, you can further limit your search and help increase relevancy. The only other search engine that has this extended ability at present is Infoseek, but for only a few fields. In AltaVista you can use this option combined with other operators and options, and it can be used within a basic or advanced search. One example of utilizing this feature would be to limit your search only to the title field of the document. For instance:

```
title:freud
```

Note that there is a colon but *no space* between the field you wish to search and the search term itself. This would greatly limit your search, since only those files that had the term "freud" *in their title* (capitalization here is unimportant) would be returned. I received about 1,500 documents using this method as opposed to just typing in "freud," which returned over 168,000 results from AltaVista! Using this method is no guarantee of increasing relevancy; it will exclude perfectly relevant and useful documents that simply don't have the keyword in the title. But it can be helpful when used sparingly or to narrow your search.

Another helpful tool in the AltaVista search arsenal is something called "Live-Topics." First you conduct a regular, basic search using whatever search terms you want. On the results page, you then choose the "LiveTopics" option. This will display a list of categories and subcategories that help to logically organize and arrange subjects and keywords related to your search. You can browse through these categories and choose those of interest to you. Then by pressing the "Submit" button, a new results listing will appear with more relevant and useful results than originally obtained. This is an example of the trend among search engines to make searching the World Wide Web more intuitive and easy.

Title (or descriptor):	Ask Jeeves
Owner:	Ask Jeeves, Inc.
URL (Web address):	`http://www.ask.com/`
Rating:	★★★

An interesting search engine, assembled by humans (rather than indexing software), which allows you to enter queries in normal, everyday English (known as "natural language queries"). Because Ask Jeeves is assembled by humans, it also means it's not very comprehensive or complete. Ask it about treatments for panic attacks, for instance, and it'll refer you to an unrelated, general encyclopedia article on panic. Ask Jeeves is best for general, everyday queries when you don't want a lot of choices to sift through—you just want the answer to a question quickly and somewhat authoritatively.

Title (or descriptor):	Excite
Owner:	Excite, Inc.
URL (Web address):	`http://www.excite.com/`
Rating:	★★★

Excite claims that its database is the largest: but so do other search engines online. What matters is the retrieval software. While making claims of greater accuracy, Excite's software often didn't measure up during some simple tests I ran (e.g., for depression resources). This is probably because its indexing software is fooled by some tricks Webmasters use to obtain a higher listing in a search engine's results. This translates into your getting less-useful results. Excite unfortunately doesn't provide the ability to search individual fields within a Web document (as AltaVista and Infoseek do), but it does offer full use of Boolean operators (such as **and**, **or**, and **not**). Some of the Web resources listed within Excite's database are reviewed by its editorial staff, but it is not clear who writes the reviews or how often (if at all) they are updated.

Title (or descriptor):	FAST Search
Owner:	Fast Search & Transfer ASA
URL (Web address):	http://www.alltheweb.com/
Rating:	★★★

A newcomer to the search engine world, FAST has quickly gotten people's attention with its claim to index over 250 million Web documents (whittled down from an amazing 450 million documents, weeding out the duplicates). This would make it the largest index currently available. Time will tell if quantity equals quality, but it wouldn't hurt to try it out. My experiences with it were mixed.

Title (or descriptor):	Google
Owner:	Google, Inc.
URL (Web address):	http://www.google.com/
Rating:	★★★★

An innovative search engine in a field that is in need of some innovation. The relevancy of results returned is determined by the document's importance. The more additional pages with high importance in the Google database point to the document, the more likely it will show up in a user's results. My experiences with the search engine have resulted in mixed outcomes, but the underlying technology appears sound.

A minor annoyance in using this and the "FAST Search" engines is that neither supports Boolean searches. This may provide some frustration to more experienced Web users used to such options, but most people won't notice the loss.

Title (or descriptor):	HotBot
Owner:	Wired, Inc.

URL (Web address):   `http://www.hotbot.com/`

Rating: ★★

HotBot is a run-of-the-mill search engine with few additional features to recommend its use over other engines. It allows searching on both the World Wide Web and Usenet newsgroups (explained later in this chapter), with a variety of search options available through a user-friendly but simplistic form. It supports the use of Boolean operators and phrases, as well as a number of other unique search tools. These include the ability to search by the date a particular Web page was indexed by the search engine, the media type (e.g., if you're searching for an audio file or a particular image), among others. Results, however, were often disappointing and generally less relevant than those found by its peers. You will either love or hate the lime green background and the sometimes cryptic graphics found throughout the site.

ADVERTISING ONLINE

Advertising online is now as commonplace as it is on television. Most of the advertising is generally innocuous—a small graphic that runs at the top or on the side of each page. On search engines, however, there may be more at work to produce that ad than meets the eye. Using an advertising technique called "targeted marketing," search engines display advertisements directly related to the search terms entered. For example, if you enter the term, "computer buying" into a search engine, you might receive an advertisement on the search results page for a computer maker, such as Gateway or Dell.

Another trend in online advertising is a change in how advertisers pay for their ads. Traditionally, advertisers paid Web developers based upon how many times their ad was shown on a page. More and more advertisers are backing away from this business model, however, and are moving toward paying based upon the number of people who actually click on the ad. A "click-through," as they are called, means a person is more likely interested in the product or service being sold. But since click-throughs account for only 1–2% of the people who actually see the ad, advertisers and developers are working on still more intrusive strategies to increase advertising revenue and sales. One such strategy used to try and enhance people's interest in a product or service is to make the advertisement nearly indistinguishable from editorial content on the Web site. This type of online advertising is another disturbing trend which will hopefully be short-lived. When content becomes blurred with advertising in this manner, the usefulness of the online world as an information medium diminishes substantially. Yet another form of online revenue generation is an "association" with a book or music retailer. These associations return 5–25% of any purchases made online through them to the Web site's owner.

Title (or descriptor):	Infoseek
Owner:	Infoseek Corporation
URL (Web address):	`http://www.infoseek.com/`
Rating:	★★★★

Infoseek offers a larger database, more accurate and relevant results, and better search retrieval tools than Excite does. Infoseek is a thorough and reliable search engine. Infoseek also offers an extensive advanced searching area. Infoseek allows you to form your search query in plain language (e.g., `When was B. F. Skinner born?`), which is called a "natural language query." Out of all of the search engines available today, Infoseek does the best job in answering such queries. For instance, the answer to the above question was found in the second result listed. No quotation marks are needed around phrases in Infoseek.

Infoseek offers a wide array of value-added services, at no additional charge. For example, it provides daily world and national news stories and a personalized news service. This allows you to choose which types of news you'd like to read (national, international, business, entertainment, etc.). Also offered by Infoseek are business Yellow Pages and a handy "Fast Facts" area. This section offers links to online dictionaries, *Roget's Thesaurus, Bartlett's Quotations,* stock tickers, phone books, e-mail address finders, street maps, and government agencies on one page. It's a handy reference source.

Title (or descriptor):	Lycos
Owner:	Lycos, Inc.
URL (Web address):	`http://www.lycos.com/`
Rating:	★★

Lycos is best known for being one of the oldest and largest Web search engines available online. It indexes not only all the words of all the Web pages it finds, but also the links found on each Web page. This is positive if you're looking for comprehensiveness, but many of the results it gives may not be relevant. Lycos's search form and retrieval software is also old, and by current standards, sorely lacking in powerful features. For instance, it doesn't support the ordinary use of Boolean or inclusion/exclusion operators. It's a good search engine for quick-and-dirty, general searches online. Lycos also offers two search guides, a2z and Point, which are reviewed below.

Title (or descriptor):	Northern Light
Owner:	Northern Light Technology, LLC
URL (Web address):	`http://www.northernlight.com/`
Rating:	★★★

Northern Light's index is just slightly smaller than FAST Search's, but as history has taught us, size doesn't matter as much as accuracy and relevancy. Northern Light tries to accomplish this by offering "Customized Search Folders" next to your results. So a search on depression treatment brings up not only the usual 200,000+ results, but also a list of folders with labels such as "mental health," "psychotherapy," "prozac," and "diseases and disorders." Clicking on one of these folders allows you to explore more on that related topic. Some "related topics" seemed pretty unrelated, however, such as the appearance of a folder entitled "Latinos" while searching for depression treatment. It is probable that this technology will improve over time, and for now, it offers an interesting alternative way of looking at search results.

Title (or descriptor):	Webcrawler
Owner:	Excite, Inc.
URL (Web address):	`http://www.webcrawler.com/`
Rating:	★

Webcrawler is one of the oldest search engines online and the first to index the full text of each Web page in its database. Unfortunately, due to its inability to keep up with its tremendous growth in 1995, it has fallen behind both technologically and in the smallish size of its database. Make sure you choose to "View Summaries" on the results page if you wish to use this search engine, otherwise results are difficult to interpret and use.

ASSEMBLED BY HUMAN HANDS: SUBJECT/SEARCH GUIDES AND DIRECTORIES

As discussed earlier (see Chapter 1) subject or search guides rely on human editors rather than software to find information on the Internet and index it. There are two primary types of search guides: general and specific. General guides act like a library's card catalog organized by broad subjects.

They cover everything under the sun, from computers to entertainment, from hobbies to psychology, from cars to clothing, and a whole lot more. The specific guides limit themselves to particular online topic areas. So there might be a guide to psychology online, or neuropsychology, or depression. These latter types of guides tend to be smaller, by definition, but more comprehensive within the subject they cover than the general-purpose guides. Both types of these guides are included in the alphabetical list below.

Title (or descriptor):	healthfinder™
Owner:	U.S. Department of Health and Human Services
URL (Web address):	`http://www.healthfinder.gov/`
Rating:	★★★★

This informative and extensive search guide from the U.S. Department of Health and Human Services offers links to health and mental health information found on hundreds of Web sites, but most of them are overseen by the U.S. federal government. The site has grown considerablly since its inception, and continues to improve weekly. This site is unique in that it not only provides you with the usual hypertext links to other sites, but in many cases to their real-world contact information, such as phone numbers and addresses. Descriptions are brief but helpful and the site has a simple yet effective design.

Title (or descriptor):	Lycos Top 5%
Owner:	Lycos, Inc.
URL (Web address):	`http://point.lycos.com/`
Rating:	★★★

Lycos offers the ubiquitous "Top 5%" award badge to Web sites it deems the most popular. It is also one of the oldest Web search guides online. Because it offers links and listings only to those sites it has reviewed, it is somewhat limited in scope. Similar to most search guides, it isn't a very good place to do a serious research query. However, it does offer an idea of some of the best places to find more information online and can therefore act as a good stating point. Its reviews, which are updated on a regular schedule, tend to be more creative (and just as accurate) than other reviews I've seen. One doesn't have to be boring to get one's point across online.

Title (or descriptor):	Magellan Internet Guide
Owner:	Excite, Inc.
URL (Web address):	`http://magellan.excite.com/`
Rating:	★★★

This search guide reviews and rates Web sites much like Point (see below) but is newer and, hence, smaller. It offers a mix of reviewed and nonreviewed Web sites in its database. Although I list it as a subject guide (and it bills itself as the "Internet Guide"), it is actually a search engine that allows you to search it by browsing through subjects. Its reviews are written by general staff writers who, as in Excite and Point, may have little or no specific knowledge or experience in reviewing and rating Web sites on any given topic. This is something you should be wary of—professionals in the field are not the persons rating professional sites in these guides. Its reviews are generally well written, but the reviews are undated. With no date available, readers have no way of knowing whether the information is timely and accurate.

Title (or descriptor):	Medical Matrix
Owner:	Medical Matrix, LLC
URL (Web address):	
	`http://www.medmatrix.org/_SPages/Psychiatry.asp`
Rating:	★★

Updated regularly, this is a peer-reviewed guide to a wide variety of medical resources online, including a section devoted to psychiatry. Each subcategory is arranged by Medical Subject Headings (MeSH), a medical standard for arranging information developed by the U.S. National Library of Medicine, and includes news, abstracts, reviews, articles, meeting reports, major resources, indices, reference documents, learning modules, practice guidelines, cases meetings, textbooks, diseases, forums, and patient education. Listings are relatively short and incomplete, and some were quite out-of-date. An internal search engine and logical layout of resources make navigation through the Matrix a breeze. Good for use mainly as a quick-start guide to the world of online medical resources.

Title (or descriptor):	Mental Health Net
Owner:	Mental Health Net & CMHC Systems, Inc.

URL (Web address):   `http://mentalhelp.net/`

Rating: ★★★★

Mental Health Net is an example of a field-specific search guide that I cofounded. It covers resources only within the mental health, psychological, and psychiatric fields. Because it limits itself to those professions and is maintained by a staff of professionals, it can be quite good about maintaining a comprehensive catalog of relevant resources. Unlike general-purpose guides, Mental Health Net offers large listings of professional and lay resources online in specific subcategories (e.g., cognitive, assessment, psychopharmacology, etc.) and disorders (e.g., major depression, anxiety, PTSD, etc.). Like other guides, it also has an internal search engine that searches within the Web site, to make it easier to find topics quickly. Mental Health Net uses a unique combination of software, human editors, and reader feedback to find, rate, and review the resources found within its database.

While I can't be completely neutral in evaluating this site, I believe there are a number of features that make Mental Health Net stand out. Not only are resources reviewed, but they are rated (much in the way I rate resources throughout this book). A number of additional databases are available on the site, including one that keeps track of the over 1,600 journal Web sites online. Others include a Clinicians Yellow Pages and a calendar of events, workshops, continuing education courses, and conferences for all disciplines. Mental Health Net also publishes its own quarterly refereed electronic journal, *Perspectives*, and is actively involved in many other professional areas online. These areas include providing a research mailing list for discussing online psychology and behavior, promoting the usefulness of self-help topics through discussion forums and the publication of two self-help books online, and developing online continuing education for mental health professionals. The Web site's more recent attempts at advertising and branding have been confusing and less successful.

Title (or descriptor):   Online Dictionary of Mental Health

Owner: Centre for Psychotherapeutic Studies,
University of Sheffield

URL (Web address):

    `http://www.shef.ac.uk/~psysc/psychotherapy/`

Rating: ★★

This is an eclectic offering from the Centre for Psychotherapeutic Studies, incorporating both the *Online Dictionary of Mental Health* and the *Online Dictionary of Ideas*. Basically replicating guides and resources already found on the Web, this guide allows both alphabetical and subject browsing and provides an internal search engine. Descriptions for many resources are provided. Nothing stands out about this resource except its unique inclusion of links to information and resources on philosophers and thinkers throughout history (through its *Online Dictionary of Ideas*). Some of its graphics seem amateurish and less than obvious in their meaning. North American users may find the site slow to load since it is located in the United Kingdom; European users will appreciate the site's proximity, however. The Guide to Psychotherapy is easy to navigate and logically arranged. Infrequently updated.

Title (or descriptor):	Open Directory Project
Owner:	Netscape
URL (Web address):	http://www.dmoz.org/
Rating:	★★★★

Billing itself as the "largest human-edited directory of the Web," it's not hard to see how it lives up to its reputation—over 17,000 of its volunteer editors are keeping track of over 1 million sites that the directory indexes. This is far more than the hundreds of editors Yahoo! employs, and ideally, leads not only to more diversity in the sites listed, but ultimately more sites listed. The volunteer editors only manage categories in which they are experienced. Because of its open, noncommercial nature, the Open Directory Project has the potential to be one of the largest and most interesting collaborative online projects in history. It has the best chance of being able to keep up with the Internet's enormous growth.

Title (or descriptor):	PsychREF—Resources in Psychology on the Internet
Owner:	LeMoyne College Psychology Department
URL (Web address):	http://www.psychref.com/
Rating:	★★★

Maintained by Vincent W. Hevern, SJ, PhD, PsychREF is a well designed and attractive offering oriented toward professionals within the mental health field. Extensive resources range from teaching topics in psychology, clinical and abnormal psychology, to specific disorders and specialty fields such as behavioral science and neuropsychology. I especially liked its clean layout, brief summaries, and proper attributions found for each resource. The drawbacks are its lack of an internal search engine to find resources more quickly and the large size of the resource files themselves, which will take most people a while to load.

Title (or descriptor):	Psych Web
Owner:	Russell A. Dewey, PhD
URL (Web address):	http://www.psychwww.com/
Rating:	★★★

Located in Georgia Southern University's Psychology Department, Russell Dewey developed one of the older and more popular online guides to mental health and psychology. Arranged in a topical hierarchy, resources are generally easy to find although an internal search engine for a site of this size would be appreciated. Unique contributions to the online world include the complete text of two classics, *The Interpretation of Dreams* (3rd edition) by Sigmund Freud and *Varieties of Religious Experience* by William James. The site not only hosts a wide variety of professional and lay resources, but also includes specific categories for psychology students, links to brochures and articles in psychology, and a psychology of religion section. All in all, Psych Web is a useful guide, which is updated regularly.

Title (or descriptor):	Yahoo!
Owner:	Yahoo!, Inc.
URL (Web address):	http://www.yahoo.com/
Rating:	★★★★

Easily the most popular and well known of the search guides, Yahoo! is also one of the oldest search methods available online. The reason Yahoo! has become and remained so popular is its ease-of-use, simple and fast-loading pages, and its ever-expanding database. Yahoo! staffers review each site listed, and award a set of sunglasses (considered one of the premier online awards) to the sites they deem the best. Yahoo! reviews Web sites for inclusion or exclusion within its catalog, but it doesn't provide actual reviews to sites it indexes. It relies on the individuals who submit their Web sites to provide a short, one-line description to include with their site if it ends up being listed in Yahoo!. Yahoo!'s criteria for inclusion into its guide are unclear, and some Web developers of perfectly good sites complain of not being included. But for an easy-to-navigate, general-purpose subject guide, this is still the best and largest online today. Even professionals will find much to explore on this site, which also offers the ability to customize your own search method. This allows you to receive personalized news summaries, sports scores, and other tidbits.

DOING THE LEGWORK FOR YOU: META-SEARCH ENGINES

The last category covered in this chapter is perhaps one of the most interesting developments online today and a portent of the future. Meta-search engines offer the ability to send a search query across all the search engines previously listed. The meta-search engine then intelligently collates the results, removing duplicatons and broken links. The downside to this wonderful technology is long wait times. Some search sites on the Web are more popular (and therefore slower to respond) than others. It can also be difficult at times to access the meta-search engine Web site itself, since these are becoming increasingly popular as they become better known among Web users.

Just because you're searching six or eight search engines at the same time doesn't mean you're more likely to get more relevant results, either. You're just saving yourself the hassle of having to visit the six Web sites yourself and do the same search six times. However, it is sometimes more productive to visit the sites individually because of the lack of uniformity of search tools of each engine. Meta-search engines can't be as specific or as powerful in their searches because not every search engine understands the same syntax (as discussed earlier).

One other caveat about these types of search engines. Some of them listed below may be somewhat experimental. While I have made every attempt to verify their existence and stability, by the time this book is published, some of these may have been superseded by others.

Title (or descriptor):   All-4-One

Owner: John E. Haag

URL (Web address):   `http://www.all4one.com/`
Rating: ★

Both All-4-One and SuperSearch (below) are not true meta-search engines. All they provide is an interface to the search engines they link to. In the case of All-4-One, the query is sent to only four search engines. While it may be somewhat convenient to send out a single set of search criteria (and cull through the results of all four engines at the same time), it's not a pretty thing to watch! It doesn't do any cross-checking to ensure the results are not repetitions from other search engines. (Inference Find and MetaCrawler both do this.) All-4-One also cannot check for bad links. Because each of the four search engine's own graphics need to load when you get your result back, it takes forever to see. I can't see any reason for using a service like this instead of the true meta-search engines.

Title (or descriptor):   Inference Find
Owner: Inference Corporation
URL (Web address):   `http://www.infind.com/`
Rating: ★★★★

Certainly one of the most intriguing of the meta-search engines, this one is also the fastest and most thorough I've used. Inference Find claims to be the first and only search tool that calls out in parallel all the best search engines on the Internet, merges the results, removes redundancies, and clusters the results into neat understandable groupings. It is the ability to do this last task—logically grouping its results—that makes Inference Find stand out from other meta-search engines. It also does an excellent job of removing duplicate links, so while a few duplications still pop up, most are automatically removed.

Inference Find queries six search engines on the Web: AltaVista, Excite, Infoseek, Lycos, Webcrawler, and Yahoo!. Each of these search engines is automatically called *in parallel,* and Inference Find retrieves the maximum number of results each engine will allow. Some engines will return 250 documents; some as few as 10. Other less-sophisticated meta-search engines (which are not reviewed here) may query each search engine in succession, which dramatically increases the time it takes to receive results. After Inference Find has retrieved the hundreds or thousands of results, it groups similar items together based on its own internal logic. Sometimes this works very well, and other times the clusterings it chooses are questionable. Usually, though, it does a pretty intelligent job and makes your task of sorting through the results much easier.

Title (or descriptor):   MetaCrawler
Owner: go2net, Inc.
URL (Web address):   http://www.go2net.com/
Rating: ★★★

MetaCrawler sends your queries to five search engines, which currently include AltaVista, Excite, Lycos, Webcrawler, Infoseek, Thunderstone, Looksmart, Direct Hit, and Yahoo!. MetaCrawler tends to be slower to respond than Inference Find, and the results are viewed in a standard rank order. Rank-ordering results makes less sense in this kind of searching, though, because typically there are so many results obtained. Inference Find's clustering approach seems to work much better. Originally developed by researchers for researchers at a university, MetaCrawler was one of the first parallel Web search engines of its kind (much like Lycos). But technology has advanced and threatens to leave MetaCrawler behind.

Both MetaCrawler and Inference Find offer the ability to utilize standard search operators (like the plus and minus signs). MetaCrawler offers a unique feature not available through Inference Find, which is the ability to specify where MetaCrawler should conduct its search. If you are only interested in finding information in a specific country, this is easily specified. MetaCrawler uses domain names (e.g., .com, .edu, .net) to categorize results, which I found to be less useful than Inference Find's broader grouping methods.

In an effort to stay ahead of the technology, MetaCrawler also offers a Java version of its search forum. (Java is an Internet-based computer programming language and different from the previously mentioned Javascript.) If you have a Java-enabled Web browser, MetaCrawler will display its status as it conducts your search, keeping you updated on what it's doing. The downside to using the Java interface is that the search will actually take longer to conduct the first time than the non-Java interface.

Title (or descriptor):   SavvySearch
Owner: Daniel Dreilinger
URL (Web address):   http://www.savvysearch.com/
Rating: ★★★★

The most interesting and useful aspect of this meta-search engine is the number of languages in which it's available (Français, Deutsch, Italiano, Português, Español, Nederlands, Norsk, Korean, Russian, Suomi, Esperanto, Svenska, Nihongo, and

Dansk). Like other meta-search engines, SavvySearch is designed to simultaneously send your query to multiple Internet search engines and return a complete set of rank-ordered results. Unlike other meta-search engines, SavvySearch can search over 200 search engines, guides, auctions, Usenet newsgroup archives, e-mail address directories, reference Web sites, and even software archives! You can request anywhere from 10 to 50 results from each engine that you query. SavvySearch also lets you restrict your searches to particular types of information (e.g., Web resources, people, and academic topics).

Title (or descriptor):	SuperSearch III
Owner:	Robert Olsson
URL (Web address):	`http://www.robtex.com/search.htm`
Rating:	★★

Like All-4-One above, this is not a true meta-search engine, but rather a simple interface to shuttle your query to a large number of search engines simultaneously. Unlike All-4-One, SuperSearch III doesn't limit you to just four search engines, but has over a dozen to choose from! It suffers from the same drawbacks as All-4-One, however, including extremely slow loading time of results (because of the graphics on each search engine's results page). It displays the results of each engine in tiny frames on one page. Needless to say, while it may be useful on a rare occasion, it is likely to be more annoying than helpful. Since it utilizes both frames and Javascript, you'll need a Javascript- and frames-enabled browser.

HOW TO FIND AND SEARCH DISCUSSION FORUMS: MAILING LISTS AND USENET NEWSGROUPS

There is no inherent advantage to searching for information in newsgroups or mailing lists, since most of these forums are simply ongoing conversations among many people. But you can use this type of search in a unique way. For example, you could search for individuals discussing a particular topic to find out where to go to join in on the discussion. Or you might use these tools to find another professional somewhere in the world who's interested in the same research questions (or clinical topics) as you are. Anything that anybody has ever written or contributed to a newsgroup or, sometimes, mailing lists, is stored—for a short time anyway. It's all available for your searching, allowing for vast communicative and collaborative possibilities!

The search engines listed in this section are for finding information on the Internet's discussion forums (Usenet newsgroups) or on specific mailing lists. Many of the search engines reviewed earlier also allow searching within Usenet newsgroups.

I have also listed a few services that help you *find* mailing lists and newsgroups. The software you use to read newsgroups also keeps a listing of all the current newsgroups. There is an advantage to using a subject guide in lieu of a search engine for simply finding a newsgroup or mailing list. These forums are typically more subject-specific, making it easier to locate an appropriate discussion. Such guides also generally offer a brief description of the newsgroup, whereas the software does not.

Most mailing lists' messages are not stored anywhere. This means you usually won't be able to find an archive of messages sent to that mailing list. This is actually quite a shame, because a lot of useful and meaningful discussion takes place in these forums—most of this is lost forever. For the few mailing lists that do keep archives, I will tell you how best to find those archives if they are on the Web. Some archives are found on the Web, while others can only be accessed through cryptic commands to the mailing list software. For the latter, the only sure method of finding out if an archive exists and how to access it is to contact the mailing list's owner. To help in this process, I have provided mailing lists owners' names and e-mail addresses in Chapter 6.

Resources below allow you to search for a specific subject found within a newsgroup, look for archives of mailing lists on the Web, find the name and address of a mailing list on a specific topic, or find a professional mailing list or newsgroup quickly.

Searching within Newsgroups

Title (or descriptor):	AltaVista
Owner:	AltaVista
URL (Web address):	`http://www.altavista.com/`
Rating:	★★★

That's right . . . That very powerful and useful Web search engine also allows you to search for information in newsgroups. Simply clisk on the "Usenet" link in the "Useful Tools" section. Use all the usual parameters and operators you would for a Web search on AltaVista. The one drawback to using AltaVista for this search, however, is that it only searches newsgroup articles for the past month or so. Anything written before that on the newsgroups won't be found by using this search method. A separate help section is available on AltaVista to search on fields specific to newsgroups.

Title (or descriptor):	Deja.com
Owner:	Deja.com, Inc.
URL (Web address):	`http://www.deja.com/`
Rating:	★★★★

The main alternative to AltaVista is Deja.com, and a better alternative it is. Deja.com was designed from the ground up to search only within newsgroups. So it has a lot of features and capabilities not found in typical search engines. For example, it allows you to specify a filter to help limit your searches (to one specific newsgroup, to a specified date range, etc.). Deja.com keeps its newsgroup articles in two databases—current and old. The default setting uses the current database, which includes the previous few weeks of articles. The old database includes articles since mid-1995. You can use Deja.com to do a much more thorough search of newsgroups than is possible with other search tools.

Deja.com has many other unique features as well. It allows you to browse through newsgroups, post to newsgroups, view a particular author's posting profile (e.g., what newsgroups they've posted to, how many of those articles are followups to other articles), and conduct a "power search" (an advanced search). This last feature is useful for conducting in-depth searches on subjects.

Searching for Archives of Mailing Lists on the Web

Title (or descriptor):	AltaVista
Owner:	AltaVista
URL (Web address):	`http://www.altavista.com/`
Rating:	★★

You can utilize almost any Web search engine to look for mailing list archives that are kept on the Web. But there is no reliable way to conduct a search on a mailing list through this method: The software that keeps the mailing list archives varies from site to site. One tip is to use the plus sign (+) in your search on the name of the list itself. For instance, one mailing list I administer is "Psychology of the Internet: Research and Theory" and the name of the list is simply "research." So your query might look like:

```
+psychology +Internet +research
```

You can also search for a mailing list by its name, by using quotes:

```
"Psychology of the Internet"
```

Searching for a Mailing List

Title (or descriptor):   List of Lists

Owner: Vivian Neou

URL (Web address):

```
http://www.catalog.com/vivian/interest-group-
search.html
```

Rating: ★

The List of Lists is one of the older collections of mailing lists online and unfortunately, its database is outdated and full of errors. I would not recommend using this site unless you have already tried one of the other methods for locating a mailing list.

Title (or descriptor):   Liszt

Owner: Liszt

URL (Web address):   http://www.liszt.com/

Rating: ★★★★

Liszt is the place to go when you want to find a mailing list on any topic under the sun. A large, comprehensive, and useful database of tens of thousands of mailing lists on hundreds of topics, it relies on a variety of methods to keep its database current and accurate. Much as search engines have software that traverses the Web looking for new and updated Web sites, Liszt has software that queries mailing list servers on the names of mailing lists hosted by them. This method ensures a relatively accurate and up-to-date listing, depending on how accurate those servers are. (A mailing list may still be in existence technically but may have no subscribers or no traffic on it, for instance.)

Liszt also can let individuals add new mailing lists to Liszt's database. Its searching capability is excellent and about as powerful as most regular search engines, handling most of the common options for limiting and expanding searches (see their "Options" file for full descriptions and examples.) Liszt currently has over 65,000 mailing lists cataloged in their database. Use their search engine rather than "Liszt Select" (a categorical browsing list somewhat like Yahoo!), because the latter gives you very few listings in almost every category.

Liszt's Web site is often slow, based on my experiences. This may just be an indication of how valuable and popular a resource this Web site has become. Liszt has a lot of graphics as well as banner ads, which can slow down access even further. But combining the use of my listing of mailing lists with Liszt will make it more than likely you will find a discussion group on a topic you're interested in.

Liszt also has drawbacks. Although it is a great way to find a list with its large database, it still relies heavily on mailing list owners to add new or updated information about their lists. This is a poor way of maintaining a large database: some of the addresses listed are out-of-date and invalid. For most lists, no further information is available other than how to subscribe and the list's name. Information provided often was nothing more than the mailing list's header (a technical, less-than-helpful file).

Searching for a Professional Mailing List or Newsgroup

Title (or descriptor):	Psych Central
Owner:	John M. Grohol, PsyD
URL (Web address):	`http://psychcentral.com/`
Rating:	★★★

In my humble opinion, Psych Central offers one of the better and more up-to-date listings of professional mailing lists and newsgroups in the areas of mental health, psychology, psychiatry, and social work. While not as comprehensive as Liszt, it is easier to use, allowing you to locate lists more quickly. Since the index is updated twice a month, it is also current and accurate. I would recommend checking out a guide like this first. Then, if you haven't found what you need, go wrestle search engines such as Liszt for the information.

PART

II

Getting Answers to Your Professional Questions

In this section of the book, I'll tell you how to find answers to commonly asked professional questions. Out of the hundreds of questions that have come to me via e-mail throughout the years, I've chosen some of the most interesting. Not only do I show you where to look online for these answers, but in most cases, I also tell you how I found this information in the first place. You can then conduct your own intelligent searches for information beyond that covered within this book.

3

Finding Disorders, Subspecialties, Clinical and Treatment Information Online

This chapter tells you where to find basic information online about mental disorders, diagnosis, treatment and subspecialty areas of professional interest. Such areas contain not only Web resources about alcoholism and substance abuse, neuropsychology, and trauma, but also social work, managed care, personality, and medication information.

As of this writing, there is no central Internet location for up-to-date, comprehensive treatment information; it is scattered throughout the online world. This is partly due to the multiple professions involved in the mental health field. While the lack of a central location may be disappointing at first, in truth it means that you can find a diversity of refereed opinions online from which to read and choose.

ARE DIAGNOSTIC CODES, CRITERIA, AND INFORMATION ONLINE FOR THE DSM-IV, ICD-9-CM, AND ICD-10?

It is very handy to have diagnostic categories, codes, and information on diagnoses available through online resources. Various Web sites, therefore, have made such information available at no cost to you. The *International Classification of Diseases* (ICD) is used widely except in the United States to diagnose and treat mental disorders. The latest version is the ICD-10, but the ICD-9-CM is still in common use. The *Diagnostic and Statistical Manual of Mental Disorders* (DSM) is utilized in the United States and elsewhere and is published by the American Psychiatric Association (APA). Through the "fair use" provision of U.S. copyright court decisions, parts of it have been made available online. The APA apparently has little intention of putting the entire manual online, though, because it is a primary income source for the association (much as PsycLIT and PsychINFO are income sources for the American Psychological Association). Understanding the economics behind organizations helps us understand why some reference material and databases are online when others are not.

Title (or descriptor):	Diagnostic Related Groups (DRGs)
Owner:	Health Services Research Group
URL (Web address):	
	`http://www.fec.newcastle.edu.au/hsrg/hypertexts/andrg.html`
Rating:	★★★

Need to look up a diagnostic related group code? This quick index of DRGs is one page long and very easy to use.

Title (or descriptor):	DSM-IV Diagnoses and Codes
Owner:	Dr. Bob's Virtual En-psych-lopedia (Robert Hsiung, MD)
URL (Web address):	`http://www.dr-bob.org/tips/dsm4a.html` (Alphabetical listing)

URL (Web address):	`http://www.dr-bob.org/tips/dsm4n.html` (Ordered by diagnostic code)
Rating:	★★★

Straightforward presentation of the DSM-IV listing of mental disorders, either al-phabetized by disorder or arranged by diagnostic code.

Title (or descriptor):	ICD-9-CM
Owner:	National Center for Health Statistics
URL (Web address):	

`http://www.cdc.gov/nchswww/datawh/ftpserv/ftpicd9/`
`ftpicd9.htm`
(Rich text format [RTF] file)

Owner:	Health Services Research Group
URL (Web address):	

`http://www.fec.newcastle.edu.au/hsrg/`
`hypertexts/icd9cm.html`
(Diagnostic codes only)

Owner:	Division of Medical Informatics, University of California–Davis
URL (Web address):	

`http://www-informatics.ucdmc.ucdavis.edu/`
`CodingHome.htm`

Rating:	★★
Owner:	Central Office on ICD9-CM
URL (Web address):	`http://www.icd-9-cm.org/`
Rating:	★★
Owner:	Yaki Technologies
URL (Web address):	`http://www.eicd.com/`
Rating:	★★★

Need an ICD-9-CM code? The first two of the above sites will allow you to find a diagnostic code, although the first resource, has only a very large RTF (rich text for-mat, readable by most word processing software) file; you'd have to download it first in order to display it. The second site, which is much more useful, offers the complete set of ICD-9-CM codes online. It is completely text based and except for the length of some of the pages, should load relatively quickly. The third site in this listing provides information about coding manuals and ICD9-CM itself. The fourth site listed provides a keyword- or code-searchable database of the ICD9-CM.

Title (or descriptor):   ICD-10 (Chapter V(F))

Owner: Medical University of Lübeck, Department of Psychiatry
                                & Fachhochschule Lübeck, Germany

URL (Web address):
    `http://www.informatik.fh-luebeck.de/icd/welcome.html`

Owner: Internet Mental Health

URL (Web address):
    `http://www.mentalhealth.com/` (by disorder)

Owner: World Health Organization

URL (Web address):   `http://www.who.int/whosis/icd10/`

Rating: ★★★

The first ICD-10 resource listed is a work-in-progress. When first visited, they had only completed the first two categories of the ICD-10's mental health section. Little progress had been noted in subsequent visits. Internet Mental Health hosts complete ICD-10 descriptions of 52 mental disorders on its site and is the best place to look for such information. The World Health Organization's site not only offers the complete categorical codes for the ICD-10's mental health section, but also ordering information for the ICD-10 itself.

Title (or descriptor):   Mental Disorders—Symptoms & Treatment

Owner: Mental Health Net & CMHC Systems, Inc.

URL (Web address):   `http://mentalhelp.net/disorders/`

Rating: ★★

Mental Health Net houses symptom lists summarized from the DSM-IV symptom criteria. These symptom lists are in a different format and may not list all of the criteria for each disorder (e.g., often missing is the caveat that the disorder may not be caused by a preexisting medical condition). Also missing from these lists are more in-depth descriptions of each of the disorders.

HOW CAN I FIND UP-TO-DATE TREATMENT INFORMATION ONLINE?

There are places online where you can go to keep up with the latest interesting developments within the treatment field. There are two main types of resources: (1) those that directly provide you with treatment information through peer-reviewed research studies, articles, or news; and (2) those that can help you locate such research studies, articles, or news resources. Research articles and studies generally appear only in professionals journals, newspapers, or newsletters. Locating professional journals online to h 'p track down treatment information, among many other uses, is described in Chapter 9.

Additional information resources include a number of online news services. News articles tend to be more watered-down and won't provide much useful content, but they may provide guidance on where to find additional information. Such news articles or press releases can also make you aware of development or government approval of new psychotropic medications. You can also use a search engine to find specific treatment information, using the steps outlined in Chapter 2.

Finding Clinical Information Directly on the Web

Title (or descriptor):	Internet Mental Health
Owner:	Phillip W. Long, MD
URL (Web address):	`http://www.mentalhealth.com/`
Rating:	★★★★

A general place to find treatment information is Internet Mental Health, which offers research citations and suggested bibliographies for many mental disorders. This Web site is a virtual encyclopedia of information related to mental disorders, their possible causes, and some treatments. It offers a relatively short list of links to other

Web sites, organized by category and carrying "popularity ratings" (see box). Under certain disorders (the information available, such as diagnostic criteria, treatment guidelines, bibliographies, research abstracts, etc., varies greatly), readers will also find the ICD-10 criteria for the disorder, as well as Dr. Long's own diagnostic criteria for each. This latter section is of questionable value to most professionals, since we all conceptualize disorders quite differently. Furthermore, in the United States the DSM is the book used to diagnose mental disorders in most hospitals, institutions, and universities.

Internet Mental Health is vast, and is filled with tidbits from the "Harvard Mental Health Letter," "Medical Post," and other publications. It links to publications put out by the National Institute of Mental Health and others on disorders as well. It is one of the top mental health sites online today because of its cornucopia of knowledge on mental disorders. Readers will probably find some interesting and useful information on specific disorders nearly every time they visit the site.

Internet Mental Health is very much medically oriented and talks at great length about various medications and their use with some mental disorders. But be careful about taking the resource as a peer-reviewed and general mental health guide, because the information comes from a lone psychiatrist in Canada. While I didn't find anything overtly harmful in his general treatment guidelines, I did find his omission of social science research in general (which would not support some of his treatment recommendations) somewhat disturbing. The site itself is very large but lacks any search options. Its reliance on frames (dividing the Web browser's screen into smaller sections) to lay out information is unfortunate. For people who use small screens, this choice will make the Web site difficult to read and navigate. Its reliance on numerous but tiny graphics can also make the site slow to load.

Title (or descriptor):	Lifescape.com
Owner:	Lifescape.com
URL (Web address):	http://www.lifescape.com/
Rating:	★★

A newcomer to the world of online mental health, lifescape.com nonetheless brings a wealth of free, in-depth content on mental health, relationship, parenting skills, and aging issues. Covering major mental disorders, content comes from various academic institutions, such as the University of Florida's Brain Institute. In addition to

AWARDS, BADGES, AND POPULARITY RATINGS ON THE WEB

"Popularity ratings" for various sites are featured on Internet Mental Health and on other places on the Web. Such ratings are one way Web sites try to distinguish themselves in a crowd. The myriad Web "badges" or "awards," handed out by dozens of different (and often competing) Web reviewers is an example of a similar phenomenon. Bestowing an "award badge" for a popular Web site goes back to the early days of the World Wide Web. One young upstart company called Point (now owned by Lycos) was looking for a way to make a name for itself online and ultimately become more marketable as a company. The Point "Top 5% of the Web" award badges were an instant success when they were first launched. They garnered Point the expected publicity and increased the volume of visitors to its own Web site. But this started an "award" phenomenon that has resulted in the creation of hundreds of award badges. The more awards given out, the less meaningful they—as a whole—become.

How strong a recommendation is such an award and how are they really chosen? Point relied on the badge's name ("Top 5% of the Web") to obtain its respectability, rather than a top-drawer editorial staff to do the actual reviews and ratings. The badge's claim of "Top 5%" should not be taken literally. It would be impossible to actually conduct such a rating service without in-depth statistical analyses of popularity, usability, quality, etc. Point instead relies on an editorial staff to make the ratings determinations. They may just as well be the top 2%, the top 10%, or the top 30% of the Web. There's no actual way of measuring such a percentage.

Internet Mental Health and other Web sites are beginning to look for additional ways to "prove" their uniqueness online, in much the same way. One way to determine a Web site's popularity is by counting the number of links that point to that site. The number of links to any given Web site, not including the site's own pages, can be estimated using the AltaVista and Infoseek search engines. These derived "popularity ratings" are inaccurate and misleading for a number of reasons: (1) Search engines do not index all of the World Wide Web; it is not clear exactly how inclusive they really are. The amount of the Web indexed by each search engine also varies widely. (2) Some search engines, like AltaVista, are dynamic. This means that they are constantly changing (new entries are being added and deleted all the time), so the numbers returned will never be reliable. (3) Web sites themselves are dynamic and may change their Web addresses from time to time as they move (just like you change your home address from time to time). They may also offer different Web addresses that go to the same site. Popularity ratings are inaccurate and invalid if they don't address all of these concerns.

I suggest you forgo putting any serious weight into such ratings at the present time, until search engines can become more accurate in their numbers and are cross-validated with one another.

offering coverage of mental disorders' symptoms and treatments, the Website provides large sections covering recovery and addiction issues; life events such as mar-
riage, having children, and growing older; and learning life skills, such as improving
coping skills, improving communication at work or at home, and more.

Title (or descriptor):	Mental Disorders: Symptoms and Treatment
Owner:	Mental Health Net & CMHC Systems, Inc.
URL (Web address):	`http://mentalhelp.net/disorders/`
Rating:	★★

A subset of the large Mental Health Net site, this listing is notable for its relatively
more balanced view of treatment options open to people who suffer from a mental
disorder. It won't tell professionals information they don't already know, for the
most part, nor will it provide them with peer-reviewed articles or article summaries
about new and upcoming treatments. But for a broad-based overview of treatment
for many particular disorders, this site does have a fair amount of information.

Using Guides to Find Additional Clinical Information Online

Unlike the two sites reviewed in the above section, the Web sites below simply link to other online resources that may provide additional clinical information on a wide range of subjects.

Title (or descriptor):	Dr. Bob's Mental Health Links
Owner:	Robert Hsiung, MD
URL (Web address):	`http://www.dr-bob.org/mental.html`
Rating:	★★

An infrequently updated, single page of mental health links that may be of benefit to
professionals. Subcategory listings include psychiatry departments, university student counseling centers and organizations.

Title (or descriptor):	Cognitive & Psychological Sciences
Owner:	Ruediger Oehlmann

URL (Web address):

`http://www-psych.stanford.edu/cogsci.html`

Rating: ★★

A very large, but plain, listing of online resources in the cognitive and psychological sciences. Includes everything from academic programs, organizations, discussion forums, and journals to software, announcement lists, and related Web links. When last visited, the site hadn't been updated in nearly 2 years, minimizing its accuracy and usefulness.

Title (or descriptor):	Hanover College Psychology Department
Owner:	John Krantz, PhD
URL (Web address):	`http://psych.hanover.edu/`
Rating:	★★★

This site hosts a great deal of psychology information. Included is a journal index, a listing of other psychology departments, an index to psychological societies, tutorials in psychology, links to software archives and other psychology-related sites. A good resource for college-level psychology courses.

Title (or descriptor):	Knowledge Exchange Network
Owner:	U.S. Department of Health and Human Services, Substance Abuse and Mental Health Services Administration, and the Center for Mental Health Services
URL (Web address):	`http://www.mentalhealth.org/`
Rating:	★★★★

An excellent U.S. government-sponsored Web site devoted to a wide range of mental health issues. The site includes links to mental health and substance abuse databases, a wealth of statistical data, as well as an extensive list of publications (many of which are available for downloading directly from the Web site, or may be ordered from the

Web site). Site design suffers from cryptic graphics on the home page, which is also difficult to read.

Title (or descriptor):   Medical Matrix–Psychiatry
Owner: Healthtel Corporation
URL (Web address):
   `http://www.medmatrix.org/_SPages/Psychiatry.asp`
Rating: ★★

Reviewed in-depth in Chapter 2, this site hosts a select list of psychiatric resources with brief descriptions.

Title (or descriptor):   MedWeb
Owner: Emory University Health Sciences Center Library
URL (Web address):   `http://www.medweb.emory.edu`
Rating: ★★

Although its interface has improved, MedWeb as a directory still lacks the organization and refinement found in other online directories. Hundreds of links are listed in alphabetical order in broad categories. The descriptions provided are brief and often uninformative (and sometimes inaccurate). The descriptions also lack information on when the site was last reviewed or when it was added to the directory, so the reader has no idea of how often the directory is updated. A partner Web site, Med-WebPlus (`http://www.medwebplus.com/`) seeks to build upon MedWeb's architecture, and so suffers from the same problems.

Title (or descriptor):   Mental Health Net–Professional Resources
Owner: Mental Health Net & CMHC Systems, Inc.
URL (Web address):   `http://mentalhelp.net/prof.htm`
Rating: ★★★★

Reviewed in-depth in Chapter 2, this catalog of online resources is one of the most comprehensive subject guides in the field.

Title (or descriptor):	Psych Web
Owner:	Russell A. Dewey, PhD
URL (Web address):	http://www.psychwww.com/
Rating:	★★★

Reviewed in-depth in Chapter 2. Extensive lists of links to other mental health and psychological resources make this a good place to start a search for treatment and clinical information.

Finding Treatment Information through a Search Engine

You can use a search engine (see also Chapter 2) to find references to articles or online documents that contain the actual treatment information. I'll use a simple example (treatment techniques for posttraumatic stress disorder) to guide us through this section. You may substitute nearly any disorder (e.g., depression, panic attacks, etc.) or treatment technique (EMDR, relaxation exercises, cognitive restructuring, hypnosis, NLP, etc.) to get similar results. I will use AltaVista (http://www.altavista.digital.com/), since it's my search engine of choice. Here's a couple of search terms I used in my search:

```
"treatment of PTSD"
"treatment of posttraumatic stress disorder"
"PTSD treatment"
"posttraumatic stress disorder treatment"
+PTSD +"new treatment"
```

You'll want to use quotation marks as noted, since these are specific phrases we're searching. (Note that there is no space between the plus sign and the quotation mark in the last example.) And since these are all different phrases, they will yield slightly different search results. You can probably think of a few others to try as well, if these don't provide you with the necessary information. We're in luck with this search, however. The third and fifth searches yield a lot of the same results, a few of which seem to be what we're looking for about treatment of PTSD.

Using one of the methods discussed above, whether it be looking through journal listings, looking through the journals themselves from time to time, using search engines, or keeping track of health-related topics through news-oriented sites, you should be able to stay on top of the latest medical, health, and mental health developments in the treatment field. I would explore all of these options and find one that is reliable and works best for you. As with most things in life, there is no one "right" answer, only myriad competing but equally useful ones. Try them out and find the one right for you—the one that fits within your online habits and skills.

Keeping Up-to-Date with Online News Services

There are a few news services you can search and/or visit on a regular basis to keep abreast of the latest treatment developments. These news sites generally offer press releases and tidbits of information, which may or may not help the practicing clinician. If nothing else, they can keep the professional on top of the kind of "news" the general public is reading about mental health disorders and issues. This may be invaluable the next time a client walks into your office and asks, "So what do you think about that study announced yesterday that mental disorders are all biological?" You can become more prepared to answer such questions if you know the kinds of information that is being publicly disseminated. Reviewed below are the few that I recommend and visit regularly. "Access restrictions," found in some descriptions below, note any type of registration process and/or fee required before you can access the information found on that Web site.

Title (or descriptor):	CNN Health Section
Owner:	CNN
URL (Web address):	`http://www.cnn.com/HEALTH/`
Rating:	★★★

The health section is updated daily with health and mental health-related stories.

Title (or descriptor):	drkoop.com
Owner:	drkoop.com

URL (Web address):	`http://www.drkoop.com/news/`
Rating:	★★★

Combine a solid newsfeed with a talented team of health writers and editors and you get an informative news section updated daily.

Title (or descriptor):	Medscape
Owner:	Medscape, Inc.
URL (Web address):	`http://www.medscape.com/`
URL (Web address):	
	`http://www.medscape.com/Home/News/Medscape-News.html`
Rating:	★★★
Access restrictions:	Registration required, free

Medscape, as its name implies, is oriented toward physicians and medical topics, but it carries a fair amount of information relevant to the field of psychology and mental health in its "Psychiatry" section.

Title (or descriptor):	NewsPage
Owner:	Individual, Inc.
URL (Web address):	`http://www.newspage.com/`
Rating:	★★★

Like other news services, NewsPage has a general "Healthcare" area, which is then further divided into additional subcategories of information. Under "Clinical Areas," you will find a "Psychiatry & Psychology" category. News stories in this category are often nothing more than press releases from pharmaceutical companies or some U.S. government agency.

Title (or descriptor):	Reuters Health
Owner:	Reuters, Inc.
URL (Web address):	`http://www.reutershealth.com/`
Rating:	★★★
Access restrictions:	Registration required; free and subscriptions sections

Although mainly oriented toward general health and medical topics, Reuters often publishes relevant and useful clinical information on mental disorders. News briefs are updated daily. Reuters Medical News, a subsection of the site oriented toward healthcare professionals, is available for an annual subscription.

Title (or descriptor):	USA Today
Owner:	USA Today
URL (Web address):	

`http://www.usatoday.com/life/health/health.htm`

Rating: ★★★

This Web site includes daily news, as well as in-depth reports, such as *USA Today*'s objective look at the use of electroconvulsive therapy (ECT) as a treatment for depression.

WHERE CAN I FIND CLINICAL INFORMATION ONLINE IN SUBSPECIALTY AREAS?

Hundreds of professionals maintain Web sites devoted to specific professional topics, ranging from alcohol resources and neuropsychology, to managed care and dealing with childhood trauma. Many other Web sites are maintained by government or academic organizations. The authors of these sites have put considerable resources and effort into providing not just information about their particular organization or interests, but also about a wide range of clinical and research topics. Most of these sites are of high quality (or I wouldn't bother listing them here) and are relatively stable. This means you can visit them and will probably find useful information, pointers to additional resources in that topic area (both online and in the real world), and you can trust that the information is reasonably accurate.

Most of the resources for specific areas listed next in this chapter have been gathered from the various large indexes (found in Chapter 2 and earlier in this chapter). You may use such indexes, search engines, and search guides to find other specific sites on areas covered below or other topics of interest. The balance of this chapter is just a small sampling of the hundreds of useful and valuable Web sites maintained by professionals for professionals.

Adler, Freud, Jung, Personality, and Psychoanalysis Online

Title (or descriptor):   Classical Adlerian Psychology

Owner: Henry T. Stein, PhD

URL (Web address):

`http://ourworld.compuserve.com/homepages/hstein/`

Rating: ★★★

A robust site on Adlerian psychology, including dozens of articles on theory, philosophy, theology, and practice. It offers biographical information on Adler and others in a simple but well-designed site, which is updated frequently.

Title (or descriptor):   FreudNet

Owner: Abraham A. Brill Library of the New York Psychoanalytic Institute

URL (Web address):   `http://www.interport.net/nypsan/`

Rating: ★★★

A great deal about Sigmund Freud and psychoanalysis may be discovered on this solid Web site.

Title (or descriptor):   C. G. Jung Home Page

Owner: Donald Williams, LPC

URL (Web address):   `http://www.cgjung.com/`

Rating: ★★★

Everything about Jung, including a glossary of Jungian terms, abstracts, articles, and links to many other analytic and Jungian resources.

Title (or descriptor):   Personality and Consciousness

Owner: Eric Pettifor

URL (Web address):   `http://www.wynja.com/personality/`

Rating: ★★★★

An excellent site devoted to discussing the major theorists in personality psychology, including Alfred Adler, Sigmund Freud, Carl Jung, George Kelly, Abraham Maslow, Carl Rogers, B. F. Skinner, and Charles T. Tart. The Web site offers not only their respective theories and philosophies on psychotherapy, but recommends related and worthwhile books.

Title (or descriptor):   Psychoanalysis

Owner: Wolfgang Albrecht

URL (Web address):

    `http://userpage.fu-berlin.de/~albrecht/psa.html`

Rating: ★★

A page full of psychoanalysis-related links and resources.

Alcoholism and Substance Abuse Online

Title (or descriptor):   Dual Diagnosis Website

Owner: Kathleen Sciacca

URL (Web address):   `http://www.erols.com/ksciacca/`

Rating: ★★★

With over a half-dozen articles about the treatment of dually diagnosed patients (substance or alcohol abuse with an existing mental disorder), a bibliography, links to other online resources, a discussion forum, and an interactive chat area, this is a well-designed, informative site.

Title (or descriptor):   Join Together

Owner: Join Together

URL (Web address):	`http://www.jointogether.org/`
Rating:	★★★★

One of the premier sites online today for alcohol, substance abuse, and gun violence information, legislative alerts, resources, news, and updates. A well-designed and attractive site makes finding information (including news headlines, grants, and community organizations) on alcohol, substance abuse, and drug violence easy.

Title (or descriptor):	PrevLine: National Clearinghouse for Alcohol and Drug Information
Owner:	Center for Substance Abuse Prevention, Substance Abuse and Mental Health Services Administration, and Center for Substance Abuse Treatment
URL (Web address):	`http://www.health.org/`
Rating:	★★★★

In a crowded field of excellent substance abuse resources online directed toward professionals, PrevLine still manages to stand out. Includes fact sheets, research news and updates, and a wealth of online resource guides. A powerful search engine makes any topic easy to find, and the pleasant, consistent look of the site makes it easy to navigate.

Title (or descriptor):	Substance Abuse and Mental Health Services Administration
Owner:	Substance Abuse and Mental Health Services Administration (SAMHSA)
URL (Web address):	`http://www.samhsa.gov/`
Rating:	★★★★

This site provides a starting point to jump to a number of important government resources related to not only substance abuse but mental health in general. These include the Center for Mental Health Services (CMHS), the Center for Substance
Abuse Prevention (CSAP), the Center for Substance Abuse Treatment, the National
Clearinghouse for Alcohol and Drug Information (PrevLine, above), and the
National Mental Health Services Knowledge Exchange Network (KEN). Reports,
data, statistical information, grants, and further resources may be found at each of
these sites.

Title (or descriptor):	Web of Addictions
Owner:	Andrew L. Homer, PhD, and Dick Dillon
URL (Web address):	`http://www.well.com/user/woa/`
Rating:	★★★

A large, comprehensive site where information on drug and addiction topics is easily
found. A global listing of fact sheets on addictions residing on over a dozen different
Web servers around the world is especially invaluable. A meeting and conference calendar and links to other addiction resources online, such as Alcoholics Anonymous
and lots of recovery-oriented sites, are also available.

Forensic Psychiatry and the Law Online

Title (or descriptor):	Psychiatry & the Law
Owner:	James F. Hooper, MD, University of Alabama and the Alabama Department of Mental Health and Mental Retardation
URL (Web address):	`http://bama.ua.edu/~jhooper/`
URL (Web address):	`http://mentalhelp.net/law/`
Rating:	★★★

A very large and well-maintained resource of law decisions related to mental health,
psychiatry, and psychology.

Managed Care Online

Title (or descriptor):	Policy Information Exchange (PIE) Online
Owner:	Missouri Institute of Mental Health (MIMH)

URL (Web address):   `http://www.pie.org/`

Rating: ★★★

This service acts as a central clearinghouse for mental health and behavioral health-care policy data, information, legislative and policy updates, and press and news releases. Links and news are regularly updated, and include updates of legislative developments on both the federal and state levels. A searchable calendar of related conferences and events is available, as is a literature search service (for a fee) through the MIMH library. PIE Online's main database is fully searchable, and the site is easy to navigate. The site unfortunately lacks information about PIE's purpose and history.

Title (or descriptor):   Psychotherapy Finances Online

Owner: Psychotherapy Finances

URL (Web address):   `http://www.psyfin.com/`

Rating: ★★★

Although largely designed to help sell new subscriptions to their two publications, *Psychotherapy Finances* and *Managed Care Strategies*, this site provides numerous news updates every month from each of these newsletters. The publisher also offers weekly-updated news links, the table of contents of each newsletter online, and hosts a discussion forum and provider directory on the site. This is a growing site which provides some good business resources for behavioral health providers.

Medications and Psychopharmacology References Online

Title (or descriptor):   drkoop.com

Owner: drkoop.com

URL (Web address):

      `http://www.drkoop.com/hcr/drugstore/interactions/`

Rating: ★★

An overly complicated user-interface makes it sometimes difficult to actually get information from this online drug database. One of its key features is the ability to check drug interactions by entering in more than one drug name, separated by commas. Drug reports include indications, contraindications, precautions while taking the medication, and possible adverse side effects.

Title (or descriptor):   HealthAnswers.com

Owner: HealthAnswers.com

URL (Web address):   `http://www.healthanswers.com/`

Rating: ★★★

HealthAnswers provides general health information geared mostly toward consumers. Simply type the name of a drug (brand or generic name, but no misspellings) into the database and you will receive informative reports include indications, contraindications, proper dosing, precautions while taking the medication, and possible adverse side effects.

Title (or descriptor):   *The Merck Manual of Diagnosis and Therapy*

Owner: Merck & Co, Inc.

URL (Web address):   `http://www.merck.com/`

Rating: ★★★

Sections of the venerable Merck Manual are available for free reading online. While not specifically a psychopharmacology book, it does offer some treatment guidelines and recommendations for all the major mental disorders. It is also a good overall psychiatric resource for mental health professionals to understand more about mental disorders in general.

Title (or descriptor):   Pharmaceutical Information Network (PharmInfoNet)

Owner: VirSci Corporation

URL (Web address):   `http://pharminfo.com/`

Rating: ★★★★

A very good reference guide to medications, full of drug references, frequently asked questions, (FAQs), and questions answered by a staff of experts. This Web site also includes articles archived from the newsgroup, `sci.med.pharmacy`. The Web site is large and extensive, offering a handful of their own publications, discussion forums and specific "disease centers" (including one on mental health). The search engine could use some improvement to help list and categorize its results more effectively.

Title (or descriptor):	Psychopharmacology & Drug References
Owner:	Mental Health Net
URL (Web address):	`http://mentalhelp.net/guide/pro22.htm`
Rating:	★★

Not a drug reference in itself, but an index of currently available drug and psychopharmacology information online. Arranged by drug name (generic and brand), it provides links to a variety of online databases maintained by different Web sites for each medication. This allows you to compare information and see how opinions and thoughts about prescribing a drug may differ. Most reference information includes indications, side effects, and typical dosing levels for adults.

Title (or descriptor):	Psychopharmacology Tips
Owner:	Robert Hsiung, MD
URL (Web address):	`http://www.dr-bob.org/tips/`
Rating:	★★

Offers a wealth of knowledge to professionals looking for some of the lore about how best to prescribe psychotropic medications. Arranged according to types of medications, as well as problem areas, this site is relatively easy to use. Information found here is rarely updated any longer. The tips were originally drawn by Dr. Hsiung from the psychopharmacology professional mailing list. The addition of an internal search engine makes finding the "tips" much easier than by having to browse through the Web site.

Title (or descriptor):	RxList
Owner:	Neil Sandow, PharmD
URL (Web address):	`http://www.rxlist.com/`
Rating:	★★★★

A complete reference of over 4,000 drugs available for searching. The results give only the brand name, generic name, and class of drug. The "Top 200 Prescriptions" are available with generic prescribing information. Professional and growing, this is usually a reliable and stable source of basic medication information.

Neurophysiology, Neuropsychology, Neuroscience, and Biofeedback Online

Title (or descriptor):	Association for Applied Psychophysiology and Biofeedback
Owner:	Association for Applied Psychophysiology and Biofeedback
URL (Web address):	http://www.aapb.org/
Rating:	★★★

General information can be found on this Web site on biofeedback, clinical psychophysiology, and links to related resources online.

Title (or descriptor):	Books and Articles on the Brain & Neurophysiology
Owner:	William H. Calvin
URL (Web address):	http://www.WilliamCalvin.com/
Rating:	★★★

A large home page (which will take most computers a long time to load) offers a confusing array of choices. But many of the books William Calvin has written over the years on the brain, evolution, and future directions may be found here. Not just to purchase, mind you, but to read the full text of these books online.

Title (or descriptor):	Neuropsychology Central
Owner:	Jeff Browndyke
URL (Web address):	http://www.neuropsychologycentral.com/
Rating:	★★

A site largely made up of links to a great deal of neuropsychology resources online. The site's content is often eclipsed by its design, however, especially with its large home page graphics (which will take most computers a long time to load). Categories include assessment, geriatric, forensic, neuroimaging, treatment, and cognitive resources, among many others. Online discussion forums are also provided.

Title (or descriptor):	Neurosciences on the Internet
Owner:	Neil A. Busis, MD
URL (Web address):	`http://www.neuroguide.com/`
Rating:	★★★★

Offering a searchable database as well as extensive resources about the neurosciences, neuropsychology, and neuropsychiatry. The resources are well categorized and easy to find, and an internal search engine is included. The site is updated regularly with new resources and links to valuable information. Three international mirror sites are also available.

Title (or descriptor):	Neuroscience Web Search
Owner:	Fred K. Lenherr, PhD
URL (Web address):	

`http://tamora.acsiom.org/nsr/neuro_new.html`

Rating:	★★★

This amazing Web site contains a full-text index of over 130,000 Web pages related to neuroscience. "Neuroscience," as used here, is broadly defined. While the site isn't much to look at, it worked very well in my use of it.

Posttraumatic Stress Disorder and Trauma Resources Online

Title (or descriptor):	National Center for PTSD
Owner:	National Center for PTSD, U.S. Department of Veterans Affairs
URL (Web address):	`http://www.dartmouth.edu/dms/ptsd/`
Rating:	★★★★

A simple but accessible site for clinical and research information on posttraumatic stress disorder (PTSD). The PILOTS database ("Published International Literature on Traumatic Stress") is also maintained here. This database includes over 11,000 article titles and abstracts on trauma-related literature. National Center Fact Sheets available on this site offer information on selected aspects of PTSD, mainly for laypeople.

Title (or descriptor):	Trauma Information Pages
Owner:	David Baldwin, PhD
URL (Web address):	`http://www.trauma-pages.com/`
Rating:	★★★★

Updated regularly, this site focuses primarily on emotional trauma and traumatic stress, including PTSD. Details not only the possible causes and treatments of trauma, but also includes extensive lists of additional online resources in the trauma field.

Title (or descriptor):	Trauma Treatment Manual
Owner:	Ed Schmookler, PhD
URL (Web address):	
	`http://users.lanminds.com/~eds/manual.html`
Rating:	★★

An online treatment manual that gives professionals an overview of trauma treatment from one psychologist's viewpoint. Includes treatment guidelines and examples.

School Psychology and Teaching Resources Online

Title (or descriptor):	School Psychology Resources Online
Owner:	Sandy Steingart
URL (Web address):	`http://www.schoolpsychology.net/`
Rating:	★★★

An excellent compendium of resources for school psychology, including resource lists of common disorders and problems studied in this field.

Title (or descriptor):	Teaching Clinical Psychology
Owner:	John Suler

URL (Web address):

    `http://www.rider.edu/users/suler/tcp.html`

Rating: ★★★

A great deal of information may be found on this well-constructed site about teaching clinical psychology, including in-class exercises, projects, suggested course syllabi, and reading materials. Essays and links to other related resources round out this site.

Social Work and Social Psychology Resources Online

Title (or descriptor): Clinical Social Work Homepage

Owner: Pat McClendon, MSSW, CSW

URL (Web address): `http://www.ClinicalSocialWork.com/`

Rating: ★★

Articles of interest to social workers and assorted mental health resources, all of which are updated regularly, make this a good page to visit.

Title (or descriptor): Social Psychology Network

Owner: Scott Plous, PhD

URL (Web address): `http://www.socialpsychology.org/`

Rating: ★★★

Provides a variety of links to psychology organizations, U.S. schools with psychology PhD programs, and social psychology topics of the day.

Title (or descriptor): Social Work Access Network (SWAN)

Owner: College of Social Work at the University of South Carolina

URL (Web address): `http://www.sc.edu/swan/`

Rating: ★★★★

An excellent resource for social workers, offering resources and links to associations and additional, general social work information.

Statistical Help Online

Title (or descriptor):	SurfStat Australia
Owner:	Department of Statistics, The University of Newcastle—Australia

URL (Web address):

`http://surfstat.newcastle.edu.au/surfstat/`

Rating: ★★★★

SurfStat is a very nicely constructed general statistics resource and tutorial, providing all the basics of statistical analysis. Both framed and unframed versions are available from the above URL. Practice exercises and links to other statistical online resources are also available. A great online starting point for statistical information.

4

Locating Employment Opportunities through the Web

At one time or another, most of us seek new employment opportunities. It may be because we're moving for family reasons, or just looking for a change of pace, or we've been "downsized" out of a job. Going online is an excellent place to begin your search for a new job. There are dozens of large and useful employment databases online today, as well as a few hidden gems, which are a bit more difficult to find.

As with treatment information, there is no central online clearinghouse that lists all the available jobs for all mental health–related professions. You will, therefore, have to do some jumping around and visit a number of Web sites to ensure a thorough search. This situation is unlikely to change in the near future because of the vast variety of competing interests in listing employment opportunities, as well as the great number of differences among professions, which keeps such listings as scattered in the real world.

HOW DO I FIND JOB OPPORTUNITIES IN MENTAL HEALTH ONLINE?

Begin your search with an employment guide; a human-compiled collection of employment-related Web sites. Employment guides contain listings of databases for various online employment classified ads. Then select and visit the most relevant databases to see the actual employment ads themselves. I recommend two broad job guides to get you started; one specific to the mental health field and the other more general. Alternatively, you could go directly to one of the employment and career databases that I also list. It was through the employment guides that I discovered these services. This list is by no means comprehensive. I have, however, tried to choose from among the oldest, largest, and most interesting sites available.

Searching the Employment Guides

Title (or descriptor):	Open Directoy Project: Business: Jobs
Owner:	Netscape
URL (Web address):	`http://www.dmoz.org/Business/Jobs/`
Rating:	★★★

A smaller, less comprehensive listing than Yahoo's (below), the Open Directory Project provides another list of employment guides that may be of help.

Title (or descriptor):	Professional Employment Resources
Owner:	Mental Health Net & CMHC Systems, Inc.
URL (Web address):	
	`http://mentalhelp.net/guide/pro04.htm`
Rating:	★★★

The guide is a compilation of a number of various employment and career databases available online. Like all resources on Mental Health Net, it offers an up-to-date listing of online sites as well as reviews, rating many of the sites to help you decide where to concentrate your online travels. It includes not only employment sites specific to the mental health and related academic fields, but general employment sites as well. This is a good solid employment resource.

Title (or descriptor):   Yahoo! Business and Economy: Employment: Jobs

Owner: Yahoo!, Inc.

URL (Web address):

```
http://www.yahoo.com/Business_and_Economy/
Employment_and_Work/
```

Rating: ★★★★

Yahoo! is known for its quality listings of online resources in myriad categories. Their resource lists are updated regularly by their large editorial staff, and their simple rating system ("cool" versus "not cool") may help you decide where to begin your search. This listing of employment databases is much larger than Mental Health Net's, but it includes many that will be of no relevance to mental health professionals. As with anything found on Yahoo!, there are one-line descriptions next to most resources, and the site itself is very well organized and usually quick to load (if not overly busy, as it often is in the later afternoon and evening hours).

Reading the Classified Ads Online: Employment and Career Databases

There are a lot of other, smaller, and more difficult-to-find databases of various employment opportunities also online. While you might find them with a search engine, the best way is to use one of the above guides as a starting point. I've listed below a few I found from the guides that are likely to be the most relevant to you.

Title (or descriptor):   Academe This Week

Owner: The Chronicle of Higher Education

URL (Web address):   `http://chronicle.com/jobs/`

Rating: ★★★

Access restrictions: Optional registration

One of the more comprehensive job databases for the academic world, it offers a variety of flexible search methods to allow you to find relevant employment opportunities quickly and easily. It allows readers to either browse through listings, or search via keywords, and it offers one of the largest listings of positions available today. The version available to unregistered readers (registration is optional) is a compilation of employment listings that are 1 week old, but the most current version of the database is open to current subscribers to *The Chronicle of Higher Education*. Since this Web site is updated weekly and academic positions tend to be advertised for months, even the week-old listings are timely and probably current enough for most readers. Browsing through the job listings keeps you on their Web site, where the graphics are clean and the site is fast. If you're seeking an academic position, this is the place to visit regularly.

Title (or descriptor):	America's Job Bank
Owner:	United States Department of Labor and local state public Employment Service Agencies
URL (Web address):	http://www.ajb.dni.us/
Rating:	★★★★

This classified ad service is nationwide and allows you to search under any profession. My searches for "psychologist" and "mental" (as in "mental health professional" or "mental health counselor" or the like) both turned up over dozens of listings. This Web site is easy to use with appropriate graphics and a logical layout. It is one of the better large, nonspecific job sites. Information is presented in a familiar, standard format that includes the job title, location, salary, education and experience required, hours, and schedule (e.g., full time). As with all of the larger nationwide databases, America's Job Bank also allows searching by individual state, profession, and offers a self-directed occupational search. Using the latter method, I chose the "counseling" category and discovered over 250 jobs nationwide! One of the most useful government-sponsored sites on the Web today.

Title (or descriptor):	CareerMosaic
Owner:	CareerMosaic
URL (Web address):	http://www.careermosaic.com/
Rating:	★★

CareerMosaic's home page is cluttered, and its organization leaves something to be desired. CareerMosaic came up short in offerings compared to other services. The word "psychologist" found no listings, and the keyword "counseling" found fewer than a dozen. With the Web site's less-than-intuitive interface and poor organization, this is one of those Web sites that should be lower on your list to visit.

Title (or descriptor):	CareerPath.com
Owner:	Various newspapers
URL (Web address):	`http://www.careerpath.com/`
Rating:	★★★

CareerPath takes a different approach to offering classified employment announcements. Over five dozen newspapers have compiled their classified ads sections into one, easy-to-search database. You find ads by choosing which newspapers you'd like to search, choosing a general category (such as "Health/Medical"), then listing any additional keywords you'd like to use to further limit your search. Sample searches turned up a few relevant jobs in various geographical locations. The great benefit of this Web site is that it allows you to search a newspaper's employment classified ads without actually having to get the newspaper! This can be a boon to those looking to relocate to a specific geographical location. Graphics tend to be a bit on the larger side, but overall the site is simple to use and fast. Results are given as one large file displayed in your Web browser, so pay particular attention to limiting your search. You can use your Web browser's "Find" function (usually located under the "Edit" menu) to search for terms or keywords within this file. Other large job sites usually display an index listing first, where you can look at jobs based on the job title or summary description.

Title (or descriptor):	JobLink
Owner:	Mental Health Net & CMHC Systems, Inc.
URL (Web address):	`http://mentalhelp.net/joblink/`
Rating:	★★

The Mental Health Net JobLink is a searchable database of employment opportunities. Its database is culled from online contributions by employers, postings found on mailing lists, and advertisements found on newsgroups and in other publications. It may be beneficial to check once or twice a month for new listings. Since the listings are oriented toward psychology, psychiatry, and the mental health profession in general, position openings may include clinical and academic positions. Listings are categorized by the date they were submitted, with the newest listings appearing first. Mental Health Net also sponsors the other half of the JobLink, which is a listing of individuals' resumes and vitas online. You may also search through the employment listings using an internal search engine.

Title (or descriptor):	MedSearch
Owner:	TMP Worldwide, Inc.
URL (Web address):	http://www.medsearch.com/
Rating:	★★★★

From the same people who bring you "The Monster Board" (see below) employment resource, this is a resource devoted specifically to medical professionals, which
includes the behavioral health care profession. I found a great number of job listings
when I did several sample searches. The site is well organized and simple to use.
Searches are conducted by entering in a desired geographical location, using a general job category, and any additional keywords you believe applicable. An international job database is available in addition to a U.S. one.

Title (or descriptor):	Mental Health Infosource–Classifieds
Owner:	CME, Inc.
URL (Web address):	http://www.mhsource.com/classified/
Rating:	★★★

These classified ads are taken from the publisher's print newspaper for psychiatrists,
Psychiatric Times, then arranged by state groupings or internationally. This is a good
place for psychiatrists to check in once a month to view the latest employment opportunities in their field. The ads are displayed as one large file in each category. But
you can then use your browser's "Find" function (usually located under the "Edit"
menu) to search the file for specific keywords or positions. The site is simple and the
graphics are professional and appropriate.

Title (or descriptor):	Monitor Classified Ads
Owner:	American Psychological Association
URL (Web address):	http://www.apa.org/ads/
Rating:	★★★

The American Psychological Association offers an online version of employment opportunities appearing monthly in the APA's newspaper, *The Monitor*. The employment classified ads are arranged by state and country. A search engine is also available, although it is less than intuitive in its current incarnation, and its search results

are somewhat difficult to interpret. These classified ads tend to be oriented toward psychologists and academic positions, as well as the occasional post-doc and internship listing. But some clinical positions usually appear as well. The Web site is fast and easy to navigate; position listings appear as one large file, based on the state or country you select.

Title (or descriptor):	The Monster Board
Owner:	TMP Worldwide, Inc.
URL (Web address):	`http://www.monster.com/`
Rating:	★★★★

With a less-than-obvious name, The Monster Board is actually one of the older job databases online. It allows you a number of search options from which to choose, including the simple "Monster Search," which allows you to select a geographical location and general job category (for instance, "Health Care–Psychology"). It returns results nearly instantly. In my sample search, it found 15 related jobs in this category. Using their "keyword" search tool, I found only 6 jobs for a "psychologist" but 120 related to the word "counseling." Your results will obviously vary, but it does offer a large job database and a good selection of search tools. As with most keyword searches online, make sure you use all the possible variants of the word in your query to ensure the most complete search possible. "`Psychology and psychologist`" will get you more results than either one by itself. Some academic jobs are listed in the database as well, and search results are viewed in batches of 10 at a time. Site layout is logical and the graphics are professional and appropriate.

Title (or descriptor):	*Psychiatric News* Classifieds
Owner:	American Psychiatric Association
URL (Web address):	
	`http://www.psych.org/pnews/classifieds.html`
Rating:	★★★

This site is an online version of the classified section of *Psychiatric News*. It is divided into simple categories by state, country, and position. Unfortunately for you, the publishers have decided to place *all* of the classifieds into one very large file, which will take a few minutes for your Web browser to load. However, once loaded, the file can be easily searched with your browser's "Find" function. *Psychiatric News* is published once every 2 weeks, and this file is updated just as often online. A good location for psychiatrists to check regularly for new employment opportunities.

Title (or descriptor):   American Psychological Society Job Listings
Owner: American Psychological Society
URL (Web address):
    `http://207.238.152.15/publications_jobs.htm`
Rating: ★★

From the American Psychological Society's *Observer,* the classified ads were searchable only by keyword when I visited the site. The keyword search makes it difficult to limit search results to certain geographical locations. You can, however, view the entire month's listings and use your Web browser's internal search function to find relevant jobs more easily.

Title (or descriptor):   Social Work and Social Services Jobs Online
Owner: Career Services Office, George Warren Brown School of Social Work, Washington University
URL (Web address):   `http://gwbweb.wustl.edu/jobs/`
Rating: ★★★

An excellent resource for social workers, jobs are listed by state or country. Hundreds of listings are available through this Web site. Date posted, job title, job location, qualifications of the applicant, salary, job description, a respond-by date, and contact information is provided for each listing.

5

Online Education and Continuing Education Resources

Professional education is available in many forms through the online world. You can find additional information about a university you're thinking of attending or look up more information on the university that employs you. Continuing education programs for clinicians are also becoming available online as an easy and cost-saving alternative to regular continuing education. Learning environments that exist only online—such as online universities—are taking advantage of the technology and the flexibility of the medium that can reach busy people or isolated professionals more easily. Learning through such courses is a new and interesting experience. It may not be right for everyone, but it may fit into your busy schedule more easily than trying to take night classes at the local community college. Or if the nearest university is 100 miles away, this may be a desirable alternative. Nearly all universities and colleges in the world have some sort of Internet presence today, most of them via Web sites.

Online education is very much in its infancy and so you should be aware of the pitfalls and limitations of such programs. Not all may be accredited to award degrees in your state, or even within the United States. Read the fine print carefully before signing up for a 6-month course or 2-year program. If the university or educational organization resides within the United States, a call to the Better Business Bureau in the locale of the university is a very good precaution. They can let you know whether there have been any complaints against the university and if they had been satisfactorily resolved. Be sure to choose a university and course based on your

QUICKLY FINDING A UNIVERSITY OR COMPANY ONLINE

While not the most reliable way to find a university, a quick method to locate a particular university's Web site is to simply type in that university's initials as the URL (or Web address), followed by the suffix, ".edu" (which stands for "educational"). For example:

New York University	http://www.nyu.edu/
Ohio State University	http://www.osu.edu/

Sometimes you will need to type in an abbreviation of the university's name:

University of Delaware	http://www.udel.edu/
University of Akron (Ohio)	http://www.uakron.edu/

And for still other universities, you will need to type in the full proper name:

Harvard University	http://www.harvard.edu/
Princeton University	http://www.princeton.edu/

Obviously there is no single way to find a university's home page through this method, but it is a quick and easy thing to try if you're in a hurry. Guides that list all the universities are reviewed below, in case you're not interested in guessing!

Corporate addresses work much the same way, except instead of adding ".edu" to the end of the name, use ".com" (which stands for "commercial"). For example:

Microsoft Corporation	http://www.microsoft.com/
IBM Corporation	http://www.ibm.com/

needs and your comfort level with the technology. If you don't enjoy accessing long reading materials through e-mail, look for an institution that provides Web access to the materials, or vice versa. The right fit between your
educational needs and what an institution has to offer is as important in the
online world as it is in the real world.

HOW DO I LOCATE A PARTICULAR UNIVERSITY'S PSYCHOLOGY DEPARTMENT OR GRADUATE PROGRAM ONLINE?

There are a number of well-established, reliable sources for finding psychology departments and graduate programs online.

Title (or descriptor): Peterson's Education Center
Owner: Peterson's
URL (Web address): `http://www.petersons.com/`
Rating: ★★★

Peterson's is the place to visit when you want to learn a lot more about a university
in general: its makeup, general tuition prices, degree offerings, and a host of other
useful items. Peterson's is a central clearinghouse of information about college programs, departments, and graduate programs in any major. Offering a comprehensive listing of over 600 graduate programs in psychology and 1,300 undergraduate
psychology programs, Peterson's online guide to these programs is unsurpassed. In
my sampling, it did, however, miss a few psychology departmental Web pages that
are available (and found through the Hanover College/APS listing below). And
while it may not be as accurate in its listing of psychology department Web pages, it
does offer a current listing of university and college main Web sites. Readers may
easily travel to such a central Web site. These then allow you to find the relevant department or program online.

Title (or descriptor): Departments and Organizations
Owner: Mental Health Net and Scott Plous
URL (Web address): `http://mentalhelp.net/guide/pro86.htm`
(Geographically)

URL (Web address):   http://mentalhelp.net/guide/pro87.htm
                            (Graduate Programs in Psychology)
Rating: ★★★

A comprehensive guide to psychology, psychiatry, and social work departments and
schools online, this guide by Mental Health Net has improved in its breadth and
quality of coverage over the years. The second link provides access to a rank-ordered
listing of graduate programs in psychology according to the results of a 1995 study
by the National Research Council. Stanford University, the University of Michigan–
Ann Arbor, Yale University, and UCLA top the list. The Graduate Programs in Psychology listing is provided and maintained by Scott Plous of the Social Psychology
Network.

Title (or descriptor):   Links to Other Psychology Departments–Alphabetical
                             Order or by Location
Owner: Hanover College and American Psychological Society
URL (Web address):

   http://psych.hanover.edu/Krantz/othera-z.html
   (Alphabetical order)

URL (Web address):

   http://psych.hanover.edu/Krantz/otherloc.html
   (By location)

Rating: ★★★★

The alphabetical listing of psychology departments is one very large file, which will
take a few minutes to load. The location index (the second URL listed above), however, is not large and is much easier to browse, by state and country. These listings
are updated regularly and are about as current as possible with the ever-changing
nature of online resource addresses. The Web site sports minimal graphics and is
logically arranged. In many cases, where a psychology or related department doesn't
yet have a Web site, an e-mail address is listed instead. This allows for online communication. Since this site had psychology departments listed when the Peterson's
Education Center didn't, I found it to be more helpful and useful in a quick look to
find a psychology department's Web site. If you're looking for a lot more information about a university in particular, though, you might want to check the Peterson's
site first.

HOW DO I FIND CALENDARS ONLINE THAT LIST PROFESSIONAL EVENTS, CONFERENCES, AND COURSES?

There are several online calendars currently available, which list conferences, courses, workshops, conventions, and events. None is comprehensive. Many calendars exist on small sites, which list only events relevant to their local organization or area. There is no easy or direct way to find these calendars, except by doing a thorough search for them. And because such calendars are often maintained irregularly and updated infrequently, they may be out-of-date and inaccurate.

If you'd like to search for your own profession's calendars, or calendars on specific subtopics not covered below, follow the Step-by-Step instructions.

Title (or descriptor):	American Psychiatric Association–Schedule of Events
Owner:	American Psychiatric Association
URL (Web address):	`http://www.psych.org/sched_events/`
Rating:	★★

Smaller than CME, Inc.'s site (see below), the APA's Schedule of Events provides members with information on upcoming annual conventions, institutes, and cosponsored events of the American Psychiatric Association. Divided into categories along those divisions, each category offers a fair amount of information on the event itself, especially the larger annual convention and institute. The graphics are professional but may take a while to load. The site's organization is logical and well developed.

Title (or descriptor):	American Psychological Association–Continuing Education Calendar /Conferences
Owner:	American Psychological Association
URL (Web address):	`http://www.apa.org/ce/cecal.html` (Continuing Education Calendar)
URL (Web address):	`http://www.apa.org/conf.html` (Conferences)
Rating:	★★★

Much like the multiple personality makeup of the American Psychological Association with its dozens of divisions, it is not surprising to find that they don't have one

STEP-BY-STEP INSTRUCTIONS: FINDING A PROFESSIONAL CALENDAR ONLINE

1. Visit a favorite search engine, such as AltaVista

```
http://www.altavista.com/
```

2. Type the following into the search query box to find a social work calendar:

```
+calendar +"social work" —undergraduate —academic —university
```

Change the term `"social work"` to `psychology` or `psychiatry` (the quotation marks aren't necessary for single words) to find related calendars.

Specifying `+calendar` ensures only those Web sites that reference a calendar appear in the results. Specifying `—undergraduate —academic —university` ensures that you don't retrieve results that are listings of academic courses. These search terms can get you started. Use other terms as needed to limit or expand your search. Remember to type all of your terms on the same line in the query box, separated only by a space in the "Simple Search" option of AltaVista.

central calendar of events readers can search. The Continuing Education Calendar offers a listing of continuing education courses approved by the American Psychological Association. The same listing often appears within the APA's *Monitor* newspaper. The online version is updated anywhere from four to five times a year and lists about 8 months at a time. Since each file contains an entire month's worth of continuing education course listings (usually dozens), the APA's search engine isn't that helpful in narrowing down a reader's search to courses on specific topic areas. The Conferences section lists information on upcoming cosponsored conferences of the APA, as well as their annual convention. The site has minimal graphics but its organization is not easy to navigate.

Title (or descriptor):	Behavioral HealthCare Meeting, Organization, and Resource Index
Owner:	Myron Pulier
URL (Web address):	`http://www.umdnj.edu/psyevnts/`
URL (Web address):	`http://mentalhelp.net/calendar/` (Searchable version)
Rating:	★★★★

Easily the best and most comprehensive calendar online today, this one covers organizational meetings, events, conferences and courses across disciplines. The calendar is generated through a large and well-maintained database, which means it is up-to-date and accurate. The only drawback to the calendar is that there is no easy way to search it. You have to choose either to view it by a particular month during the year, or by the sponsoring organization's name for the workshop. While both methods are helpful, the ability to search it through keywords would be invaluable and the only improvement on an already great online resource. The site is well organized and has minimal graphics.

Title (or descriptor):	CME Conferences
Owner:	CME, Inc.
URL (Web address):	`http://www.mhsource.com/edu/conf/`
Rating:	★★★

Organized by topic, location, and date, this calendar index is directed toward psychiatrists and lists only those conferences sponsored by the large psychiatric continuing education corporation, CME, Inc. An excellent place for psychiatrists to go to keep up-to-date on upcoming conferences and continuing education workshops of relevance to their field or specialty. The site is well designed and easy to navigate, with professional graphics.

Title (or descriptor):	PsychScapes Worldwide–Mental Health Workshops & Conferences Registry
Owner:	PsychScapes Worldwide, Inc.
URL (Web address):	
	`http://www.mental-health.com/PsychScapes/mhwr.html`
Rating:	★★

An archive of between 5,000 and 7,000 workshop listings, which is no longer being maintained. Searches of the registry database are limited to only viewing 10 listings at a time, without any way to view the next 10 results. The search page is very confusing and poorly organized.

ARE THERE APPROVED ONLINE CONTINUING
EDUCATION COURSES THAT I CAN TAKE?

The world of online continuing education offerings has undergone a shake-up in recent years, with providers either shutting down or redesigning their efforts. Too few professionals signed up for these courses to make them viable businesses. Some programs are sticking it out, however, and others are trying more integrated and larger multimedia approaches.

Continuing education courses online typically take three forms—text-based, discussion-based, and multimedia. Text-based courses typically take a tutorial format. Information is organized on a course Web page with related links to other, independent Web sites. The user reads the information at their leisure and takes a quiz at the end to test for knowledge and gain their continuing education credit. This is the least innovate online course method, similar to traditional home-based continuing education. The major difference is that the participant reads from a computer screen rather than paper.

Discussion-based courses revolve around an expert-led professional discussion, generally in an online private, closed space such as a mailing list. Participants contribute to the discussion in an interactive learning process. This is more innovative than text-based courses, as it leverages community technologies to offer a unique way of learning.

The third type of online course is the most innovative of them all. It leverages the full capabilities of the Internet's multimedia potential by integrating audio, video, a slide presentation, and discussion. The range of multimedia offerings online varies. Some services offer audio and synchronized slide presentations, with an asynchronous discussion forum. Others offer a synchronous, classroomlike environment with audio, a slide presentation, and real time chat.

Title (or descriptor):	audioPsych: Online Continuing Education in Mental Health
Owner:	Mental Health Net, Behavior OnLine, various authors
URL (Web address):	http://www.audiopsych.com/
Rating:	★★★

SENDING CREDIT CARD INFORMATION ONLINE

Never send credit card information online unless you "encrypt" it first. There are two common ways to encrypt (or encode information to prevent easy access to it, except by the authorized recipient) information online: (1) a special encryption program (such as Pretty Good Privacy programs) to use through e-mail; or (2) a Web site's encryption software, which is activated automatically by your Web browser. The first option is more complicated than I can go into here. The second option is what you will most often come across while browsing the Web.

A Web site supports encryption of your credit card information when your browser lets you know it has entered a "secure" page on a Web site. This usually includes a visual cue in the browser (e.g., in Netscape Navigator, the small picture of an open lock or broken key in the lower left-hand corner of the browser window will become a closed, highlighted lock or a whole key). It may also include a warning box that is automatically displayed when you enter or leave the secure area on the Web site.

Web developers who are concerned about your privacy and security of your financial information will be aware of these issues and let you know whether they support encryption of your credit card information. If they do not, *do not enter your credit card information online*. When in doubt, don't do it. A telephone number is usually provided as an alternative method of paying for the product or service. Do not even consider using a Web site that requests credit card information and that isn't aware of these basic security measures.

Access restrictions: Fees: $12.00–$15.00/credit hour (courses generally range from 4 to 12 credit hours)

With an innovative use of online technology, this site provides approved continuing education courses for psychologists and other mental health professionals. Offering a choice of a half-dozen courses initially, lectures are delivered through a piece of software called RealAudio, which is freely available for any computer system. Unlike some other online audio formats available, there is no need to download the audio file before hearing it. You listen to it as it plays (much like listening to a tape cassette on your car radio). While the lecturer of a course speaks, synchronized slides and other information appear automatically on your Web browser. All of this can be heard and used with as little as 28.8 Kbps modem connection. Information and extensive help for first-time users of this software is available on the site, as are good descriptions of each course's content and material. I am directly involved in the development of this service.

The downside to this service is that it requires a relatively more powerful computer than typically is required just for online browsing. A 28.8 Kbps modem connection is also recommended, although not required. Specific minimum computer requirements are noted on the Web site.

Courses include not only audio delivery of the lecture across the Internet (the quality of the audio varies according to your online connection speed), but also a course outline, review questions (which provide immediate feedback and results), a course evaluation, suggested readings and references, biographies on course authors, and additional reading materials for each course. At the end of the course, you may also choose to engage in an ongoing discussion forum on the Web with other participants who have also taken the course. The course's author may even participate online. Lectures may be listened to at any time. Continuing education credit is granted when the participant successfully completes the review questions found within each course. This Web site also supports the use of secure credit card transactions. This allows users to safely pay for the course online.

Title (or descriptor):	Interactive Testing in Psychiatry
Owner:	New York University Department of Psychiatry and the New University Post-Graduate Medical School
URL (Web address):	`http://www.med.nyu.edu/Psych/itp.html`
Rating:	★★★
Access restrictions:	Fees: $20.00/credit hour (up to 7 hours available)

This very user-friendly program allows you to answer Board-style questions just by clicking on buttons. The Web site automatically calculates your score and can give you the correct answer to every question. Seven modules are available, consisting of 30 questions each. Individuals are welcome to take the modules for free, or they can apply for continuing education credit in psychiatry by submitting a $20.00 fee for each module. There are, however, no online reading materials to consult, nor are there any Web links to additional reference materials. All that is available to readers is a "References" category, which lists books for further reading (and contains the answers to the questions in each module).

Modules are arranged in no particular order, nor are the questions contained within each module. Questions cover the full breadth of psychiatry, but tend to focus on pharmacology and diagnosis.

Title (or descriptor):	PsyBC
Owner:	Psy Broadcasting Corporation
URL (Web address):	http://www.psybc.com/
Rating:	★★★
Access restrictions:	Fees: $7.50/credit hour (courses typically range from 6 to 8 credit hours)

The Psy Broadcasting Corporation is a Web site offering a service akin to a professional mailing where the participants are charged to listen in on the conversation. The "broadcasting" referred to in the name is simply the use of a mailing list to carry on a conversation among panels of selected professionals in certain fields, such as cognitive behavioral therapy, mood disorders, and psychopharmacology. An interesting concept that could be potentially very useful in the future for professionals looking for high-quality discussions.

WHERE DO I LOOK TO FIND REGULAR UNIVERSITY PROGRAMS AND COURSES OFFERED ONLINE?

This idea, which is commonly termed "distance learning," has been around for decades. Many people confuse such educational programs with universities or institutions that just hand out degrees for a fee ("degree mills"). Most distance-learning institutions, though, are not degree mills and many are associated with a larger, well-known university to ensure quality and standards. As recommended at the start of this chapter, check out an institution through the Better Business Bureau before signing up for courses. If you're still wary, ask for references from individuals who have already completed courses and e-mail them asking about their experiences. Such precautions can help reduce the possibility of disappointment.

Searching Guides to Online Education

The best way to find out more about online education is by browsing through the guides listed below and sample some of the Web-site offerings by the many institutions listed.

Title (or descriptor):   Yahoo! Education: Distance Learning

Owner: Yahoo!, Inc.

URL (Web address):

`http://www.yahoo.com/Education/Distance_Learning/`

Rating: ★★★

This is certainly the easiest place to find a listing of dozens of universities and institutions that offer some sort of distance learning, many online. Check under both the "Colleges and Universities" category as well as the "On-Line Teaching and Learning" category. Yahoo!'s descriptions are sometimes less than informative, but under the "Colleges and Universities" category, keep a lookout for those that offer courses online through the Internet or e-mail. Many such programs are available, and they cover a multitude of topics ranging from the expected (computer programming) to those relevant to mental health professionals (health, mental health, and social welfare). Like all of Yahoo!, the site is quick to load and offers simple graphics (and your typical banner advertising, which helps pay the bills).

Visiting Select University Web Sites

I've chosen just a few of the multitude of institutions that now offer some sort of education online. These sites are listed here just to give you a general idea of the types of experiences you can expect to have when enrolling in an online university. I do not personally endorse any of these sites, nor have I taken any of their courses, so I cannot vouch for their usefulness or quality; therefore rating scores have been omitted in this section.

Title (or descriptor):   Foothill Global Access

Owner: Foothill College

URL (Web address):   `http://www.foothill.fhda.edu/fga/`

Access restrictions: Yes; fee unpublished

Unlike some other online institutions, Foothill College simply offers many of its regular courses for online access. The program is not organized in any logical way to obtain a specific degree. As at the University of Phoenix, courses are not self-directed or open-ended; they start and end at specific times throughout the year, based on a quarter schedule (fall, winter, spring, and summer). Teaching is done entirely through group e-mail (a mailing list), as are testing and other regular class activities. The course credit is as transferable as regular course credit to other universities, the college claims, but that will largely be dependent on the university to which you want to transfer the credit. Each class is taught by a regular instructor, and courses are offered on a wide variety of subjects ranging from computers and art, to economics and business. The Web site offers little information beyond the basics and leaves a lot of obvious questions unanswered.

Title (or descriptor):   Online Education
Owner: Online University and the University of Paisley (Scotland)
URL (Web address):   `http://www.online.edu/`
Access restrictions: Yes; fee unpublished

The Online University is a unique institution. It offers degrees such as an MBA in marketing, a BSc in health studies, an MSc in quality management, Postgraduate Certificate in business development, an MSc in computer-aided engineering, an MBA in real estate management, and an MBA in total quality management. Fully accredited in its United Kingdom home base to offer degree courses in these areas, it has brought the concept of online learning to your home. The site appears to be marketed and oriented toward Hong Kong professionals, but the courses are available to anyone internationally.

Title (descriptor):   Open Directory Project: Business: Jobs
Owner: Netscape
URL:
    `http://dmoz.org/Reference/Education/Distance_Learning/`
Rating: ★★★

Similar to Yahoo!'s directory listing of distance learning opportunities, the Open Directory Project offers similar choices and categories. As with all of the Open Directory Project, the site is quick to load and offers simple graphics, and, refreshingly, no banner advertising.

Title (or descriptor):   University of Phoenix
Owner: University of Phoenix
URL (Web address):   http://www.uophx.edu/online/
Access restrictions: $410/credit hour for graduate courses and $335/credit hour for undergraduate courses

One of the leading online institutions, the University of Phoenix offers Bachelor of Science degree programs in business/administration, business/information systems, business/management; Master of Arts in organizational management; Master of Business Administration, Master of Business Administration/Technology Management, and Master of Business Administration/Global Management. The Web site is fast and offers professional graphics as well as copious information, including a frequently asked questions file (also called an "FAQ"), which answered all of my immediate questions. This institution appears to take education seriously. It lets prospective students know that it will take anywhere from 2 to 3 years to complete a program. Course tuition is also not cheap; comparable community college courses within your local area probably cost much less. Unlike other online institutions, the courses are not self-paced or open-ended; they are scheduled much like regular real-world classes. Most of the work is done through reading assigned texts, either offline or through the university's online library. It all appears to be well organized and many students have already successfully completed the programs.

6

Networking with Other Professionals Online

The Internet allows professionals to keep in touch with others around the world at a fraction of the cost of regular telephone use, and in a much more timely manner than going through thc postal scrvice. The online tools range from the mundane (e-mail directories) to cutting-edge technology (Internet telephone and videoconferencing, discussed in Chapter 10). This chapter examines how to participate in online case conferences and ongoing discussion groups with other professionals, how to quickly find someone's e-mail address, and how to track down other professionals conducting particular kinds of research.

Professional discussion areas are among the most popular and widely used online resources. Such discussions usually take place through mailing lists, which are basically a form of group electronic mail. In these forums, like-minded clinicians and researchers can discuss specific issues on a wide range of professional topics. Most such discussion areas are focused on specific topic areas, such as forensic psychology, clinical psychology, clinical social work, psychopharmacology, and so forth. Professionals may use such forums for reading or posting announcements of workshops, conferences, or employment; engaging in theoretical, research-oriented, or clinical discussions; and exchanging information about valuable books, journal references, or online resources that may benefit other professionals. It is in these kinds of discussion areas where most professionals tend to gather online and probably the first area you should go to if you're new online. Why? Because most of these discussion areas are mailing lists, which are simple to subscribe to and easy to use. These will be covered later in this chapter.

An additional use of many discussion areas online is the presentation of a formal or informal case conference. I will illustrate this example in depth, because it is one of the most useful to a wide variety of practitioners.

WHERE CAN I PARTICIPATE IN ONLINE CASE CONFERENCES?

There are many areas online where you can participate in a case conference. Before I discuss specific online resources, however, I will first present an overview of the purpose of online case conferences. Case conferences exist online for a number of the same reasons they do in the real world. First and foremost, they allow professionals to present current cases that may be presenting some difficulty in treatment. The difficulty may arise because of a unique or rare disorder, the clinician's lack of experience in treating a particular type of disorder, or an abnormal presentation of a disorder, which the therapist would like to gain some additional insight on and clarify his or her own conceptualization of it. When presenting cases, clinicians usually discuss explicitly their reasons for asking for input on the case. Second, professionals will also present cases for comment when they have treated a particularly difficult case. By sharing the case and treatment approach, other professionals may gain some benefit from the ensuing discussion. Third, clinicians who are isolated from their colleagues (for instance, due to working in an independent practice or in remote or rural areas) benefit from case conferences, keeping them in touch with current trends in treatment and outcomes. There are many additional benefits (such as research and training) in case conferences, but these are the central ones. As discussed in Chapter 8, professionals should exercise the same care when presenting cases in any online forum as they would in real life. Identifying information should be omitted or changed enough so that someone who may be reading the case presentation and know the person being presented could not easily identify that person through your online description.

Types of Online Case Conferences

Case conferences online are of two basic types: formal and informal. In formal case conferences, invited faculty—usually well-known figures in their particular subspecialty area—present a difficult case from their history. Other invited faculty are then encouraged to comment on aspects of the case from their particular theoretical perspectives. Other professionals may participate in the ensuing discussion or simply sit back and read it as it enfolds. These formal presentations are most often made in a Web-based discussion area, because the messages don't expire and the discussion threads are simple to follow and read. This easily allows newcomers to "get up to speed" on the discussion thus far. There is no reason these presentations can't be made in a live, interactive chat group online, or through some related medium such as audio or video, except that such technologies are not as well known as the Web or e-mail are to most professionals or may not be readily available to them.

Informal case discussions are far more prevalent. They often take place through mailing lists rather than in Web-based discussion areas. Mailing lists are simple; the e-mail technology involved is available to anyone online. You must first sign up or "subscribe" to a mailing list, but this is easy to do for most people (see the "Step-by-Step: Subscribing to a Mailing List" on page 112). In an informal case presentation, a professional who has subscribed to the particular mailing list simply sends an e-mail to the list describing the patient or client (keeping confidentiality in mind), his presenting problem, a little bit about his background and relevant personal history, and treatment to date. The clinician may also talk about her conceptualization of the case before getting feedback from other professionals, or she may decide to withhold it until after she has elicited others' opinions. Additional questions may be asked of the professional who presents the case online, and they are usually quickly answered.

The elegance and beauty of case conferences online is that opinions come from many different people with vastly different backgrounds, professional orientations, and experiences from around the world. A wealth of knowledge and information exists in these online discussion areas that cannot exist easily or often in the real world. This is one of the best examples of an online experience that is actually quantitatively and qualitatively better than a similar experience in the real world. Every organization I have worked in as a clinician has held case conferences. But most organizations are closed systems; new information rarely permeates the outer "walls" that have been built up over years within the organization. Universities and graduate schools can often be notable exceptions, when the programs are larger and encourage diversity within their clinical tracks.

Online case conferences suffer no such limitations because the online world is inherently an open system. There is an easy experiment you can conduct to test this observation. Present the same case both to your colleagues in a staff meeting or case conference, and also to one of the online conferences. Ask for treatment suggestions and conceptualizations. I will bet that you will receive a much more diverse and rich response from those individuals in the online conference than from your real-world colleagues.

So where do you find these conferences? There is one Web site I am aware of that offers formal presentations, and that is Behavior OnLine (described in detail below). Formal case presentations in the real world are often made in association with universities, so you might also keep tabs on schools that have a strong online presence to see if they offer case conferences. (Quite frankly, I don't know of any who currently do.) Informal case conferences exist most often on professionally oriented mailing lists. For instance, the clinical psychologists mailing list (listed under "Psychologists, Clinical" on page 139) sometimes features discussions among psychologists about specific cases.

The next section gives details on mailing lists and includes how to find those that may have informal case conferences. I also keep an index of such lists on my Web site, as well as on Mental Health Net.

A Formal Case Conference

Title (or descriptor):	Behavior OnLine
Owner:	Behavior OnLine
URL (Web address):	http://www.behavior.net/
Rating:	★★★★

Behavior OnLine, the online gathering place for professionals, started out as a small, well-designed Web site that featured conversations (actually, interviews) with five well-known professionals within their specific subspecialty areas. Some of these professionals also went on to participate in ongoing discussion forums on the same site. Behavior OnLine expanded them further and made use of their unique features and attributes. These include the ability to keep discussions around for as long as they remain relevant, as well as offering a format that makes reading easy and logical: Through a process called "threading," responses to an original message appear directly under that first message.

Behavior OnLine launched its first formal case conference in June of 1996 and has since followed up with a handful of additional presentations. Invited faculty present their cases, and a lively and interesting discussion then ensues. Participants may simply follow along or offer their own insights and opinions on the presented case.

The Web site itself is extremely well-designed and professional, offering the ideal mix between sensible graphics and a logical layout. Behavior OnLine hosts a number of organizations on its site as well, and allows readers an optional membership at no cost. A book store rounds out this eclectic offering by Gil Levin, PhD. I am an associate editor of this site.

WHERE DO I FIND TOPIC-ORIENTED DISCUSSIONS WITH OTHER PROFESSIONALS ONLINE?

Mailing List Discussions

Naturally, case conferences are just one aspect of using discussion forums online. There are dozens of professional mailing lists from which to choose, all of which may be relevant to you as a professional, depending on area of expertise or interest. While I have endeavored to list all I know of below, I am certain that more have been added since this book went to press. That is why by using such resources as Liszt and Psych Central, you can easily to identify newer mailing lists that may not appear here. As reviewed in Chapter 2, these resources specialize in helping you find lists in your areas of interest.

Mailing lists are the most popular way for professionals to network with one another online, largely because of their ease of use. Many professional mailing lists are *credentialed*, which means you might have to first submit proof of your professional status before the facilitators will allow you to subscribe. This protects the professionals currently subscribed to the list from off-topic conversations from nonprofessionals; it ensures that you are who you say you are. It is relatively easy for unscrupulous individuals to pretend they are someone else online or pretend to expertise and credentials they don't have. Most professional mailing lists are also *closed*. A closed list means that only subscribers to the list can actually send messages to it. Open mailing lists, on the other hand, allow even nonsubscribers to post to the list. The advantage of a closed mailing list is that it won't often be used for off-topic advertisements. Some professionals still post the occasional employment opportunity or conference announcement, but these notices are usually relevant to the list's topic and occur so rarely that it is not bothersome. Closed mailing lists are just as easy to join as open mailing lists, and they are the preferred standard in the online world for professional discussions.

Mailing lists, like newsgroups, may also be moderated. "Moderated" means that before an article is published to the list, a human being (the "moderator") approves its content. This ensures that only those articles that are on-topic for that particular mailing list make it out to the hundreds of other list members. Most professional mailing lists are not moderated because they are closed. The list owner can ensure only professionals subscribe to their list at the outset, which then makes a task like moderating largely unnecessary.

Mailing lists tend to be subject-specific, and those oriented toward mental health professionals are no different. A list for professional discussion of addictions is different from the one for the discussion of affective disorders; some topics may even have multiple lists. List quality and traffic (how much e-mail you will receive each day from the list) varies greatly. My suggestion is that you subscribe to one list at a time and see if it suits you in terms of quality and traffic. Allow a week or two to go by before you make your decision.

If you can't locate a mailing list on a topic that interests you, you may want to consider starting one on your own. Mailing lists are relatively easy to create and simple to maintain in most cases. Many well-equipped Internet Service Providers have the facilities to allow you to host a mailing list or two if you'd like. For further information on this topic, speak to a customer service representative at your Internet Service Provider.

An alternative to creating a new mailing list through your service provider is to use one of the many free and low-cost mailing list service

MAILING LIST ETIQUETTE

Mailing list etiquette varies from forum to forum. On low-traffic, smaller lists, it is often considered polite to introduce yourself after you have subscribed, telling list members a bit about your background and interest in the list's topic. High-volume lists frown on such introductions, since there is already so much (and often times, too much!) e-mail being exchanged on the list. If you're unsure what to do, you can always privately e-mail the list's owner and ask.

Never send mailing list commands (e.g., subscribe or unsubscribe) to the list address! They don't work if you send them to the wrong address and you end up annoying hundreds of other subscribers on the list. That's why I've included *all the information* you will need to both subscribe and unsubscribe from a mailing list. I have also hunted down the list's description and list owner's name and e-mail address so if you have any further questions about the list, you can write that person directly.

Once subscribed to a mailing list, you will start receiving e-mail messages that are distributed to everyone on the list. Typically when you want to reply to a message on a list, you just choose your e-mail software's "Reply" feature. Your response will usually automatically be sent to every other member on the list as well. It is a good idea to differentiate between replies you'd like to send to the entire list (hundreds of people) and those you'd like to send only to the original author of a message (e.g., a regular, private e-mail). It is always a good idea, therefore, to double-check the "To:" line of your reply e-mail to ensure it is being sent to the correct addressee.

STEP-BY-STEP: SUBSCRIBING TO A MAILING LIST

1. Create a new e-mail message. Ensure the message is sent as *plain text,* not HTML. Turn off any fancy stationary options.

2. Address it to the e-mail address in the "Commands to:" listed below for that specific mailing list.

3. Don't fill in anything for the "Subject" of your e-mail message (or use a single space if your e-mail software requires the subject line to be filled in).

4. In the body of your e-mail, write *exactly* what is listed below in the "Subscribe" field for that mailing list. This is the command you use to tell the mailing list software to add you to the list.

5. If needed, as noted in each listing below, replace the phrase "Your-name" with your actual name (e.g., `John Grohol`); or, alternatively, replace the phrase "Your-email-address" with your actual e-mail address (e.g., `grohol@netscape.com`). If neither is noted in the listing, then the subscription command will look simply like "subscribe name-of-mailing-list" (without the quotes).

6. Do not write anything else in the e-mail.

7. Send the e-mail and wait for an automated reply, which should confirm your subscription request within 24 hours. Some mailing lists may also require you to respond to the automated reply to confirm your subscription. Instructions for doing so are included in the automated reply if this is required.

---

providers. Free service providers include Onelist (`http://www.one-list.com/`), eGroups (`http://www.egroups.com/`), and Topica (`http://www.topica.com/`). These are full-service providers, offering your mailing list a Web page to host archives and a description of the list, as well as a simple Web-based interface for both your subscribers and administrative functions. But nothing in life is truly free; services typically place advertising in every message sent to the list in order to offset the costs of running the service. For a small monthly fee, these ads can be removed. A low-cost mailing list service is Esosoft (`http://www.esosoft.com/`),

UNDERSTANDING MAILING LIST RESOURCE HEADINGS

Title (or descriptor): Name or description of the mailing list.

Web site: `http://psychcentral.com/`
Some mailing lists also have Web sites, which can give you additional information about the list. The Web site may also house the list's archives. This heading only appears when a mailing list has a known Web site.

Commands to: `listserv@nowhere.com`
This is the e-mail address to which you address all of your subscribe and unsubscribe requests.

Subscribe: `subscribe Listname Your-name`
This is the subscribe command you place in the body of your e-mail message, substituting "Your-name" or "Your-email-address" with the appropriate name or address. The "Listname" is the proper name of the mailing list.

Unsubscribe: `unsubscribe Listname`
This is the unsubscribe command you place in the body of your e-mail message. Notice you *do not* include your name or e-mail address in this request.

List: `Listname@nowhere.com`
This is the address of the mailing list itself, to which you may send your messages to get distributed to all the list's subscribers after you have become a member of the list.

List owner: John Smith (E-mail: `johnsmith@nowhere.com`)
This is the person responsible for maintaining the list and helping people subscribe and unsubscribe. He or she may also participate in and lead the list's discussion.

which offers mailing list hosting for as low as $5/month at this writing. Because it is easier than ever to create one of these lists, I strongly encourage you to consider starting a mailing list on a professional topic of interest to you.

Once you have subscribed to a mailing list, you will remain subscribed to it and continue receiving e-mail from the list for as long as it exists. For any of a number of reasons (e.g., you may be receiving too much e-mail from the list, you are changing e-mail accounts, you are going on vacation), you may wish to unsubscribe from that mailing list. You follow the same steps you used to subscribe to the list, except you substitute the "unsubscribe" command for the "subscribe" command (see the box, "Unsubscribing from a Mailing List").

STEP-BY-STEP: UNSUBSCRIBING FROM A MAILING LIST

1. Create a new e-mail message. Ensure the message is sent as *plain text,* not HTML. Turn off any fancy stationary options.

2. Address it to the e-mail address in the "Commands to:" listed below for that specific mailing list.

3. Don't fill in anything for the "Subject" of your e-mail message (or use a single space if your e-mail software requires the subject line to be filled in).

4. In the body of your e-mail, write *exactly* what is in the "Unsubcribe" field for that mailing list. This is the command you use to tell the mailing list software to remove you from the list.

5. Do not write anything else in the e-mail.

6. Send the e-mail and wait for a reply e-mail, which should confirm your unsubscription request within 24 hours. If you have any difficulties, contact the list owner directly through his or her own e-mail address.

7. If you ever lose the unsubscription instructions to a particular list that you are subscribed to, try this handy tip:

    A. Note the name of the mailing list and its domain. This is typically the e-mail address that appears in the "To:" line of e-mail sent to the list. For example, a list's "To:" line might read "To: research@cmhc.com." Everything before the "@" sign is the mailing list's name, and everything after the "@" sign is the list's domain. In this case, the name of the list is "research" and its domain is "cmhc.com."

Below, I've given a brief summary description of some relevant and interesting mailing lists. The descriptions are gleaned from the list's owner or publicly available information. Sample topics may also be included in the description. These may not be the topics currently under discussion on the list but are *examples* of topics that *may* be discussed on it. Mailing list addresses change from time to time (although usually not too often). If you have difficulty with any of the addresses below, check the book's Web site for a complete up-to-date listing of these addresses

B. Compose a new e-mail message and address it to the following three addresses:

```
listserv@domain.name
listproc@domain.name
majordomo@domain.name
```

Replace "domain.name" with the list's actual domain. In the example from above, we would compose our e-mail to the following three addresses:

```
listserv@cmhc.com
listproc@cmhc.com
majordomo@cmhc.com
```

C. *Leave the subject line of the e-mail message blank.*

D. In the body of your e-mail message, write:

```
unsubscribe listname
```

where "listname" is the name of the list we discovered in step A. In the example from above, this would look like:

```
unsubscribe research
```

E. Send the e-mail message.

What will now happen is that your e-mail will be sent to all three e-mail addresses. More than likely, two of them will be invalid and the e-mail will be returned to you as "undeliverable." Delete those messages when they arrive. But one of those e-mails you sent will be successful in unsubscribing you from the mailing list 99.99 percent of the time. I have never had this trick fail.

(`http://www.insidemh.com/`), or consult the updated lists at Psych Central (`http://psychcentral.com/`). Nearly all of the mailing lists discussed below are maintained by professionals, with some maintained by *the* leading figures within the field. Individuals who maintain mailing lists are referred to as "list owners" because they "own" the list. These people are responsible for creating the list in the first place and are typically in charge of ongoing administration as well. If you have any questions or problems subscribing to a mailing list below, the list owner can often help you properly subscribe to the list.

Professional Mailing Lists

Title (or descriptor):	Addiction Medicine
Commands to:	`listserv@maelstrom.stjohns.edu`
Subscribe:	`subscribe ADD_MED Your-name`
Unsubscribe:	`unsubscribe ADD_MED`
List:	`ADD_MED@maelstrom.stjohns.edu`
List owner:	Peter E. Mezciems (E-mail: `mezciems@wat.hookup.net`)

A closed list for professionals and students interested in a discussion on research, diagnosis and treatment of addiction disorders.

Title (or descriptor):	Addictions
Commands to:	`listserv@listserv.kent.edu`
Subscribe:	`subscribe Addict-L Your-name`
Unsubscribe:	`unsubscribe Addict-L`
List:	`addict-L@listserv.kent.edu`
List owner:	`ddelmoni@kentvm.kent.edu`

A list for the academic and scholarly discussion of addiction related topics.

Title (or descriptor):	Affective Disorders
Commands to:	`listserv@maelstrom.stjohns.edu`
Subscribe:	`subscribe AFFECTD Your-name`
Unsubscribe:	`unsubscribe AFFECTD`
List:	`AFFECTD@maelstrom.stjohns.edu`
List owner:	Steven Dubovsky (E-mail: `steven.dubovsky@uchsc.edu`)

A forum for discourse on all aspects of affective disorders, including depression, mood, and bipolar disorders.

Title (or descriptor):	Against the Medical Model of Behavior
Commands to:	`listserv@maelstrom.stjohns.edu`
Subscribe:	`subscribe NUVUPSY Your-name`
Unsubscribe:	`unsubscribe NUVUPSY`
List:	`NUVUPSY@maelstrom.stjohns.edu`
List owner:	Jeffrey Schaler (E-mail: `jschale@american.edu`)

This is a forum to share points of view critical of the "therapeutic state" (Thomas Szasz) and institutional psychiatry. Discussions often focus on the relationship between liberty and responsibility and its implications for clinical, legal, and public policy.

Title (or descriptor):	Aggression, Psychology of
Commands to:	`listserv@maelstrom.stjohns.edu`
Subscribe:	`subscribe Your-name`
Unsubscribe:	`unsubscribe aggress`
List:	`aggress@maelstrom.stjohns.edu`
List owners:	Juan Carlos Garelli (E-mail: `lagare@attach.edu.ar`)
	Seymour Feshbach (E-mail: `ekchsyf@mvs.oac.ucla.edu`)

This list is devoted to the study and discussion of the antecedents, development, manifestations, regulation, and reduction of aggressive behavior. Aggression in this context is broadly defined. Consideration of prosocial behaviors of cooperation and conflict resolution in the context of constructive alternatives to aggression is appropriate.

Title (or descriptor):	American Association of Applied and Preventive Psychology (ΛΛΛPP)
Commands to:	`listserv@LSV.UKY.EDU`
Subscribe:	`subscribe AAAPP Your-name`
Unsubscribe:	`unsubscribe AAAPP`
List:	`AAAPP@LSV.UKY.EDU`
List owner:	(E-mail: `AAAPP-request@LSV.UKY.EDU`)

For members of the American Association of Applied and Preventic Psychology
(AAAPP).

Title (or descriptor):	Anxiety Disorders
Commands to:	`listserv@maelstrom.stjohns.edu`
Subscribe:	`subscribe ANX-DIS Your-name`
Unsubscribe:	`unsubscribe ANX-DIS`
List:	`ANX-DIS@maelstrom.stjohns.edu`
List owner:	Andrew Baillie (E-mail: `andrewb@crufad.unsw.edu.au`)

A scholary forum for mental health professionals to discuss anxiety disorders.

Title (or descriptor):	Attachment Issues
Commands to:	`listserv@maelstrom.stjohns.edu`
Subscribe:	`subscribe attach Your-name`
Unsubscribe:	`unsubscribe attach`
List:	`attach@maelstrom.stjohns.edu`
List owner:	Chuck Hollister (E-mail: `gauguin@ix.netcom.com`) Phil Shaver (E-mail: `prshaver@ucdavis.edu`)

This list emphasizes socio-affective and defensive processes, as well as unconscious
representations. Discussion includes Bowlby-Ainsworth's theory of attachment.

Title (or descriptor):	Behavioral Sciences
Commands to:	`listproc@sti.nasa.gov`
Subscribe:	`subscribe scan-53 Your-name`
Unsubscribe:	`unsubscribe scan-53`
List:	`scan-53@sti.nasa.gov`
List owner:	Unknown

For the general discussion of behavioral science topics.

Title (or descriptor):	Bodywork Practitioners
Commands to:	`listproc@echonyc.com`
Subscribe:	`subscribe bodywork Your-name`
Unsubscribe:	`unsubscribe`
List:	`bodywork@echonyc.com`
List owner:	Greg Tobias (E-mail: `gtobias@interport.net`)

For the professional discussion of bodywork therapies, such as Swedish massage, Trager approach, trigger point therapy, Rolfing, polarity therapy, Reiki, reflexology, Alexander technique, Jin Shin Do, acupuncture, and Shiatsu. Physical therapy and training issues are also appropriate topics.

Title (or descriptor):	Business Consultation for Professionals (PsyBUS)
Web site:	
	`http://www.shpm.com/selfhelp/ppc/psybus.html`
Commands to:	`listserv@maelstrom.stjohns.edu`
Subscribe:	`subscribe PsyBUS Your-name`
Unsubscribe:	`unsubscribe PsyBUS`
List:	`PsyBUS@maelstrom.stjohns.edu`
List owner:	Marlene Maheu (E-mail: `drm@cybertowers.com`)

This list facilitates a discussion among practicing psychotherapists across disciplines interested in the development and marketing of practice-related products and services. There are no fees to join or participate.

Title (or descriptor):	Case Managers
Commands to:	`CASEMGR-request@cue.com`
Subscribe:	`subscribe`
Unsubscribe:	`unsubscribe`
List:	`CASEMGR@cue.com`
List owner:	Al Todak (E-mail: `prnmed@halcyon.com`)

This forum has been created to facilitate communications between case managers and utilization review (UR) and quality assurance (QA) professionals about the

problems and concerns unique to their role in the delivery of health care and mental
health services.

Title (or descriptor):	Child and Adolescent Psychiatry
Commands to:	`listserv@maelstrom.stjohns.edu`
Subscribe:	`subscribe child-psych Your-name`
Unsubscribe:	`unsubscribe child-psych`
List:	`child-psych@maelstrom.stjohns.edu`
List owner:	Amber Robey (E-mail: `akrobey@acs.ucalgary.ca`)

Research, clinical, and developmental issues having to do with children and adolescents.

Title (or descriptor):	Clinical Psychophysiology and Biofeedback
Commands to:	`majordomo@listp.apa.org`
Subscribe:	`subscribe PSYPHY`
Unsubscribe:	`unsubscribe PSYPHY`
List:	`PSYPHY@listp.apa.org`
List owner:	Arnon Rolnick (E-mail: `telhome@netvision.net.il`)

This forum is for the discussion of all aspects of psychophysiology and biofeedback.
This includes techniques and treatment methods in the fields of medicine, psychology, psychiatry, social work, education, and sports medicine.

Title (or descriptor):	Cognitive Science
Commands to:	`listserv@nic.sufnet.nl`
Subscribe:	`subscribe COGSCI Your-name`
Unsubscribe:	`unsubscribe COGSCI`
List:	`COGSCI@nic.sufnet.nl`
List owner:	Michel Weenink (E-mail: `weenink@psych.kun.nl`)

This list is an open, unmoderated discussion about all aspects of cognitive science.
Topics may include artificial intelligence, linguistics, philosophy, connectionism, psychology, conferences, lectures, and publications.

Title (or descriptor):   Community Psychology

Commands to: `listserv@maelstrom.stjohns.edu`

Subscribe: `subscribe commpsy Your-name`

Unsubscribe: `unsubscribe commpsy`

List: `commpsy@maelstrom.stjohns.edu`

List owners: Juan Carlos Garelli (E-mail: `lagare@attach.edu.ar`)

Bob Dick (E-mail: `bd@psy.uq.edu.au`)

This moderated list is for the discussion of community psychology. Community psychology as a field is devoted to helping psychologists understand and improve communities in ways that are helpful, cooperative, and culturally appropriate.

Title (or descriptor):   Computer Use in Social Services Network (CUSSNet)

Web site: `http://www.uta.edu/cussn/`

Commands to: `listserv@utarlvm1.uta.edu`

Subscribe: `subscribe cussnet Your-name`

Unsubscribe: `unsubscribe cussnet`

List: `cussnet@listserv.uta.edu`

List owner: Dick Schoech (E-mail: `schoech@uta.edu`)

An informal association of professionals interested in exchanging information and experiences on using computers in the human services.

Title (or descriptor):   Computers in Mental Health

Commands to: `listserv@maelstrom.stjohns.edu`

Subscribe: `subscribe CIMH Your-name`

Unsubscribe: `unsubscribe CIMH`

List: `CIMH@maelstrom.stjohns.edu`

List owner(s):   Martin Briscoe
(E-mail: `M.H.Briscoe@exeter.ac.uk`)

Carl Littlejohns
(E-mail: `csljohns@cix.compulink.co.uk`)

A closed list primarily aimed at professionals interested in computer and software applications in the field of mental health.

Title (or descriptor):	Controlled Drinking (CD)
Commands to:	`listserv@maelstrom.stjohns.edu`
Subscribe:	`subscribe CD Your-name`
Unsubscribe:	`unsubscribe CD`
List:	`CD@maelstrom.stjohns.edu`
List owner:	Martin Smith (E-mail: `mws@metis.no`)

This list is devoted to discussion of controlled drinking and controlled drug use. From the list's public description, "The beliefs and values likely to be shared by subscribers to this list include the following: Alcohol and drug use are behaviors, not diseases. [. . .] Behavior is a function of free will and moral values. It is not determined. Drug prohibition as a response to drug use has not been a successful policy."

Title (or descriptor):	Creative Arts Group Psychotherapy
Web site:	`http://www.artswire.org/asgpp/talk4.htm`
Commands to:	`majordomo@albie.wcupa.edu`
Subscribe:	`subscribe grouptalk`
Unsubscribe:	`unsubscribe grouptalk`
List:	`grouptalk@albie.wcupa.edu`
List owner:	Tom Treadwell (E-mail: `ttreadwell@albie.wcupa.edu`)

This list offers discussion of all types of creative arts group psychotherapy among professionals—for instance, psychodrama and group psychotherapy—among other relevant and related topics.

Title (or descriptor):	Current Issues in Psychology and Psychiatry
Commands to:	`listserv@maelstrom.stjohns.edu`
Subscribe:	`subscribe PSYCH-CI Your-name`
Unsubscribe:	`unsubscribe PSYCH-CI`
List:	`PSYCH-CI@maelstrom.stjohns.edu`

List owner:	Ian Pitchford (E-mail: `I.Pitchford@sheffield.ac.uk`)

For the general discussion of topical issues in research and clinical practice in psychology, psychiatry, and related fields.

Title (or descriptor):	Dependency & Self-Criticism in Psychological Health & Psychological Functioning
Commands to:	`listserv@maelstrom.stjohns.edu`
Subscribe:	`subscribe DEPEN-CRIT Your-name`
Unsubscribe:	`unsubscribe DEPEN-CRIT`
List:	`DEPEN-CRIT@maelstrom.stjohns.edu`
List owner:	Alan J. Lipman (E-mail: `ajlipman@clam.rutgers.edu`)

This is a discussion forum for mental health professionals and researchers interested in how personality variables, such as self-criticism and dependency, may influence a person's psychological health and well-being. While Blatt's introjective-analytic theory is emphasized, other approaches are also welcomed.

Title (or descriptor):	Disabilities, Social & Relational Context
Commands to:	`listserv@maelstrom.stjohns.edu`
Subscribe:	`subscribe disabled Your-name`
Unsubscribe:	`unsubscribe disabled`
List:	`disabled@maelstrom.stjohns.edu`
List owner(s):	D. S. Marks (E-mail: `d.s.marks@sheffield.ac.uk`) Ian Pitchford (E-mail: `I.Pitchford@sheffield.ac.uk`)

This list focuses on examining disability within a social and relational context. A dialectical approach to the body and psyche is emphasized.

Title (or descriptor):	Dissociative Disorders
Commands to:	`listserv@maelstrom.stjohns.edu`
Subscribe:	

`subscribe dissociative-disorders Your-name`

Unsubscribe:	`unsubscribe dissociative-disorders`
List:	
	`dissociative-disorders@maelstrom.stjohns.edu`
List owner:	Peter Barach (E-mail: `pbarach@sprynet.com`)

For the discussion of dissociative disorders in adults and children.

Title (or descriptor):	Dual-Diagnosis
Web site:	`http://users.erols.com/ksciacca`
Commands to:	`listserv@maelstrom.stjohns.edu`
Subscribe:	`subscribe dualdiag Your-name`
Unsubscribe:	`unsubscribe dualdiag`
List:	`dualdiag@maelstrom.stjohns.edu`
List owner:	Kathleen Sciacca (E-mail: `ksciacca@erols.com`)

This is a mailing list for co-occurring mental illness and substance disorders. Discussion regarding the theory, practice, treatment, research, and improved services for persons who have dual disorders is invited. This is a closed list for professionals only.

Title (or descriptor):	Eating Disorders
Commands to:	`listserv@maelstrom.stjohns.edu`
Subscribe:	`subscribe EAT-DIS Your-name`
Unsubscribe:	`unsubscribe EAT-DIS`
List:	`EAT-DIS@maelstrom.stjohns.edu`
List owner:	David H. Gleaves (E-mail: `dhg@psyc.tamu.edu`)

This list is for the discussion of causes, treatment, theory, and research of eating disorders such as bulimia nervosa, obesity, and anorexia. Clinicians and researchers are welcomed.

Title (or descriptor):	Emergency Psychiatry
Commands to:	`listserv@maelstrom.stjohns.edu`
Subscribe:	`subscribe ERPSYCH Your-name`

Unsubscribe:	`unsubscribe ERPSYCH`
List:	`ERPSYCH@maelstrom.stjohns.edu`
List owners:	Robert Buckley (E-mail: `bbuck@itsa.ucsf.edu`)
	Nancy Tice (E-mail: `72241.2676@compuserve.com`)

The topics appropriate to this list include medical, psychotherapeutic, social, and legal issues relating to the practice of emergency psychiatry.

Title (or descriptor):	Evolutionary Approach to Human Development
Commands to:	`listserv@maelstrom.stjohns.edu`
Subscribe:	`subscribe sociobio Your-name`
Unsubscribe:	`unsubscribe sociobio`
List:	`sociobio@maelstrom.stjohns.edu`

A professional discussion forum focused on the evolutionary approach to human development.

Title (or descriptor):	Family Networker
Commands to:	`majordomo@intr.net`
Subscribe:	`subscribe FTNetwork`
Unsubscribe:	`unsubscribe FTNetwork`
List:	`FTNetwork@intr.net`
List owner:	Laura Markowitz (E-mail: `LMarkowitz@aol.com`)

This is a mailing list for therapists who want to have an open conversation about issues that appear in *The Family Therapy Networker* magazine (the list's sponsor) or other issues of relevance. Members of the Forum Groups—regional small-group meetings of therapists to discuss the nature of current practice—also converse about their experiences and share ideas.

Title (or descriptor):	Forensic Psychiatry/Psychology
Commands to:	`listserv@maelstrom.stjohns.edu`
Subscribe:	`subscribe forensic-psych Your-name`
Unsubscribe:	`unsubscribe forensic-psych`

List:	`forensic-psych@maelstrom.stjohns.edu`
List owner:	Ron Schlensky (E-mail: `3004rs@west.net`)

Discussion of criminal and civil forensic psychiatry/psychology, including treatment issues, trial issues, disability insurance, and ethics.

Title (or descriptor):	Geriatric Neuro
Commands to:	`listserv@maelstrom.stjohns.edu`
Subscribe:	`subscribe G-NEURO Your-name`
Unsubscribe:	`unsubscribe G-NEURO`
List:	`G-NEURO@maelstrom.stjohns.edu`
List owner:	Mike Usman (E-mail: `MikeUsman@aol.com`)

This list discusses neurobehavioral disorders in older adults, such as Alzheimer's, frontal lobe degenerations, vascular dementia, and delirium. It is geared toward the topics of neuropsychology, neuropsychiatry, gerontology, behavioral neurology; psychosocial issues may also be discussed.

Title (or descriptor):	Grants and Foundation Resources
Web site:	`http://charitychannel.com/forums/`
Commands to:	`listserv@philanthropy-review.com`
Subscribe:	`subscribe grants Your-name`
Unsubscribe:	`unsubscribe grants`
List:	`grants@philanthropy-review.com`

A forum that focuses on all aspects of grants and foundations.

Title (or descriptor):	Grants in Substance Abuse and Gun Violence
Web site:	

    `http://www.jointogether.org/about/jtodirect/email/`
    `frameset.html`

An announcement-only mailing list with national news, research, and alerts, and funding news and grant announcements for topics related to gun violence and substance abuse.

Title (or descriptor):	Group Psychotherapy
Commands to:	`listserv@lists.apa.org`
Subscribe:	`subscribe group-psychotherapy`
Unsubscribe:	`unsubscribe group-psychotherapy`
List:	`group-psychotherapy@lists.apa.org`
List owner:	Haim Weinberg (E-mail: `haimw@netvision.net.il`)

For any clinician who works with a group psychotherapeutic modality and for the discussion of group work and group psychotherapy.

Title (or descriptor):	Holistic and Alternative Medicine
Commands to:	`listserv@citadel.net`
Subscribe:	`subscribe holistic-L Your-name`
Unsubscribe:	`unsubscribe holistic-L`
List:	`holistic-L@citadel.net`
List owner:	Leonard A. Manion (E-mail: `ceo@citadel.net`)

The purpose of the list is to discuss alternative health concepts and possible solutions for patient care. This is a closed list for health professionals only.

Title (or descriptor):	Human Relations, Authority, and Justice
Commands to:	`listserv@maelstrom.stjohns.edu`
Subscribe:	`subscribe HRAJ Your-name`
Unsubscribe:	`unsubscribe HRAJ`
List:	`HRAJ@maelstrom.stjohns.edu`
List owners:	Robert Young (E-mail: `robert@rmy1.demon.co.uk`)
	Ian Pitchford (E-mail: `I.Pitchford@Sheffield.ac.uk`)

Designed to encourage the application of psychoanalytic and related psychodynamic approaches to the understanding of group, institutional, cultural, and political processes.

Title (or descriptor):	Human Resources Development
Commands to:	`listserv@yorku.ca`
Subscribe:	`subscribe HRD-L Your-name`
Unsubscribe:	`unsubscribe HRD-L`
List:	`HRD-L@yorku.ca`
List owner:	Al Doran (E-mail: `dorana@yorku.ca`)

Intended to promote the exchange of information on human resource development.

Title (or descriptor):	Human Resources Network (HRNET)
Commands to:	`listserv@cornell.edu`
Subscribe:	`subscribe HRNET Your-name`
Unsubscribe:	`unsubscribe HRNET`
List:	`HRNET@cornell.edu`
List owner:	Hope Tinsley (E-mail: `hope@academy.pace.edu`)

This list is for those professionals interested in research and the practice of human resource management. Topics can include almost anything, including research ideas, statistical methods, research measures, teaching methods, and requests about member activity in particular topic areas. Forum topics may include labor law developments and interchanges by members on teaching, research, and practical issues related to the field.

Title (or descriptor):	Human Rights in Psychiatry (Dendrite)
Web site:	`http://www.efn.org/~dendron/`
Commands to:	`majordomo@efn.org`
Subscribe:	`subscribe dendrite`
Unsubscribe:	`unsubscribe dendrite`
List:	`dendrite@efn.org`
List owner:	David Oaks (E-mail: `dendron@efn.org`)

This resource is a one-way mailing list, which sends periodic announcements (about twice a month) to list members about human rights in—and alternatives to—psychiatry. A service of Support Coalition's Web site.

Title (or descriptor):   Hypnosis

Commands to: `listserv@maelstrom.stjohns.edu`

Subscribe: `subscribe hypnosis Your-name`

Unsubscribe: `unsubscribe hypnosis`

List: `hypnosis@maelstrom.stjohns.edu`

List owner: Irving Kirsch (E-mail: `IRVINGK@uconnvm.uconn.edu`)

This forum is for the discussion of hypnosis and the broader topics of suggestion and suggestibility. It is a closed list, open to researchers and scientifically minded clinicians who would like to exchange ideas and information on these topics.

Title (or descriptor):   Industrial and Organizational Psychology (IOOB-L)

Commands to: `listserv@uga.cc.uga.edu`

Subscribe: `subscribe IOOB-L Your-name`

Unsubscribe: `unsubscribe IOOB-L`

List: `IOOB-L@uga.cc.uga.edu`

List owner: John L. Cofer (E-mail: `coferjl@utk.edu`)

A discussion list dedicated to industrial/organizational psychology and organization behavior (IOOB).

Title (or descriptor):   International Society for Mental Health Online

Web site: `http://www.ismho.org/`

Commands to: `listproc@cmhc.com`

Subscribe: `subscribe ismho Your-name`

Unsubscribe: `unsubscribe ismho`

List: `ismho@cmhc.com`

The open discussion forum for the International Society for Mental Health Online, an organization formed in 1997 to promote the understanding, use, and development of online communication, information, and technology for the international mental health community.

Title (or descriptor):   Internships, Psychology
Commands to: `listserv@utkvm1.utk.edu`
Subscribe: `subscribe INTERN-L Your-name`
Unsubscribe: `unsubscribe INTERN-L`
List: `intern-L@utkvm1.utk.edu`
List owner: Victor W. Barr (E-mail: `barr@utkux.utcc.utk.edu`)

This forum is designed to foster discussion of the psychology internship process and is open to all current and prospective interns, as well as internship program staff.

Title (or descriptor):   Joint Commission Accreditation
Commands to: `listserv@usa.net`
Subscribe: `subscribe JCAHO-WATCH Your-name`
Unsubscribe: `unsubscribe JCAHO-WATCH`
List: `JCAHO-WATCH@usa.net`
List owner: Unknown (E-mail: `dhernan@ucg.com`)

For discussions on the process of obtaining Joint Commission Accreditation.

Title (or descriptor):   Latin Psych
Commands to: `listserv@maelstrom.stjohns.edu`
Subscribe: `subscribe lat-psy Your-name`
Unsubscribe: `unsubscribe lat-psy`
List: `lat-psy@maelstrom.stjohns.edu`
List owner: Hector R. Biaggi
                             (E-mail: `Biagfi@pcpsych1.fla.ccf.org`)

This list is to encourage communication among Latin mental health professionals around the world. Its main languages are Spanish, Portuguese, and English, in that order. It has a significant South American representation and a strong clinical orientation.

Title (or descriptor):   Learned Helplessness

Web site:

    `http://www.psych.upenn.edu/~fresco/helplessness.html`

Commands to: `listserv@lists.apa.org`

Subscribe: `subscribe helplessness`

Unsubscribe: `unsubscribe helplessness`

List: `helplessness@lists.apa.org`

List owners: Martin Seligman
     (E-mail: `seligman@cattell.psych.upenn.edu`)

     David Fresco
     (E-mail: `fresco@cattell.psych.upenn.edu`)

This forum is for the discussion of research on learned helplessness and explanatory style. Topics may include biological substratum, depression, anxiety, preventions, CAVE, politics, children, personal control, health, battering, bereavement, PTSD, sex differences, pessimism, work, and heritability issues.

Title (or descriptor):   Learning—Behavior, Models, Theory

Commands to: `listserv@maelstrom.stjohns.edu`

Subscribe: `subscribe learning Your-name`

Unsubscribe: `unsubscribe learning`

List: `learning@maelstrom.stjohns.edu`

List owner: Garry A. Flint (E-mail: `gaflint@junction.net`)

This list is for the discussion of human behavioral and experiential phenomena and developing models of learning. It is opened to researchers and clinicians interested in a discussion of learning models of human behavior or experiential phenomenon.

Title (or descriptor):   Managed Behavioral Healthcare

Commands to: `listserv@maelstrom.stjohns.edu`

Subscribe: `subscribe MBHC Your-name`

Unsubscribe: `unsubscribe MBHC`

List: `MBHC@maelstrom.stjohns.edu`

List owners: Greg Alter (E-mail: `alter@surf.com`)
                          Deborah Teplow (E-mail: `debtep@ix.netcom.com`)

This list is for the discussion of the managed behavioral health care field. Topics may include health care reform, best clinical practices, insurance benefits, group practice structures, outcome research, and informatics. This list can get very busy at times.

Title (or descriptor):   Medical Informatics

Commands to: `maiser@usa.net`

Subscribe: `subscribe MDINFO`

Unsubscribe: `unsubscribe MDINFO`

List: `MDINFO@usa.net`

List owner: Alexandre Aguiar (E-mail: `asaguiar@opus.com.br`)

Hosts a discussion list on medical informatics, computer, and technology topics.

Title (or descriptor):   Medical Records Automation

Commands to: `listserv@usa.net`

Subscribe: `subscribe MEDREC-L Your-name`

Unsubscribe: `unsubscribe MEDREC-L`

List: `MEDREC-L@usa.net`

List owner: Robert J. M. Long (E-mail: `rlong@ucg.com`)

This discussion list provides an online forum for health information management (HIM) professionals to exchange department-management and systems-implementation strategies with their peers. It may also offer periodic articles and survey results.

Title (or descriptor):   Medicare Part-B Billing

Commands to: `listserv@usa.net`

Subscribe: `subscribe PARTB-L Your-name`

Unsubscribe: `unsubscribe PARTB-L`

List: `PARTB-L@usa.net`

List owner: Unknown

For the discussion of issues related to Medicare Part-B billing.

Title (or descriptor):	Mental Health in the Media
Commands to:	listserv@lists.apa.org
Subscribe:	subscribe PSY-MEDIA
Unsubscribe:	unsubscribe PSY-MEDIA
List:	PSY-MEDIA@lists.apa.org
List owner:	Les Posen (E-mail: lposen@ozonline.com.au)

Features a broad discussion of public perception and portrayal of mental health and mental health issues.

Title (or descriptor):	Net Dynamics
Web site:	http://www.enabling.org/ia/netdynam/
Commands to:	listserv@maelstrom.stjohns.edu
Subscribe:	subscribe netdynam Your-name
Unsubscribe:	unsubscribe netdynam
List:	netdynam@maelstrom.stjohns.edu

This list examines online group dynamics, covering topics such as the perceptions of the other list participants, the dynamics of flame wars, power and persuasion, and what is effective communication and why.

Title (or descriptor):	Neuro-Psych
Commands to:	majordomo@psycom.net
Subscribe:	subscribe neuro-psych
Unsubscribe:	unsubscribe neuro-psych
List:	neuro-psych@psycom.net
List owner:	Ivan Goldberg (E-mail: psydoc@psycom.net)

A forum for the professional discussion of clinical neuropsychiatry and neuropsychology. Topics appropriate to this list include assessment of brain disorders, MRI and PET imaging scans, case presentations, prevention, and theory and research behind the latest testing instruments and causative factors.

Title (or descriptor):	Personality Assessment Inventory (PAI-NET)
Commands to:	`majordomo@teleport.com`
Subscribe:	`subscribe PAI-NET`
Unsubscribe:	`unsubscribe PAI-NET`
List:	`PAI-NET@teleport.com`
List owner:	Robert B. Basham (E-mail: `rbasham@teleport.com`)

This is a closed list for psychologists interested in the Personality Assessment Inventory (PAI). The forum allows for open exchange of scientific, scholarly, and clinical ideas regarding the test and its applications. News, research findings, literature summaries, comments on the test's methodology, discussion of clinical applications, and case studies of the test are all welcomed.

Title (or descriptor):	Philopsychy Society
Web site:	`http://www.hkbu.edu.hk/~ppp/ppp/PPS.html`
Commands to:	`majordomo@listserver.hkbu.edu.hk`
Subscribe:	`subscribe PPS-L`
Unsubscribe:	`unsubscribe PPS-L`
List:	`PPS-L@listserver.hkbu.edu.hk`
List owner:	Stephen Palmquist (E-mail: `stevepq@hkbu.edu.hk`)

This serves as a forum for discussing issues of interest to members of the Philopsychy Society. Topics may include the interface between philosophy and psychology, any philosophical or psychological topics that are likely to enhance our understanding of the theory and practice of "soul-loving" ("philopsychy"), topics from any area of academia (or life in general) that are likely to accomplish the latter goal.

Title (or descriptor):	Political Science–Psychology/Psychiatry
Commands to:	`listserv@maelstrom.stjohns.edu`
Subscribe:	`subscribe POLI-PSY Your-name`
Unsubscribe:	`unsubscribe POLI-PSY`
List:	`POLI-PSY@maelstrom.stjohns.edu`
List owner:	Robert White (E-mail: `rwhite@ccs.carleton.ca`)

A forum for the discussion of political aspects, theories, and research of psychology and psychiatry.

Title (or descriptor):	Psy-Language
Commands to:	`listserv@maelstrom.stjohns.edu`
Subscribe:	`subscribe PSY-LANG Your-name`
Unsubscribe:	`unsubscribe PSY-LANG`
List:	`PSY-LANG@maelstrom.stjohns.edu`
List owner:	Jack Gerber (E-mail: `jack@netaxs.com`)

This list is for the discussion of language and psychopathology by interested clinicians and researchers. Topics may include theories of language and speech and their relevance for the study of psychopathological phenomena; research methodologies and findings; and ethical and practical issues of the study of psychopathological speech.

Title (or descriptor):	Psybernet
Commands to:	`listserv@home.ease.lsoft.com`
Subscribe:	`subscribe PSYBER-L Your-name`
Unsubscribe:	`unsubscribe PSYBER-L`
List:	`PSYBER-L@home.ease.lsoft.com`
List owner:	Walter Logeman (E-mail: `wlogeman@ch.cyberxpress.co.nz`)

This is a forum devoted to the experiential exploration of the psyche in cyberspace. Topics may include leadership skills in the administration of mailing lists, list dynamics, depth psychology on the Internet, and professional services on the Internet.

Title (or descriptor):	Psychiatric Nurses
Commands to:	`listserv@maelstrom.stjohns.edu`
Subscribe:	`subscribe PSYNURSE Your-name`
Unsubscribe:	`unsubscribe PSYNURSE`
List:	`PSYNURSE@maelstrom.stjohns.edu`

List owners:	Mike Carter and Bert Vortman (E-mail: `psynurse-request@maelstrom.stjohns.edu`)

For the discussion of issues facing psychiatric nurses, centering around clinical practice topics.

Title (or descriptor):	Psychiatric Social Workers
Commands to:	`listserv@maelstrom.stjohns.edu`
Subscribe:	`subscribe PSYC-SOC Your-name`
Unsubscribe:	`unsubscribe PSYC-SOC`
List:	`PSYC-SOC@maelstrom.stjohns.edu`
List owner:	Beverly Jamison (E-mail: `bjamison@puffin.marymount.edu`)

For the discussion of issues of interest to psychiatric social workers.

Title (or descriptor):	Psychiatry
Commands to:	`listserv@maelstrom.stjohns.edu`
Subscribe:	`subscribe PSYCHL Your-name`
Unsubscribe:	`unsubscribe PSYCHL`
List:	`PSYCHL@maelstrom.stjohns.edu`
List owner:	Ian Pitchford (E-mail: `I.Pitchford@Sheffield.ac.uk`)

This is a list primarily for mental health professionals to discuss theories of psychopathology, methods for critical assessment of theories and practices, relevant research with emphasis on the interrelationship of theory, fact, and practice. This list also encourages the exchange of views on research and theory regarding psychopathology with particular emphasis on application to practice of all sorts.

Title (or descriptor):	Psychiatry, Child and Adolescent
Commands to:	`listserv@maelstrom.stjohns.edu`
Subscribe:	`subscribe child-psych Your-name`
Unsubscribe:	`unsubscribe child-psych`
List:	`child-psych@maelstrom.stjohns.edu`

List owners:	Amber K. Robey (E-mail: `akrobey@acs.ucalgary.ca`) Nathan Munn (E-mail: `nathanmt@aol.com`)

This list is dedicated to the discussion of issues regarding child and adolescent psychiatry. Topics may include family therapy, residential and in-patient care, attention deficit disorder (ADD/ADHD), child psychiatric disorders and treatment, case studies, and journal discussions. This is a closed forum for professionals only.

Title (or descriptor):	Psychiatry and the Law
Commands to:	`listserv@maelstrom.stjohns.edu`
Subscribe:	`subscribe PSYLAW-L Your-name`
Unsubscribe:	`unsubscribe PSYLAW-L`
List:	`PSYLAW-L@maelstrom.stjohns.edu`
List owners:	Roy Malpass and Douglas Narby (E-mail: `psylaw-L-request@maelstrom.stjohns.edu`)

For discussion of all areas of the interface of psychology and law in the global context of varying legal systems and approaches to psychology.

Title (or descriptor):	Psychiatry, Philosophy, and Society
Commands to:	`listserv@maelstrom.stjohns.edu`
Subscribe:	`subscribe PSYPHIL Your-name`
Unsubscribe:	`unsubscribe PSYPHIL`
List:	`PSYPHIL@maelstrom.stjohns.edu`
List owners:	Nick Crossley (E-mail: `n.g.crossley@sheffield.ac.uk`) Ian Pitchford (E-mail: `I.Pitchford@Sheffield.ac.uk`)

Offers a unique interdisciplinary forum that encourages a critical analysis of psychiatric, psychotherapeutic, and psychological practices.

Title (or descriptor):	Psychiatry Resources
Commands to:	`listserv@maelstrom.stjohns.edu`
Subscribe:	`subscribe P-SOURCE Your-name`

Unsubscribe:	`unsubscribe P-SOURCE`
List:	`P-SOURCE@maelstrom.stjohns.edu`
List owner:	Myron Pulier (E-mail: `mpulier@interport.net`)

A resource exchange forum for those interested in gaining maximum use of psychiatric and related resources of the Internet, off-the-Internet, conference, and job information and announcements.

Title (or descriptor):	Psychoanalysis
Commands to:	`listserv@maelstrom.stjohns.edu`
Subscribe:	`subscribe psychoan Your-name`
Unsubscribe:	`unsubscribe psychoan`
List:	`psychoan@maelstrom.stjohns.edu`
List owner:	Robert Galatzer-Levy (E-mail: `gala@midway.uchicago.edu`)

A forum to host issues of psychoanalytic practice, theory, politics, history, and the application of psychoanalysis to other disciplines.

Title (or descriptor):	Psychoanalysis and the Public Sphere
Commands to:	`listproc@sheffield.ac.uk`
Subscribe:	`subscribe psa-public-sphere Your-name`
Unsubscribe:	`unsubscribe psa-public-sphere`
List:	`psa-public-sphere@sheffield.ac.uk`
List owners:	Robert Young (E-mail: `robert@rmy1.demon.co.uk`) and Mark Alexander (E-mail: `m.alexander@wellcome.ac.uk`)

For discussion of wider social, cultural, political, ideological, institutional, and related aspects of psychoanalysis and other psychodynamic approaches.

Title (or descriptor):	Psychoanalytic Studies
Web site:	

`http://www.shef.ac.uk/uni/academic/N-Q/psysc/psastud.html`

Commands to:	`listproc@sheffield.ac.uk`
Subscribe:	`subscribe psychoanalytic-studies` `Your-name`
Unsubscribe:	`unsubscribe psychoanalytic-studies`
List:	`psychoanalytic-studies@sheffield.ac.uk`
List owners:	Sean Homer (E-mail: `s.i.homer@sheffield,ac.uk`) and Tim Kendall (E-mail: `t.j.kendall@sheffield.ac.uk`)

For scholarly discussion of psychoanalysis and related psychodynamic approaches; topics may include anything that has a psychoanalytic or psychodynamic dimension.

Title (or descriptor):	Psychodrama
Commands to:	`listserv@maelstrom.stjohns.edu`
Subscribe:	`subscribe psychodrama Your-name`
Unsubscribe:	`unsubscribe psychodrama`
List:	`psychodrama@maelstrom.stjohns.edu`

A forum to discuss, act, and develop old and new ideas, projects, suggestions on Moreno's psychodrama, role-playing, cathartic narration, and other kinds of educational and therapeutical dramalike interaction.

Title (or descriptor):	Psychoeducational Assessment
Commands to:	`listserv@listserv.arizona.edu`
Subscribe:	
`subscribe psychoeducational_assess Your-name`	
Unsubscribe:	`unsubscribe psychoeducational_assess`
List:	
`psychoeducational_assess@listserv.arizona.edu`	
List owner:	R. Dean Cloward (E-mail: `cloward@u.arizona.edu`)

For those interested in psychoeducational assessment and school psychology.

Title (or descriptor):	Psychological Assessment and Psychometrics
Commands to:	`listserv@maelstrom.stjohns.edu`

Subscribe:	`subscribe ASSESS-P Your-name`
Unsubscribe:	`unsubscribe ASSESS-P`
List:	`ASSESS-P@maelstrom.stjohns.edu`
List owner:	David L. DiLalla (E-mail: `ddilalla@siu.edu`)

This is a forum for scholarly discussion of psychometric theory and applications, as well as psychological and psychiatric assessment in clinical and research settings. It is also relevant for discussion of relationships between normal personality characteristics and psychopathology.

Title (or descriptor):	Psychological Types
Related Web site:	`http://www.egroups.com/group/psych-type/`
Commands to:	`majordomo@sacam.oren.ortn.edu`
Subscribe:	`subscribe psych-type Your-email-address`
Unsubscribe:	`unsubscribe psych-type`
List:	`psych-type@sacam.oren.ortn.edu`
List owner:	Joe Butt (E-mail: `jabutt@sacam.oren.ortn.edu`)

Focused on the discussion of psychological personality typing, especially using the Myers-Briggs Type Indicator (MBTI).

Title (or descriptor):	Psychologists, Clinical
Commands to:	`listserv@listserv.nodak.edu`
Subscribe:	

`subscribe clinical-psychologists Your-name`

Unsubscribe:	`unsubscribe clinical-psychologists`
List:	

`clinical-psychologists@listserv.nodak.edu`

List owner:	Joseph Plaud (E-mail: `Joseph_Plaud@brown.edu`)

This forum is the central online discussion area for clinical psychologists to congregate and share ideas that occupy the broad area of clinical psychology. Clinical case conferences are welcomed, as are discussion on treatment and research within clinical psychology and closely related areas.

Title (or descriptor):	Psychologists, Division 12 of APA
Commands to:	`listserv@listserv.nodak.edu`
Subscribe:	`subscribe DIV12 Your-name`
Unsubscribe:	`unsubscribe DIV12`
List:	`DIV12@listserv.nodak.edu`
List owner:	Joseph Plaud (E-mail: `Joseph_Plaud@brown.edu`)

This is the official mailing list for members of Division 12 (Clinical Psychology) of the American Psychological Association. Its primary function is to serve as a means of communication and rapid dissemination of knowledge on issues ranging from the governance of clinical psychology to research and clinical issues relating to the science and practice of clinical psychology.

Title (or descriptor):	Psychologists, National List (PsyUSA)
Commands to:	`listserv@maelstrom.stjohns.edu`
Subscribe:	`subscribe PsyUSA Your-name`
Unsubscribe:	`unsubscribe PsyUSA`
List:	`PsyUSA@maelstrom.stjohns.edu`

This long-standing and popular list was formed to network practicing psychologists. Topics include the dissemination of announcements on practice management, treatment resources, insurance companies and HMOs, job openings, computer software (clinical, office, and billing), new practice opportunities and sale of practices, legal and liability issues, requests for consultations, referrals, treatment protocols and guidelines, business methods, practice economics, advanced training and certifications, federal and state legislation affecting psychology, issues of various psychological associations, and changes and trends in behavioral health care delivery structures. Contact the list owner for additional information about the entire PsyUSA network, which consists of individual state mailing lists and two additional national lists (see below) for discussion of the latest news, trends, information, and opinions permeating the mental health care field. This list can get very busy at times.

Title (or descriptor):	Psychologists, National List (PsyChat)
Commands to:	`listserv@maelstrom.stjohns.edu`

Subscribe:	`subscribe PsyChat Your-name`
Unsubscribe:	`unsubscribe PsyChat`
List:	`PsyChat@maelstrom.stjohns.edu`

A part of the PsyUSA Network of associated mailing lists, this national list encourages informal group conversations among psychologists, light-hearted dialogue, "opportunities to develop personal relationships with other [. . .] subscribers, and other kinds of comradery" (from the public description of this list).

Title (or descriptor):	Psychologists, National List (PsyPOV)
Commands to:	`listserv@maelstrom.stjohns.edu`
Subscribe:	`subscribe PsyPOV Your-name`
Unsubscribe:	`unsubscribe PsyPOV`
List:	`PsyPOV@maelstrom.stjohns.edu`

PsyPOV (Point of View) is a part of the PsyUSA Network of associated mailing lists. This national list encourages debate among psychologists on various topical and timely issues, such as managed care, ethics, psychotherapy treatment, training issues, supervision, etc.

Title (or descriptor):	Psychologists, Practice
Commands to:	`listserv@lists.apa.org`
Subscribe:	`subscribe practice Your-name`
Unsubscribe:	`unsubscribe practice`
List:	`practice@lists.apa.org`

For psychologist members of the American Psychological Association to discuss practice issues.

Title (or descriptor):	Psychology in Behavioral Health Practice
Commands to:	`listserv@maelstrom.stjohns.edu`
Subscribe:	`subscribe psymed Your-name`

Unsubscribe:	`unsubscribe psymed`
List:	`psymed@maelstrom.stjohns.edu`

A forum for the discussion of assessment techniques and treatment methods applicable to behavioral health problems, the application of psychology to lifestyle and behavior changes in the prevention of health problems, employment opportunities in behavioral health, maintianing relationships with physicians and other health care providers, and sources of information accessible via the Internet that are relevant to behavioral health.

Title (or descriptor):	Psychology, Developmental Disabilities
Commands to:	`listserv@listserv.nodak.edu`
Subscribe:	`subscribe PSYCH-DD Your-name`
Unsubscribe:	`unsubscribe PSYCH-DD`
List:	`PSYCH-DD@listserv.nodak.edu`
List owner:	Paul Kolstoe (E-mail: `pkolstoe@plains.nodak.edu`)

The purpose of this list is to promote discussion of psychological issues of people with developmental disabilities.

Title (or descriptor):	Psychology, Theoretical and Philosophical Foundations of
Commands to:	`listserver@pmc.psych.nwu.edu`
Subscribe:	`subscribe socrates Your-name`
Unsubscribe:	`unsubscribe socrates`
List:	`socrates@pmc.psych.nwu.edu`

Devoted to discussions on the theoretical and philosophical foundations of psychology.

Title (or descriptor):	Psychology Graduate Students
Commands to:	`listserv@lists.apa.org`
Subscribe:	`subscribe PSYCGRAD Your-name`
Unsubscribe:	`unsubscribe PSYCGRAD`

List: `psycgrad@lists.apa.org`

List owner: Jason Washburn
                            (E-mail: `jwashbur@wppost.depaul.edu`)

A vehicle for graduate students in psychology to communicate ideas and share information about conferences worldwide.

Title (or descriptor):   Psychology in Law Enforcement

Commands to: `listserv@maelstrom.stjohns.edu`

Subscribe: `subscribe psycop Your-name`

Unsubscribe: `unsubscribe psycop`

List: `psycop@maelstrom.stjohns.edu`

A discussion list for police psychologists on the delivery of psychological services to law enforcement personnel.

Title (or descriptor):   Psychology of Religion

Web site:
    `http://www.lightlink.com/xine/psy_religion/`
    `psyrel-l.html`

Commands to: `majordomo@lightlink.com`

Subscribe: `subscribe psyrel-L`

Unsubscribe: `unsubscribe psyrel-L`

List: `psyrel-L@lightlink.com`

This list is for the academic discussion of the psychology of religion, its history, focus, cultural milieu, methods, and approaches.

Title (or descriptor):   Psychology of Women (Psycwomen)

Commands to: `psycwomen-request@fre.fsu.umd.edu`

Subscribe: `susbscribe psycwomen`

Unsubscribe: `signoff psycwomen`

List:	psycwomen@fre.fsu.emd.edu
List owner:	Pat Santoro (E-mail: e2pysan@fre.fsu.umd.edu)

This is a discussion list for undergraduate and graduate students who are interested in issues related to the psychology of women. Topics may include what it's like to volunteer at a women's shelter, applying to graduate school in counseling, history of psychology and psyche of women, and domestic violence.

Title (or descriptor):	Psychopharmacology
Web site:	
	http://uhs.bsd.uchicago.edu/~bhsiung/tips/tips.html
Commands to:	majordomo@psycom.net
Subscribe:	subscribe psycho-pharm
Unsubscribe:	unsubscribe psycho-pharm
List:	psycho-pharm@psycom.net
List owner:	Ivan Goldberg (E-mail: psydoc@psycom.net)

This is a forum to discuss the treatment of individuals with psychiatric disorders through the use of psychotropic medications. One of the oldest and most popular mailing lists online, it enjoys a high traffic volume and participation by a number of experts in this field.

Title (or descriptor):	Psychotherapists in Training
Commands to:	listserv@maelstrom.stjohns.edu
Subscribe:	subscribe PIT-D Your-name
Unsubscribe:	unsubscribe PIT-D
List:	PIT-D@maelstrom.stjohns.edu
List owners:	Warren Bush (E-mail: warrenb@maelstrom.stjohns.edu) and
	David Mahony (E-mail: dmahony@rdz.stjohns.edu)

A list for all psychotherapists in training—at all levels of training—for the discussion of training issues, supervisory relationships, and therapy experiences.

Title (or descriptor):	Psychotherapy Practice
Commands to:	`majordomo@psycom.net`
Subscribe:	`subscribe psychotherapy-practice`
Unsubscribe:	`unsubscribe psychotherapy-practice`
List:	`psychotherapy-practice@psycom.net`
List owner:	Ivan Goldberg (E-mail: `psydoc@psycom.net`)

This list is for fully trained practitioners who wish to discuss the techniques and outcome of psychotherapy. Mental health clinicians of all types are welcome to join this list.

Title (or descriptor):	Psychotherapy–Pharmacotherapy Comparative Outcome Research
Commands to:	`listserv@maelstrom.stjohns.edu`
Subscribe:	`subscribe PSY-PHAR Your-name`
Unsubscribe:	`unsubscribe PSY-PHAR`
List:	`PSY-PHAR@maelstrom.stjohns.edu`
List owner:	Alan J. Lipman (E-mail: `lipman@aol.com`)

This is a forum for psychologists, psychiatrists, and other mental health researchers and clinicians to discuss topics regarding psychotherapy–pharmacotherapy comparative outcome research. Empirical, theoretical, and case-based discussions are welcomed.

Title (or descriptor):	Psychotherapy Research
Commands to:	`majordomo@psycom.net`
Subscribe:	`subscribe psychotherapy-research`
Unsubscribe:	`unsubscribe psychotherapy-research`
List:	`psychotherapy-research@psycom.net`
List owner:	Ivan Goldberg (E-mail: `psydoc@psycom.net`)

For fully trained practitioners and researchers who wish to discuss outcome research in psychotherapy.

Title (or descriptor):   Research Design

Commands to: `listserv@lists.apa.org`

Subscribe: `subscribe research-design`

Unsubscribe: `unsubscribe research-design`

List: `research-design@lists.apa.org`

List owner: B. Hudnall Stamm
(E-mail: `afbhs@vms.acad2.alaska.edu`)

For researchers in the behavioral health sciences to discuss issues of research and study design and statistics.

Title (or descriptor):   Rorschach

Commands to: `listserv@maelstrom.stjohns.edu`

Subscribe: `subscribe rorschach Your-name`

Unsubscribe: `unsubscribe rorschach`

List: `rorschach@maelstrom.stjohns.edu`

List owner: Jack Gerber (E-mail: `jack@netaxis.com`)

For the general discussion of the Rorschach Inkblot test.

Title (or descriptor):   Rorchach, European

Commands to: `listserv@psychology.su.se`

Subscribe: `subscribe EURORLIST Your-name`

Unsubscribe: `unsubscribe EURORLIST`

List: `EURORLIST@psychology.su.se`

List owner: Unknown (E-mail: `hjn@psychology.su.se`)

For the distribution of information concerning workshops, seminars, ongoing research and education in Europe in the area of Rorschach and projective methods, particularly the Rorschach Comprehensive System.

Title (or descriptor):   Rural Care

Commands to: `listserv@lists.apa.org`

Subscribe: `subscribe rural-care`

Unsubscribe:	`unsubscribe rural-care`
List:	`rural-care@lists.apa.org`
List owner:	B. Hudnall Stamm
	(E-mail: `afbhs@vms.acad2.alaska.edu`)

This list is for the support of health care workers isolated in rural and bush communities, and for the continuing dialogue of those concerned with health care delivery in remote and developing areas worldwide. The forum is intended for health care workers in all types of settings.

Title (or descriptor):	Sex Offenders Treatment
Commands to:	`listserver@casconn.com`
Subscribe:	`subscribe SOTP-L Your-name`
Unsubscribe:	`unsubscribe SOTP-L`
List:	`SOTP-L@casconn.com`
List owner:	Unknown

For the discussion by mental health professionals of various treatments for sex offenders.

Title (or descriptor):	Sleep Technology
Commands to:	`listserv@dartmouth.edu`
Subscribe:	`subscribe SLPTECH Your-name`
Unsubscribe:	`unsubscribe SLPTECH`
List:	`SLPTECH@dartmouth.edu`
List owner:	Mary MacDonald
	(E-mail: `Mary.M.MacDonald@dartmouth.edu`)

A moderated discussion forum for all issues regarding sleep technology.

Title (or descriptor):	Social Science Data Discussion
Commands to:	`listproc@irss.unc.edu`
Subscribe:	`subscribe SOS-DATA Your-name`
Unsubscribe:	`unsubscribe SOS-DATA`

List: `SOS-DATA@irss.unc.edu`

List owner: Jim Cassell (E-mail: `irsslmgr@unc.edu`)

This is a forum for discussion of any topic related to social science data. Topics may include references to sources of data on some particular subject, conference announcements, new data sources, announcements of data archives, and information sources available online.

Title (or descriptor):	Social Work
Commands to:	`listproc@lists.vcu.edu`
Subscribe:	`subscribe SCIOFSLW Your-name`
Unsubscribe:	`unsubscribe SCIOFSLW`
List:	`SCIOFSLW@lists.vcu.edu`
List owner:	W. Beverly (E-mail: `wbeverly@titan.vcu.edu`)

For the discussion of issues related to social work.

Title (or descriptor):	Social Work
Commands to:	`majordomo@uwrf.edu`
Subscribe:	`subscribe SOCWORK Your-name`
Unsubscribe:	`unsubscribe SOCWORK`
List:	`SOCWORK@uwrf.edu`
List owner:	Ogden Rogers (E-mail: `owner-socwork@uwrf.edu`)

A list devoted to discussion of issues related to social work.

Title (or descriptor):	Stroke
Commands to:	`maiser@usa.net`
Subscribe:	`subscribe STROKE-BR`
Unsubscribe:	`unsubscribe STROKE-BR`
List:	`STROKE-BR@usa.net`
List owner:	Marcia Maiumi Fukujima (E-mail: `maiumi@sti.com.br`)

A moderated discussion list on stroke and cerebrovascular disease—open to professionals who work with stroke patients.

Title (or descriptor):	Telehealth
Commands to:	`listserv@maelstrom.stjohns.edu`
Subscribe:	`subscribe telehealth Your-name`
Unsubscribe:	`unsubscribe telehealth`
List:	`telehealth@maelstrom.stjohns.edu`

A professional discussion list focused on telehealth ethics, laws, research, services, and technologies amongst mental health professionals.

Title (or descriptor):	Thanatology
Commands to:	`majordomo@psycom.net`
Subscribe:	`subscribe thana-tology Your-name`
Unsubscribe:	`unsubscribe thana-tology`
List:	`thana-tology@psycom.net`
List owner:	Ivan Goldberg (E-mail: `psydoc@psycom.net`)

Topics and discussion on thanatology—the study of death and dying.

Title (or descriptor):	Therapists in Recovery from Addiction
Commands to:	`listserv@maelstrom.stjohns.edu`
Subscribe:	`subscribe TREAD Your-name`
Unsubscribe:	`unsubscribe TREAD`
List:	`TREAD@maelstrom.stjohns.edu`
List owner:	Warren Bush (E-mail: `warrenb@maelstrom.stjohns.edu`)

This is a closed mutual support list for therapists who are in recovery from addictions including alcoholism, substance addiction, and other "addictive" behaviors. The list membership is restricted to professional, licensed therapists, or therapists in professional training who consider themselves to be in recovery from an addiction.

Title (or descriptor):   Transformational Processing

Web site: `http://www.worldtrans.org/transproc.html`

Commands to: `majordomo@newciv.org`

Subscribe: `subscribe TRANSPROC-L`

Unsubscribe: `unsubscribe TRANSPROC-L`

List: `TRANSPROC-L@newciv.org`

List owner: Flemming Funch (E-mail: `ffunch@newciv.org`)

A forum for the serious student of the transformational processing system of personal counseling techniques developed by Flemming Funch.

Title (or descriptor):   Transcultural Psychology

Commands to: `listserv@listserv.nodak.edu`

Subscribe:

`subscribe transcultural-psychology Your-name`

Unsubscribe: `unsubscribe transcultural-psychology`

List:

`transcultural-psychology@listserv.nodak.edu`

List owners: Elsa R. Germain, Sunkyo Kwon (E-mail: `fu03c2dj@zedat.fu-berlin.de`), Florence Sushila Niles, Paul Pederson, Carol Stearns, and Adil Saeed Felix Qureshi

This forum is for the exchange of ideas, opinions, and information in cross-cultural research, minority issues, and "indigenous psychologies." Intended for mental health professionals and professionals-to-be in both academic and applied settings, participation of individuals in other disciplines is actively encouraged to add diversity and variety.

Title (or descriptor):   Traumatic Stress

Web site:

`http://www.shef.ac.uk/uni/projects/gpp/traumai.html`

Commands to: `listserv@lists.apa.org`

Subscribe: `subscribe traumatic-stress`

Unsubscribe: `unsubscribe traumatic-stress`

List: `traumatic-stress@lists.apa.org`

List owner: Charles Figley (E-mail: `cfigley@mailer.fsu.edu`)

The purpose of this forum is to promote the investigation, assessment, and treatment of immediate and long-term psychosocial, physiological, and existential consequences of highly stressful (traumatic) events. Includes discussion of posttraumatic stress disorder.

Title (or descriptor):   Victim Assistance

Web site: `http://www.vaonline.org/vaform.html`

The forum acts as an aid to increase communication between the many public, private, police, judicial, and governmental victim-assistance organizations that exist worldwide, as well as between individuals involved in this field. It also provides a place for support of professionals working in this area, announcements of related conferences and workshops, and a discussion forum for ideas and solutions to dealing with problems victims face.

Title (or descriptor):   WebPsych Partnership

Web site: `http://www.ismho.org/webpsych/`

Commands to: `listproc@cmhc.com`

Subscribe: `subscribe webpsych Your-name`

Unsubscribe: `unsubscribe webpsych`

List: `webpsych@cmhc.com`

List owner: John M. Grohol (E-mail: `john@grohol.com`)

This list supports the WebPsych Partnership, a coalition of Web sites that adhere to a set of standards for publishing mental health information online. Discussion topics include how to work together in a cooperative spirit to promote members' online resources, announcements of new Web sites or changes in existing Web resources, and how to create new, valuable content.

Title (or descriptor):   Youth–Anxiety–Depression

Commands to: `listserv@maelstrom.stjohns.edu`

Subscribe:	`subscribe YANX-DEP Your-name`
Unsubscribe:	`unsubscribe YANX-DEP`
List:	`YANX-DEP@maelstrom.stjohns.edu`
List owner:	Sue Spence (E-mail: `sues@psy.uq.oz.au`)

Focused specifically on anxiety and depression amongst children and adolescents.

Newsgroup Discussions

Newsgroups are the more public discussion forums available through the Internet. Their readerships typically number in the tens of thousands (compared to the few hundred on most mailing lists). In the psychology and mental health newsgroups, the readership consists largely of laypeople, not professionals. It is for these reasons that most professionals tend to stick to mailing lists, which give the appearance of more intimacy and confidentiality.

Newsgroups are accessed through software commonly provided as a part of your online account. Newsgroup software is often referred to as a "newsgroup reader," and one is built into the Netscape software. The procedure to subscribe to a newsgroup varies according to the type software you use, so there's no particular method I can describe here. Further information on how to subscribe to a new newsgroup or remove current subscriptions is available through the "Help" file in such software.

Nonetheless, newsgroups may provide a good forum for asking a general research or clinical question where a wide variety of opinions is desired. Some newsgroups are moderated, which tends to increase the quality of the discussion. The moderator ensures only those messages of relevance to the forum get posted. Table 6.1 offers a list of relevant professional newsgroups in alphabetical order by topic.

CAN I FIND A COLLEAGUE'S REAL-WORLD OR E-MAIL ADDRESS THROUGH MY COMPUTER?

There are several Web sites that will allow you to quickly and easily locate lost colleagues, friends, and even family members. There are databases of national White Page directories and e-mail directories. I list four of them. None of these directories is 100% accurate or complete, and there is no

TABLE 6.1 Professional Newsgroups

Description	Newsgroup Name	Moderated?
Adler, Alfred	`alt.psychology.adlerian`	No
Announcements of interest to psychologists and mental health professionals in general	`sci.psychology.announce`	Yes
Behavioral medicine discussion	`alt.med.behavioral`	No
Cognitive science	`sci.cognitive`	No
Consciousness	`sci.psychology.consciousness`	Yes
Jung, Carl	`alt.psychology.jung`	No
Medicine, general	`sci.med`	No
Mental health as viewed in society	`alt.society.mental-health`	No
Neurolinguistic Programming (NLP)	`alt.psychology.nlp`	No
Nursing topics	`sci.med.nursing`	No
Personality	`sci.psychology.personality`	No
Personality models and assessment measures (such as Myers-Briggs)	`alt.psychology.personality`	No
Psyche, an electronic journal	`sci.psychology.journals.psyche`	Yes
Psychobiology and psychiatry	`sci.med.psychobiology`	No
Psychological research	`sci.psychology.research`	Yes
Psychological theory	`sci.psychology.theory`	No
Psychology, general	`sci.psychology.misc`	No
Psychotherapy	`sci.psychology.psychotherapy`	No
Psychotherapy, moderated	`sci.psychology.psychotherapy.moderated`	Yes
Psycoloquy, an electronic journal	`sci.psychology.journals.psycoloquy`	Yes
Research discussion	`sci.research`	No
Transpersonal psychology	`alt.psychology.transpersonal`	No

guarantee that you will actually locate the person you're searching for in this manner. White Page listings are restricted to public listings; these online services will not find private listings. Many of the services listed below also note people who use a certain type of Internet telephone software (also known as "NetPhones," see Chapter 10).

Most of the following services require that you know, accurately, the person's first and last names. So if you're not sure how to spell someone's name, you should try a several spellings and consider using a "wildcard" operator.

Title (or descriptor):	Yahoo! People Search
Owner:	Yahoo!, Inc.
URL (Web address):	`http://people.yahoo.com/`
Rating:	★★
Access restrictions:	Registration is optional; free

What used to be a service called Four11 was gobbled up by the Internet media giant, Yahoo!, in 1998. While Four11's old database used to be one of the more accurate and up-to-date databases onlines, the new owners seemed to have dropped the ball in keeping the database that way. Yahoo!'s People Search consistently failed to find a number of people I typed in, in both its e-mail search and telephone search areas. As though two separate search areas weren't enough (e-mail and telephone), to find someone who is using an Internet telephone application ("NetPhone") requires an additional click into a third search area (these applications are discussed in-depth in Chapter 10). It would be much simpler if all of these areas were combined into one search form. Like most online directories, Yahoo!'s suffers from outdated, missing, and inaccurate entries. Listings appear to be at least 2 to 3 years behind current White Page telephone directories.

Title (or descriptor):	Infospace
Owner:	Infospace
URL (Web address):	`http://www.infospace.com/`
Rating:	★★

Greatly diversifying its online offerings, Infospace's telephone, e-mail, and NetPhone directories are only a small part of its online community. Unfortunately, the quality of its directories seem to suffer as a result. Like Yahoo!'s People Search, it supports searching for people's (again, in separate databases, which makes searches unnecessary repetitive and time consuming) telephone numbers, e-mail addresses, and Net-Phones (found, cryptically, under the Net Community listing). The database also supports reverse lookups, a feature which allows you to find a person at a particular phone number. It offers business Yellow Pages as well, to help find a business in your local area. While I found its White Pages listings to be much more accurate and up-to-date than Yahoo!'s People Search, its e-mail directory lacked the breadth and depth of Yahoo!'s People Search. Infospace often returned no results on e-mail searches, or the wrong contact information altogether. It also failed to list people whose names approximate your name query, in case you spelled it wrong. For searching for people in the real world (e.g., physical addresses), Infospace's White Pages would appear to net you better results (although it still failed to find some people I threw at it). But for online connections, you would be better off using another directory service.

Title (or descriptor):	Switchboard
Owner:	Switchboard
URL (Web address):	`http://www.switchboard.com/`
Rating:	★

Switchboard is a directory for searching for real-world phone numbers and addresses for individuals and businesses. I found its listings to be outdated (by at least a year or two) and inaccurate. It failed to list many current entries and simply was not a very useful tool. Infospace's real-world directories were much more current and accurate.

Title (or descriptor):	WhoWhere?
Owner:	Lycos?
URL (Web address):	`http://whowhere.lycos.com/`
Rating:	★★

Like all the other directory services online today, WhoWhere has branched out into creating an online community. If you thought its acquition by Lycos would help increase the resources devoted to keeping its directories accurate and up-to-date, you would be wrong. The quality of their directory is no better than any other directory reviewed, with out-of-date listings and no entries for over 60% of the people I typed in. The search capabilities are flexible, however, allowing you to search on a whole name or parts of a name. Unlike other directories, more results were often returned (even if many of them were inaccurate).

HOW DO I FIND COLLEAGUES AROUND THE WORLD WHO ARE DOING SIMILAR TYPES OF RESEARCH?

Academicians who do research in a particular subcategory of psychology have typically become aware of colleagues with similar research interests through a perusal of the psychological research literature. This works relatively well because professionals with research interests in a specific subject matter generally publish in regular peer-reviewed journals. But, this method also has its drawbacks. New researchers are more difficult to locate, since they may have no publications under their belt. Becoming published in a peer-reviewed, academic journal is an arduous and usually lengthy process. This is off-putting to some researchers who simply choose not to publish significant findings, or do so in nontraditional media (such as online). A fair amount of relevant and useful research also will be rejected from such journals, because of the peer-review process or stringent publishing standards. Many clinicians simply forgo the process of publishing their case studies and research findings altogether, because of the inherent difficulty in doing so and the time required to write up their results. Nonetheless, all of these professionals may still want to share and discuss their findings with other interested professionals around the world.

There are a number online methods that can help researchers and others interested in a specific research question find one another more quickly and easily. One method, detailed in the Step-by-Step box, is to submit an announcement about your research interests or findings to a professional mailing list or newsgroup. Another method is to examine journals' Web sites (whether they are electronic journals or otherwise) and browse through the research articles (see Chapter 9). Other methods might include browsing through some Web sites that offer databases of research in progress or researchers' field of study (see later in this section). All of these methods suffer from the same problem: the majority of professionals are not yet connected to the online world. The sample, therefore, is likely to be quite small compared to what a researcher may discover in the real world. This problem will naturally decrease in time.

STEP-BY-STEP: PUBLISHING THE ANNOUNCEMENT

1. Choose an appropriate mailing list or newsgroup. I would recommend one of the following:

A. Mailing lists:

- PsyUSA (see page 139)
- Clinical psychologists (see page 139)
- Psychotherapy research (see page 143)

B. Newsgroups:

- `sci.psychology.research` (moderated)
- `sci.med.psychobiology`

2. Write a short paragraph that briefly describes your active research interests, the findings of a study, or a case study you'd like to share with other professionals. Be sure to include a good subject line for your article. For example:

Subject: Cognitive Elaboration Rating System compiled

My name is John Grohol and I'm a psychologist interested in the cognitive elaboration model of psychotherapy interactions. I recently helped compile a rating system with some colleagues of mine to measure and record therapist–client interactions in a given therapy session. I would be happy to discuss and share this new rating system with anyone who might be interested in psychotherapy outcome research. Please e-mail me at `grohol@cmhc.com` for additional information or questions.

Browsing through Journals' Web Sites

A second potentially useful method of finding colleagues is to examine the journals' Web sites (see Chapter 9) and read through research articles online. This can be more painstaking, because the only sure-fire method of ensuring your search is accurate and complete is to visit each journal and Web site. Why? Because search engines are having an increasingly harder time keeping up with the growth and volume of the World Wide Web. Search engines also may not index new articles and research for months after they've been online.

Important points to consider:

■ Do not submit an entire study to a mailing list or newsgroup. (One exception is the `sci.psychology.research` newsgroup, which does accept completed studies for publication online.) You should keep the announcement short and to the point, giving readers all the relevant information they need to know about your interests in one or two paragraphs.

■ Do not submit your announcement to mailing lists or newsgroups where such submissions may be frowned upon. When in doubt, contact the mailing list's owner or administrator before making the submission and ask for permission.

■ Space your announcement submissions so that you don't barrage all the mailing lists and newsgroups at once. Such a barrage is frowned on in the online world. Post to no more than two mailing lists at a time, and not more than a half-dozen newsgroups. Wait a week and then post to another two mailing lists, if need be. While newsgroups have a much wider readership than most mailing lists, their readers tend to be laypeople rather than fellow professionals.

■ Do not keep submit your announcements more than once every 6 months or so. Mailing list and newsgroup readers do not change that drastically from month to month.

■ If you get no response from this method, you might try looking for more specific and appropriate mailing lists or discussion forums in which to publish your announcement. It may also be that there is no one else subscribed to that mailing list or newsgroup who is interested in your research subject matter.

■ If all else fails, try another method outlined in this section.

Searching through Online Databases

A less-painful means of locating research and current studies being conducted (and the people behind them) is through a clinical trials listing service, such as CenterWatch (listed below). Another means is looking through a database of clinicians (such as the Clinicians Yellow Pages, listed below), which includes a field for "research interests." This latter method is less reliable.

Title (or descriptor):   CenterWatch

Owner: CenterWatch, Inc.

URL (Web address):   http://www.centerwatch.com/

Rating: ★★★★

This the central clinical trials listing service online, offering researchers and clinicians descriptions of current research. Listings are arranged by general medical specialty (psychiatry/psychology being of interest to us), and within each specialty by disorder under study. Choosing a disorder gives you the name of the center or agency conducting the study, arranged by states, as well as a brief one-line description of the study. By clicking on the center's name, you may get additional information and details on the study as well as a contact person for the research. While this database is targeted toward participants, researchers may use it as well to discover current research being conducted. The Web site is well designed and easy to understand.

Title (or descriptor):   Clinicians Yellow Pages

Owner: Mental Health Net

URL (Web address):   http://mentalhelp.net/cyp/

Rating: ★★

While this directory is mainly published for clinicians to advertise their practice, one category of information a clinician may include is research interests. With over 1,600 individuals listed, it is certainly not a foolproof method, but it can be helpful (especially if you're looking to collaborate with a clinician in a research study).

Title (or descriptor):   Who's Who in Mental Health on the Web

Owner: Linda M. Chapman, MSW, LCSW

URL (Web address):   http://www.idealist.com/wwmhw/

Rating: ★★★

Who's Who in Mental Health on the Web is a professional database currently listing over 2,200 mental health professionals' networking and practice interests. Any mental health professional can register with the database at no charge, and list their contact information and research, practice and networking interests within their entry. A search engine makes the database easy to use. Type in keywords—such as "cognitive research"— into the search box first. Then choose the option, "Find all of these words" to get the best results from the search engine.

Researching Online: References and Databases

Entire books have been written about how to effectively conduct research and literature searches online. The truth of the matter is, though, that useful research discovery, references, abstracts, and information are rarely fully realized through simply getting online and browsing the World Wide Web. Serious researchers will still conduct their literature searches, for the most part, in a library, because libraries still easily outperform the online world in the depth and breadth of information available. And until every book and journal is converted into an electronic format, libraries will remain the gold standard and preferred option for conducting literature searches and doing background research.

However, you can do background research through online resources. But the quality and quantity of work you will find online will vary greatly, depending on the specific topic under study. For instance, in studying depression and looking for related statistics of this disorder for your research, you will probably find the needed information at the National Institute of Mental Health (`http://www.nimh.nih.gov/`). What you will not find, however, are references or abstracts to the majority of the social science literature done on this topic in the past decade. You can find a fair amount of medically related literature on it, through a MEDLINE search or a summary article written by a psychiatrist (see, for example, Internet Mental Health at `http://www.mentalhealth.com/`). But such information is very limited in its scope and excludes the bulk of relevant literature, such as that found in psychology, sociology, social psychology, cognitive science, and epidemiology. Topics that are even less well known (for instance, a paper about John Dewey) will probably garner even less useful information. The library is still the best place to begin and end such a search. It will probably remain so for at least the near future.

However, there can be useful aspects to online research searches. It may help you refine and better define your research ideas or hypotheses. It may also help you to look up information on topics related to your original idea that you may not have thought of to begin with. Such online research also has the potential to put you in touch with other researchers or professionals interested in ideas and topic areas similar to your own. Collaboration or at least the ability to bounce ideas off of these like-minded professionals can be accomplished through such communication.

Many professionals' current use of computer technology is limited to literature searches or similar uses to find specific information in a reference database. PsycLIT is the most popular and probably well-known example of a research database, because today's professionals used it extensively in their graduate studies. MEDLINE is another such database, as is the ERIC catalog of academic articles and papers. While these were, at one time, only available in paper format, they have long since become electronic because of the computer's ability to search through thousands of abstracts quickly for key terms or search queries. Much like Web-based search engines, all of these databases rely on a similar piece of software to index the catalog to allow for easy and fast searches on it.

It would make sense, then, that if these databases are already computerized, they should be available for searching online. All of them are, and most of them are available at the present time without cost. Examples of free databases include ERIC and MEDLINE at the present time; PsycLIT and PsycINFO are available at costs that vary from vendor to vendor. These fees may change as the American Psychological Association looks to become more competitive with similar types of databases available without charge online. It is just as possible that other vendors will begin charging for those databases that are currently available at no charge. Ultimately, the market (i.e., you) will decide what it is and is not willing to pay for online.

Diagnosis and medication are categories of reference material commonly used by both clinicians and researchers. Both of these categories, in many different forms and formats, are available online from a wide variety of sites. Some material will include much the same information found in real-world reference manuals, either quoted from that material or written from scratch, because of copyright restrictions.

HOW DO I LOCATE THE RESEARCH AND CLINICAL ABSTRACT DATABASES—SUCH AS ERIC, MEDLINE, PsycLIT, AND PsycINFO?

Below are some of the places where you can go online to find these databases.

Title (or descriptor):	ERIC Clearinghouse on Assessment and Evaluation
Owner:	U.S. Department of Education
URL (Web address):	http://www.ericae.net/
URL (Web address):	http://www.accesseric.org/
Rating:	★★★

The Educational Resources Information Center (ERIC), as noted on their Web site, is

a national information system designed to provide users with ready access to an extensive body of education-related literature. ERIC, established in 1966, is supported by the U.S. Department of Education, Office of Educational Research and Improvement, and the National Library of Education. . . . The database contains more than 850,000 abstracts of documents and journal articles on education research and practice.

The Web site provides direct online and free access to the ERIC database since 1991 (although other online ERIC databases back to 1989 are also available and accessible through this Web site). You can also fill out a document-ordering form to obtain documents you find within the database. The Web site allows readers to locate citations and reviews of educational and psychological tests and measures that The Buros Institute of Mental Measurements and ProEd (a book publisher) have included in their directories. The Web site is well designed, although the graphics look a little cheesy. This site is a good example of the power of putting database resources online, especially for researchers.

MEDLINE

MEDLINE is the medical abstract research database roughly equivalent to PsycLIT for psychology. Always available to physicians and medical students at no charge, it is now available to anyone online to search through for free. It can be accessed through a variety of Web sites. Some of these sites also offer document retrieval delivered to your home or office for a fee. MEDLINE contains over 9 million references from over 3,900 journals, and includes abstracts from the vast majority of the social sciences and psychology literature. It can be used as a free alternative to the PsycINFO products from the American Psychological Association.

Title (or descriptor):	Community of Science MEDLINE
Owner:	Community of Science, Inc.
URL (Web address):	`http://medline.cos.com/`
Rating:	★★
Access restrictions:	Registration required; fees variable

The Community of Science dropped its free MEDLINE searches and now makes its database available only to paid subscribers. No information is available on their Web site about the fees involved in subscribing. Three search forms offer the user a wide variety of options to choose from in forming everything from a quick and simple query, to a complex and detailed query.

HealthGate™

Title (or descriptor):   HealthGate MEDLINE

Owner: HealthGate Data Corporation

URL (Web address):   `http://bewell.healthgate.com/medline/`

Rating: ★★★★

Offers both advanced and simple searches. The simple searches may be powerful enough for most, while the advanced search option is easy to understand. Having an article mailed to you is an option available for approximately $25.00 (over twice the cost of most other MEDLINE search services). No registration is needed to search their MEDLINE database.

Title (or descriptor):   Infotrieve MEDLINE Service Provider

Owner: Infotrieve, Inc.

URL (Web address):   `http://www.infotrieve.com/`

Rating: ★★

Another free MEDLINE search service, which gives you the ability to form natural language or Boolean queries, which ever you prefer. Offers TOXLINE and AID-SLINE access in addition to advanced search functions. The full text of articles is available for $8.00 plus copyright fees (typically $2–$30 per article).

Title (or descriptor):   Internet Grateful Med MEDLINE Search

Owner: National Library of Medicine

URL (Web address):   `http://igm.nlm.nih.gov/`

Rating: ★★★

The Grateful Med MEDLINE database now uses the PubMed (see below) system and requires no registration to conduct searches on any of the 15 databases available. The results screen gives you more choices than usual MEDLINE databases. In addition to viewing abstracts, you can download the results to your computer, quickly retrieve the abstracts of all the results displayed in one screen, view one abstract or sets of abstracts at a time, or view articles related to a specific abstract. The only drawback to Grateful Med is pricing information for ordering the full text of an article is not available unless you register.

Title (or descriptor):	Medscape MEDLINE Search
Owner:	Medscape
URL (Web address):	http://www.medscape.com/
Rating:	★★★

Utilizing the full MEDLINE database (from 1966 to the present) along with an easy registration process and free searches helps make this one of the stonger MEDLINE search sites. The full text of articles is available by mail for $8.00 plus copyright fees. Results did not appear to be sorted in any particular order.

Title (or descriptor):	PaperChase
Owner:	PaperChase
URL (Web address):	http://www.paperchase.com/
Rating:	★★
Access restrictions:	Registration required; free trial or $150.00/year

It is questionable whether the cost of viewing abstracts through PaperChase is offset by its interactive search designed for beginners. The search feature on PaperChase is designed to help a user narrow their chosen topics in order to provide more relevant results. This may be helpful to new users, but will likely impede and frustrate experienced users. The Web site becomes confused if your try and take a shortcut by using the built-in history function of your Web browser, so you are forced to use the site's own navigation tools (another drawback to its design). The search recognizes only Boolean queries. Before using the free trial, users are requested to fill out a registration form. There is apparently no way to order the full text of articles.

Title (or descriptor):	Physician's Home Page
Owner:	Silverplatter, Inc.
URL (Web address):	http://php2.silverplatter.com/
Rating:	★★
Access restrictions:	Registration required; $19.95/month

This Web site provides an easy-to-understand search form to access its MEDLINE database, which is available from 1966 to the present (i.e., within the past week). The site is geared toward physicians, however, and membership isn't cheap. Document-delivery charges are competitive with other MEDLINE services.

Title (or descriptor):	PubMed
Owner:	National Library of Medicine
URL (Web address):	`http://www.ncbi.nlm.nih.gov/PubMed/`
Rating:	★★★★

Using the same database and similar search interfaces as its older government brother, Grateful Med, it has a simpler search interface. Like Grateful Med, it allows the user to find related articles and also does not display a price for retrieving the full text of an article unless you register. Because the National Library of Medicine maintains the MEDLINE database, this is where many users choose to start their free MEDLINE searches.

PsycINFO and PsycLIT

Title (or descriptor):	American Psychological Association
Owner:	American Psychological Association
URL (Web address):	`http://www.apa.org/psycinfo/`
Rating:	★★★

After years of outsourcing direct access to its PsycINFO database, the American Psychological Association has finally provided individuals a way to access it directly. Anybody can access it for $9.95 for 24 hours, or members of the APA who already subscribe to any APA journal can gain full access to the database for an entire year for $49.00. These rates are less expensive than access to PsycINFO from a third-party provider (listed below), because there is no per-record viewing or downloading charge. If you do not have access to PsycINFO via a university affiliation, this is the most inexpensive and fastest way to obtain such access.

For most academicians and students, such services, while convenient, are probably not very cost-effective. The databases are often found at educational institutions and are available to faculty and students free of charge.

Many universities also make them available through their own local computer network on campus, but only if you are a current student or faculty member. Using the university's existing PsycLIT database is usually cheaper and may be accessible via your university's local computer network, which you can confirm by contacting the reference librarian in the university library. The librarian can also provide you with instructions on how to access the database directly. Alternatively, some university libraries and departments offer search services for faculty and students, often for a fee.

If you don't have convenient, free access to these databases through an institution, you can still find them online for a fee. The fee will usually comprise the following:

- An initial sign-up fee
- An annual maintenance fee
- Telecommunications charges for time spent connected to the service
- Database charges for time spent searching the database
- A charge for each full research abstract record viewed or downloaded

Below, I list various information providers and I have included their most recent costs. These costs will vary from company to company, and they may have changed since this book was published. Please contact the relevant information service provider for the most recent fees and for further information about opening an account. Since all of these providers use the same PsycINFO database, they were not individually reviewed for this book. While there may be certain cosmetic differences between their search engines and technologies, they all offer virtually the same service with similar pricing structures. An updated listings of these vendors can be found at http://www.apa.org/psycinfo/olprice.html.

Title (or descriptor):	DataStar/Dialog
Contact:	Knight-Ridder Information, Inc.
	2440 El Camino Real
	Mountain View, CA 94040
	Phone: (800) 334-2564 or (415) 254-7000
	Fax: (415) 254-7070

E-mail:	customer@dialog.com
URL (Web address):	http://www.dialog.com/
Subscription fee:	DataStar—$0.90/record
	Dialog—$295.00 signup fee, $72.00/year maintenance fee
	and $0.65/record

Title (or descriptor):	DIMDI
Contact:	German Institute for Medical Documentation and
	Information
	Weisshausstrasse 27
	D-50899 Köln 41 Germany
	Phone: 0-221/47241
	Fax: 0-221/411429
E-mail:	helpdesk@dimdi.de
URL (Web address):	http://www.dimdi.de/
Subscription fee:	Sign-up fee and $0.39/record

Title (or descriptor):	HealthGate
Contact:	HealthGate Data Corp.
	380 Pleasant St., Suite 230
	Malden, MA 02148
	Phone: (800) 434-4283 or (617) 321-1199
	Fax: (617) 321-2262
E-mail:	info@healthgate.com
URL (Web address):	http://www.healthgate.com/
Subscription fee:	$0.75/record

Title (or descriptor):	IQuest
Contact:	CompuServe
	P.O. Box 20212
	Columbus, OH 43220
	Phone: (800) 848-8199 or (614) 457-0802
	Fax: (614) 529-1611

E-mail:	70006.101@compuserve.com
URL (Web address):	http://www.compuserve.com/
Subscription fee:	$9.95/month (CompuServe account), $2.95/hour, $2.00/record

Title (or descriptor):	Ovid Online
Contact:	Ovid Technologies
	333 Seventh Avenue
	New York, NY 10001
	Phone: (800) 950-2035 or (212) 563-3006
	Fax: (212) 563-3784
E-mail:	sales@ovid.com
URL (Web address):	http://www.ovid.com/
Subscription fee:	$30.00/hour (plus connection fees), $0.60/record

I'M DOING RESEARCH ON A SPECIFIC TOPIC— HOW DO I FIND INFORMATION ONLINE ABOUT IT?

There are two methods you can use to find research online. One method is to search specialized indices for research papers, such as those listed later in this section. But perhaps the easier and more common method is by beginning with a powerful search engine such as AltaVista (http://www.altavista.com/) or a meta-search engine such as Inference Find (http://www.infind.com/), as described in the Step-by-Step box on the next page.

Another, less-useful method to finding research online is to visit one of the many research archives. These reside at a number of different Web sites, and are specific to specialized research topics. In most cases, this method won't be that helpful unless you just happen to need to find research on one of these topic areas. Unfortunately, at the present time, there is no central online clearinghouse or index for such papers. You should also keep in mind the vast number of journals that host Web sites; research articles may often be found there too.

Title (or descriptor):   HeartMath Research Papers
Owner: Institute of HeartMath
URL (Web address):   `http://www.heartmath.org/`
Rating: ★★

The Institute of HeartMath is a nonprofit institution, whose research division's mission is to explore the central role of the heart's electrical system in health and well-being. A number of research papers are available through this site on these topics.

Title (or descriptor):   Journal of Neurotherapy
Owner: Society for Neuronal Regulation
URL (Web address):   `http://www.snr-jnt.org/`
Rating: ★★★

An interesting site with dozens of articles online taken directly from the *Journal of Neurotherapy*. Most of the peer reviewed articles cover topics such as EEG biofeedback and neurofeedback, the focus of the journal and society. One of the oldest such repositories online, and still updated regularly.

Title (or descriptor):   Prevention and Treatment
Owner: American Psychological Association
URL (Web address):   `http://journals.apa.org/prevention/`
Rating: ★★

An electronic-only journal that got off to a rocky start, it has irregular articles on varying psychological topics. These topics range from efficacy and outcome research in psychotherapy, to an analysis of drug treatment outcomes. At this point, the emphasis seems to be on treatment, not prevention.

Title (or descriptor):   Professional Resources
Owner: Mental Health Net & CMHC Systems, Inc.
URL (Web address):   `http://mentalhelp.net/prof.htm`
Rating: ★★

STEP-BY-STEP: FINDING RELEVANT RESEARCH ONLINE

1. Select a search engine or a meta-search engine (for example, AltaVista or Inference Find).

2. Keep your initial query as general as possible.

3. Submit multiple queries, adding additional keywords, operators, or search terms in different combinations and phrases as needed to narrow your search. Here are some examples.

Task: Find information on the cognitive elaboration likelihood model

Step 1. Choose a search engine. I'll use AltaVista.

Step 2. Form an initial, general query. I'll start with the phrase `"cognitive elaboration"` (with the quotes).

Step 3. If too many irrelevant results are obtained, resubmit the query, adding another word to the phrase. In my example, I'll add the word "likelihood" and resubmit the query as the phrase, `"cognitive elaboration likelihood"`.

Task: Find information on Prozac (fluoxetine) efficacy versus other treatment

Step 1. Choose a search engine. Again, I'll use AltaVista.

Step 2. Form an initial, general query. I'll start with the query: `prozac or fluoxetine`

Step 3. This brings up far too many results. So I'll narrow my search by adding some additional operators and a word: `(prozac or fluoxetine) and efficacy`

Task: Use AltaVista's "Advanced Search" features to limit the results of the above example

Step 1. Using AltaVista, choose the "Advanced Search" option.

Step 2. Form an initial query. The Advanced Search section refers to its search query box as the "Selection Criteria" box. In that box, I'll enter our last query: `(prozac or fluoxetine) and efficacy`. The Advanced Search Web page also has another box, which should be filled in. This is called the "Results Ranking" box and simply tells the search engine which results should be ranked higher, according to the keywords you enter into it. I'll enter: `prozac fluoxetine`.

Step 3. This brings up still too many results. So I will refine my search query one last time: `(prozac or fluoxetine) and efficacy near research`. This resulted in a reasonable number of results being returned, some of which were actual research studies reproduced online about this topic.

Divided by broad topic areas, each page in the professional resources section of this Web site includes a category for journals and research papers online. While probably not a comprehensive index, it may be a good place to browse through some research archives on a variety of professional topic areas, such as alcoholism and substance abuse, cognitive and behavioral therapy, health and sports psychology, industrial and organizational psychology, and others.

Title (or descriptor):   Psychiatry & Mental Health
Owner: Medscape
URL (Web address):

    http://www.medscape.com/Home/Topics/psychiatry/
    psychiatry.html

Rating: ★★★★

A growing repository of respectable, peer-reviewed articles in psychiatry and mental health are available at no charge from Medscape. Topics range from detailed discussions regarding the latest treatment options for specific disorders, to trends in psychopharmacological treatment and prevention. Psychiatry news, conference summaries, and practice guidelines round out this excellent resource for therapists. Overseen by a scientific advisory board led by Charles L. Bowden, M.D. and 11 other physicians, the site's central drawback is its medical focus and orientation.

Title (or descriptor):   PubMed Central
Owner: National Institutes of Health
URL (Web address):

    http://www.nih.gov/welcome/director/pubmedcentral/
    pubmedcentral.htm

Rating: Unrated

PubMed Central is a new service of the U.S. National Institutes of Health (NIH). PubMed Central is "a Web-based repository for barrier-free access to primary reports in the life sciences. [. . .] PubMed Central will archive, organize and distribute peer-reviewed reports from journals, as well as reports that have been screened but not formally peer-reviewed," according to the NIH. It will be interesting to see if this concept turns into an evolution in scientific publishing.

8

Professional Associations, Issues, and Ethics Online

Some of the best-designed and most informative Web sites online today are those created by specific professional associations. You will discover not only information related to professional issues and ethics on such sites, but membership information, contacts for the organization, calendars of workshops and events, lists of online resources, and a good deal more. Naturally, some association Web sites are more helpful than others. In general, the larger the organization the more complete the Web site.

WHAT ARE SOME IMPORTANT ETHICAL CONCERNS FOR PROFESSIONALS ONLINE?

Ethics are an important aspect of any profession. They are especially vital to the helping professions where individuals are often in emotional distress and therefore are more vulnerable. The application of ethical and professional standards to the online world is still in its formative stages. Many professional organizations are not yet certain how to translate real-world ethics to the electronic, "virtual" world. The larger professional organizations, such as the American Psychological Association and American Psychiatric Association, are taking conservative, wait-and-see stances. In the meantime, there are some unique issues I'll address in this chapter, which are not likely to be specifically addressed in any profession's ethical code or guidelines. But these issues are *vitally important* for you to understand and consider as you engage in any type of online interaction. They concern confidentiality, informed consent, and conducting therapy over the Internet.

Confidentiality Online

A special concern in the online world is confidentiality of a client's personal background and history. Just as in the real world, professionals must use care when presenting a case on a mailing list (or any other online discussion forum). Information published on the mailing list will reach hundreds, potentially thousands, of others across the world, and there is no guarantee that all of them will be professionals or bound by any ethical code of conduct. Identifying information must be left out or changed; this includes geographical locations and names of significant others in relation to the client. Professionals should never assume that because they subscribe to a professional mailing list, it is safe to discuss cases as they would in an office with the door closed. *Mailing lists are public forums*—only slightly less public than other forums online (such as newsgroups or Web-based discussion areas). In other words, exercise the same care as you would if you were presenting the case to the entire staff of your clinic or hospital. This will ensure the patient's confidentiality is not compromised as well as maintain your professional ethics and image.

Informed Consent

There are other professional issues in dealing with ordinary people in the online world. Some researchers have engaged in ethically questionable behavior online by conducting naturalistic studies through observation of a support mailing list or newsgroup. These researchers did not gain the mailing list users' consent, nor did the users have any reason to expect that their interactions on the mailing list would come under scrutiny or be used as an object of study. I find the downside of such research to far outweigh any benefits. A few months back, someone sent me e-mail about this situation. A researcher was discussing the results of such a study to a large audience. Unknown to the researcher, one of the mailing list's participants was sitting in the audience. She was aghast to discover that her behaviors on the list had been studied and were now being presented to a large group of complete strangers!

Should such naturalistic research take place online? Yes, if it is conducted in the same manner that real-world naturalistic studies are with full consensual participation by those being observed. This question was answered long ago in the real world. Just because the modality of communication has changed doesn't mean that researchers and professionals are no longer bound by the same ethical principles.

Therapy over the Internet

Another hot ethical issue is the question of conducting psychotherapy online. This question has remained largely unresolved in any codified fashion to this point. For a longer discussion of the ethical and professional issues in conducting online therapy, as well as resources offering more information, see Chapter 11. For now, suffice to say that you should think long and hard before hanging out your virtual shingle.

ARE THE ETHICAL PRINCIPLES FOR VARIOUS MENTAL HEALTH PROFESSIONS AVAILABLE ONLINE?

Yes, most such ethical principles and guidelines are available online. For ethical guidelines, the logical place to look is the appropriate professional association that writes or oversees such guidelines. For psychologists, it's the

American Psychological Association; for psychiatrists, it's the American Psychiatric Association. Other professions may also find their ethical codes online at their respective national association's Web site. State licensing in the United States doesn't require a professional to be a member of a professional guild, nor do states have their own individual ethical principles (although they often adopt the professional association's guidelines by law). So such principles may apply to practicing professionals in their respective fields in the United States, but not necessarily to international psychologists or psychiatrists.

Title (or descriptor):   American Counseling Association

Owner: American Counseling Association

URL (Web address):

    http://www.counseling.org/resources/codeofethics.htm

Rating: ★★★

The code of ethics for counselors may be found here, available as one large file (which will take most computers a few minutes to load). Use your Web browser's "Find" function (often found under the "Edit" menu) to locate specific areas of interest, or use the index at the top of the document to jump down to major categories. The "Standards of Practice" for counselors are a part of this same document, as are references for the entire document. No frequently asked questions (FAQ) file on how to report ethics violations is available.

Title (or descriptor):   American Psychiatric Association—Membership Ethics

Owner: American Psychiatric Association

URL (Web address):

    http://www.psych.org/apa_members/ethics.html

Rating: ★★★

The "Principles of Medical Ethics" make up the bulk of the content of this section within the American Psychiatric Association's Web site. The APA has adopted and annotated the American Medical Association's medical ethics to make them more applicable and relevant to psychiatry. The original and the annotated versions are available here, as are the procedure used for filing a complaint against a psychiatrist member and an FAQ file about how ethical complaints are handled. The information appears current and is certainly relevant to professionals within the psychiatric field. This section suffers from the same problem as the rest of the APA Web site, as I'll discuss in more detail later in this chapter—it is too hierarchical in structure. Finding relevant items often requires exploring layers upon layers of menu lists.

Title (or descriptor):	American Psychological Association—Ethics Information
Owner:	American Psychological Association
URL (Web address):	`http://www.apa.org/ethics/`
Rating:	★★★

The information found here could certainly be more online-friendly, as they have placed the entire listing of ethical principles into one, very large file. The same is true of the APA Ethics Committee Rules and Procedures, whose file is even larger than the principles' file itself. (If that isn't a comment about bureaucracy, I don't know what is!). The authors have at least taken the time to properly convert the ethical principles into a Web-based format so you can jump around in the large document relatively easily. Unlike the American Psychiatric Association, there is no FAQ file so members who have a complaint filed against them or are seeking to file an ethics complaint won't really know what to expect unless they call the APA directly. Statements about telephone and online therapy as well as behavioral research with animals may also be found here, as are guidelines for ethical conduct in the care and use of animals.

Title (or descriptor):	National Association of Social Workers—Code of Ethics
Owner:	National Association of Social Workers (NASW)
URL (Web address):	`http://www.naswdc.org/code.htm`
Rating:	★★

Available directly from the Association's home page, the social workers' code of ethics is neatly organized. It is divided into a number of logical categories (preamble, purpose, ethical principles, and ethical standards). No FAQ file is available for consumers or professionals on how to resolve ethical dilemmas or complaints.

WHERE ARE THE PROFESSIONAL ASSOCIATIONS ONLINE?

There are a few places you can consult for indexes of professional organizations. One place might be to use Yahoo!'s (http://www.yahoo.com/) internal search engine to find such an organization quickly and easily (by just typing the association's name into the search query box). Another resource is Mental Health Net's (http://mentalhelp.net/) listing of professional associations and organizations under their "Professional Resources" category. Yet a third online listing of such resources is Myron Pulier's index (http://www.umdnj.edu/psyevnts/psyjumps.html). I've listed some of the larger organizations below in alphabetical order, for your convenience.

Title (or descriptor):	Administrators in Academic Psychiatry (AAP)
Owner:	Administrators in Academic Psychiatry
URL (Web address):	
	http://www.kumc.edu/wichita/dept/psych/aap/home.html
Rating:	★★

As noted on their Web site, the AAP is a professional organization

founded in 1985 to provide education and networking opportunities for administrators of psychiatric programs in academic settings. AAP sponsors a Fall meeting as well as an annual Educational Conference in conjunction with the Medical Group Management Association's Academic Practice Assembly Educational Conference. Members also receive a quarterly newsletter, The AAP Grapevine.

This Web site not only offers the usual organizational information, but also select articles from their quarterly newsletter, the "AAP Grapevine." The site is of a pretty basic design, offers no graphics, and uses an unfortunate choice of colors. It does, however, appear to be updated on a regular basis.

Title (or descriptor):	Albert Ellis Institute
Owner:	Albert Ellis Institute
URL (Web address):	http://www.rebt.org/
Rating:	★★★

This page provides a lot of useful information on rational emotive behavior therapy (REBT), a specific psychotherapy and theory developed by Albert Ellis. This Web site includes a directory of REBT-trained therapists throughout the world, an FAQ file, a schedule of upcoming seminars, and a host of other resources. It is interesting to discover that Albert Ellis answers one question a month posed to him by the public through this Web site. Who would have ever guessed that one of the pioneers in the field of psychotherapy could be found on the Web.

AMERICAN ACADEMY OF CHILD & ADOLESCENT PSYCHIATRY

AACAP

Title (or descriptor):	American Academy of Child and Adolescent Psychiatry
Owner:	American Academy of Child and Adolescent Psychiatry
URL (Web address):	http://www.aacap.org/
Rating:	★★★★

As noted on their Web site,

> The Academy represents over 6,500 child and adolescent psychiatrists—physicians with at least five years of additional training beyond medical school in general and child and adolescent psychiatry. AACAP members actively research, diagnose and treat psychiatric disorders affecting children and adolescents and their families, and the Academy is dedicated to supporting this work through a variety of programs including government liaison, national public information and continuing medical education.

Their Web site reflects this dedication with sections for each of its offices. Offerings include one of the first online transplants of a helpful series of informational brochures called "Facts for Families." These brochures, available online and as regular printed publications in Spanish and French, provide concise and up-to-date material on issues ranging from children who suffer from depression and teen suicide, to stepfamily problems and child sexual abuse. It's usually a good recommendation to have parents read a relevant brochure if their child suffers from one of the topic areas covered. Press releases, legislative alerts, research and clinical information, and a calendar of events can all be found here. It has consistently been rated as one of the most popular and useful Web sites online today, which is probably due to its effective layout and easy navigation. Graphics are smaller once you get beyond the home page.

Title (or descriptor):	American Academy of Neurology (AAN)
Owner:	American Academy of Neurology
URL (Web address):	`http://www.aan.com/`
Rating:	★★★★

This Web site, providing information for both professionals and the public on neurology subjects, is large and very well designed. Once beyond the large graphics on the home page, pages are quick to load and attractively presented. The AAN is a professional organization representing neurologists worldwide. The Web site covers a multitude of information from Alzheimer's and Parkinson's diseases to stroke and migraine. Their comprehensive and well-written Fact Sheets cover topics such as Alzheimer's disease, anencephaly, Bell's palsy, boxing, brain tumors, carpal tunnel syndrome, chronic pain, epilepsy, tremor, headache, head injuries, lumbar puncture, multiple sclerosis, neuroaids, neuroimaging, Parkinson's disease, stroke, transient ischemic attack, Tourette's syndrome, and essential tremor; informational brochures on ALS and multiple sclerosis are also available. Information on neurology is also available, as is a "news" section, which highlights a different disorder every so often. This section also houses monthly news reports from the ANN journal, *Neurology*.

Title (or descriptor):	American Association of Suicidology
	See *CyberPsych*, below.

Title (or descriptor):	American Board of Examiners in Clinical Social Work
Owner:	American Board of Examiners (ABE)
URL (Web address):	`http://www.abecsw.org/`
Rating:	★★

This Web site houses information about this organization, credentialing, ethics, and the board of directors. The American Board of Examiners (ABE) issues a credential—the Board Certified Diplomate in Clinical Social Work (BCD)—to advanced clinical social workers nationwide. Currently about 13,000 social workers hold this advanced credential. The Web site is very basic, missing information, and had not been updated in nine months when I visited it. While directories are available for purchase, only the 1997 is available online (and it requires a free registration in order to use it).

Title (or descriptor):	American Counseling Association
Owner:	American Counseling Association
URL (Web address):	`http://www.counseling.org/`
Rating:	★★★★

This is an informative Web site offering a host of information about the American Counseling Association. In addition to offering general information about the association and membership, it hosts legislative and news updates, a conference and workshop calendar, as well as links to related resources and publications. *Counseling Today On-Line*, a monthly newsletter with informative articles and commentary, is also available. The code of ethics for counselors in addition to other professional information is offered. The Web site has reduced the use of overly large graphics over the years and now offers a relatively clean interface and faster Web site. The site is well designed and organized, but pages other than the home page lack information about when they were last updated.

Title (or descriptor):	American Medical Association
Owner:	American Medical Association
URL (Web address):	`http://www.ama-assn.org/`
Rating:	★★★★
Access restrictions:	Registration optional; free

The largest professional association of medical doctors in the world has a large and impressive Web site. It offers a wide range of medical information, links to their own journal (*Journal of the American Medical Association* [JAMA]), and links to a dozen other journals sponsored by the AMA, including the *Archives of General Psychiatry*. Full-text abstracts of each journal's current and past articles are available. Naturally information about the organization itself and its members is available. Advocacy, press releases, science, and education categories round out the site. Graphics are professional and usually quick to load. The site is equipped with an internal search engine, which is a good thing given its size. The graphical navigation menu (which helps you maneuver throughout the Web site) found at the bottom of some of its pages is cryptic however; the newer version appears to be more informative.

Title (or descriptor):	American Medical Informatics Association
Owner:	American Medical Informatics Association (AMIA)
URL (Web address):	`http://www.amia.org/`
Rating:	★★★

Much improved over the years, the AMIA Web site offers users information about technology in healthcare. The home page is divided into six distinct categories, including meetings and educational events, membership and services, publications, the organization's structure and operations, additional information about informatics, and background information about previous AMIA meetings. Complete abstracts are available on this site from the AMIA journal, *Journal of the American Medical Informatics Association*, dating back to 1994. A simple site, but full of useful information helpful in keeping on top of the medical informatics field.

Title (or descriptor):	American Psychiatric Association
Owner:	American Psychiatric Association
URL (Web address):	`http://www.psych.org/`
Rating:	★★★★

The Web site of the APA is so large and layered that if it didn't have its own internal search engine you might spend days trying to get to the actual abundance of information. The site is filled with a wide variety of information on mental disorders, on the professional association itself, consumer-oriented "Let's Talk Facts" brochures, and a whole lot more for psychiatrists and laypeople. It is relatively well-designed with sharp graphics. The Web site is, however, much too hierarchical in its information presentation, requiring the reader to access submenu after submenu to get to the useful content. The graphics tend to be overdone as well, and there are far too many of them. The font size used throughout the site is *large* and easy to read.

Professional information on the site includes a section for APA members, ethics, a catalog of current offerings, information on the annual Psychiatric Institute and APA convention, a number of publications, and additional links. The catalog offers links to information on APA Periodicals (*American Journal of Psychiatry, Psychiatric Services,* and *Psychiatric News*), publications ("DSM-IV & Related Products," "Practice Guidelines," "Task Force Reports," and "Ethics Booklets"), multimedia products, educational programs and seminars, a job bank, and information on their insurance and consultation services. But the majority of information on the APA site appears to consist of educational brochures and similar information on mental disorders. This includes well-written and lengthy articles on depression, anxiety, eating disorders, coping with HIV and AIDS, and substance abuse, among others. Research funding information and training manuals can also be found on the Web site.

Title (or descriptor):	American Psychiatric Nurses Association
Owner:	American Psychiatric Nurses Association (APNA)
URL (Web address):	`http://www.apna.org/`
Rating:	★★

The Web site for the APNA offers the standard organizational fare—membership information, contact information, organizational information, and past tables of contents for its own *Journal of the American Psychiatric Nurses Association*. Graphics are small and quick to load, but are from standard graphic libraries on the Web, making them less than customized or professional. Announcements and links to other related Web sites round out this site.

Title (or descriptor):	American Psychoanalytic Association
Owner:	American Psychoanalytic Association (APsA)
URL (Web address):	`http://www.apsa.org/`
Rating:	★★★

The American Psychoanalytic Association (APsA) has approximately 3,000 individual members and a Web site offering its members a great deal of information. While psychoanalysis has lagged in the United States, it still enjoys a popular worldwide following and is respected in many schools. Highlighted in a recent visit to their Web site was the APsA's annual meeting. Like many organizational sites, this Web site placed too many links to its offerings on its home page. This design blunder makes it difficult for people to reasonably choose from a short list of topics. Once you do choose, though, you will find a wealth of resources at this site, including the unique ability to send e-mail to any member who has registered an e-mail address. An extraordinary feature of this site is a searchable bibliographic database containing over 30,000 references to books, book reviews, and journal articles of a psychoanalytic orientation. It is original contributions to online resources such as this that make the

World Wide Web so valuable. Selected full-text articles from *The American Psychoanalyst* are also available, but they may be slow to update those. Overall, this is a strong Web site and a valuable resource to anyone interested in psychoanalysis.

| **Title (or descriptor):** | American Psychoanalytic Foundation |
| | See *CyberPsych*, below. |

Title (or descriptor):	American Psychological Association
Owner:	American Psychological Association
URL (Web address):	http://www.apa.org/
Rating:	★★★★

A Web site full of useful information about journals as well as consumer information, press releases, and professional information related to the psychological profession. It also serves as an online publishing "mirror" for the psychologist's monthly newspaper, the APA *Monitor*, offering listings from their events and continuing education calendar, classified ads, and select full-text articles every month (http://www.apa.org/monitor/). Design suffers from a lack of overall organization and style standards from page to page within the site, although this was slowly improving. This lack of design continuity also impairs navigation; numerous bad links were found throughout the site, including links to their own search engine.

Despite these flaws, though, the APA (with over 142,000 psychologist members) rivals the American Psychiatric Association's Web site in its breadth and depth of content. Organized around a somewhat similar hierarchical approach, the site is most effective in providing online material published in traditional media. It offers information for professionals ranging from the full text of the APA's "Ethical Principles and Guidelines" to newsletters (*Practitioner Update* and *Practitioner Focus*, for instance, although neither was up-to-date). The science section provides resources on the directorate's programs and general information, annual report, the "APA Task Force on Intelligence Releases Report," APA science advocacy, awards and funding programs, testing and assessment information, and various psychological science resources online and in the real world. The site gets low marks for not linking to related content on the Web, as most other organizations do.

The Members Services area will be of special value to APA members, as it gives them access to additional services, such as PsychINFO. Members could also search the APA's book and journal offerings and use a professional version of their PsycCrawler Web search engine.

Title (or descriptor):	American Psychological Society
Owner:	American Psychological Society and Hanover College
URL (Web address):	`http://www.psychologogicalscience.org/`
Rating:	★★★

The American Psychological Society (APS) Web site, maintained by John Krantz at Hanover College, is a cornucopia of online professional resources. Although I don't much care for the home page (which is *way* too confusing!), you will find employment listings, information about the society, federal funding updates, annual convention information, and much more. Many of the past issues of the *APS Observer* can also be found here, as well as past APS convention proceedings. The graphical buttons are a bit outdated, and some information does not appear to be updated regularly. This site is also home to many additional Internet resources of use to professionals. These include links to hundreds of psychology department Web sites throughout the world and a large listing of journal Web sites. Links are arranged by categories: teaching, research, mental health, employment, graduate student, and a host of other resources. Some areas, such as the "Teaching Resources" section, are very well done and offer a lot of topics not found anywhere else online today. The site is about average to navigate around in, but the breadth of content offered more than makes up for its navigational and design shortcomings.

Title (or descriptor):	Association for the Advancement of Gestalt Therapy
Owner:	Association for the Advancement of Gestalt Therapy (AAGT)
URL (Web address):	`http://www.g-g.org/aagt/`
Rating:	★★

The Association for the Advancement of Gestalt Therapy (AAGT) site explains the basics about the Association, including an introduction to the AAGT, a description of the special interest groups in the organization, information about their annual international conference, a simplified summary of Gestalt therapy, a listing of Gestalt, psychology, and psychotherapy online resources, and a short glossary of Gestalt terminology. I wish more time was spent expanding the Gestalt area and information sections, rather than adding links to other pages. Membership information (including the organization's bylaws) is available. It's a solid Web site with potential.

Title (or descriptor):	Association for Applied Psychophysiology and Biofeedback
Owner:	Association for Applied Psychophysiology and Biofeedback (AAPB)
URL (Web address):	http://www.aapb.org/
Rating:	★★★

This association represents clinicians who are interested in psychophysiology or biofeedback. A well-constructed site offers links to their mission statement, membership information, research, FAQ about biofeedback, conference listings, and links to other sites. Current news and events round out this attractive site.

Title (or descriptor):	The Association of Black Psychologists
Owner:	The Association of Black Psychologists
URL (Web address):	http://www.abpsi.org/
Rating:	★★★

Much improved since its inception, the Association for Black Psychologists' Web site now offers extensive information about this organization. This information includes the organization's history and vision, contact and membership information, and publications of interest.

Title (or descriptor):	Association for the Scientific Study of Consciousness
Owner:	Association for the Scientific Study of Consciousness (ASSC)
URL (Web address):	http://assc.caltech.edu/
Rating:	★★★

The Association for the Scientific Study of Consciousness (ASSC) states on their Web site that the association promotes research within cognitive science, neuroscience, philosophy, and other relevant disciplines in the sciences and humanities, directed toward understanding the nature, function, and underlying mechanisms of consciousness.

The Web site offers additional information about the organization, its bylaws, how to join as a member, and journal information. ASSC is the sponsor of the online refereed electronic journal, *PSYCHE*, as well as the regular print journal, *Consciousness and Cognition*; information about these journals and how to subscribe to them is available here.

The real depth of content at this site lies in its very extensive bibliography, put together by Thomas Metzinger and David Chalmers. This selected bibliography covers books and articles on consciousness in philosophy, cognitive science, and neuroscience since 1970. It consists of three main sections: monographs, edited collections of papers, and articles, and it is completely searchable. It is constantly updated on the Web site and is an invaluable addition to the online world.

Title (or descriptor):	Canadian Psychological Association
Owner:	Canadian Psychological Association
URL (Web address):	http://www.cpa.ca/
Rating:	★★★

The Canadian Psychological Association (CPA) Web site is a good example of an online resource with a lot of information, as well as a lot of potential. Attractively designed and well-organized, the CPA offers a wealth of background and history about the organization, a listing of staff should you wish to contact the CPA, an online searchable membership directory, and a few publications. The publications include the *Canadian Journal of Behavioural Science* as well as the CPA's official quarterly newspaper, *Psynopsis*. I was disappointed to see that although the journal offered full-text articles all the way back to 1992, the most recent issues hadn't been updated for over 8 months. Since placing full-text articles on their Web site apparently was a project of some kind, it may be that the project is over, and new articles will never be published online. Progress reports were supposed to be published quarterly, but I could only find two out of four quarters. After reading through a half-dozen files on the project, I still wasn't clear as to its outcome. Noticeably lacking on the CPA Web site are any resources or information about mental disorders for either laypeople or professionals. Their general links to other psychology Web sites is eclectic and missing a lot of popular and useful sites commonly found on other lists. Available in English and French versions.

ONLINE DOESN'T ALWAYS MEAN ON TIME

One of the most frustrating aspects of surfing the Web and looking for online information is determining how often a publisher or organization decides to place their real-world print articles on their Web site. A lot of sites place articles online without carefully deciding on a schedule for updates or further publication and without assigning the appropriate staff for this online responsibility. This short-sightedness is common among Web developers. They understand that content is important and rush to place as much of it as possible online when they first develop their Web site. But as the weeks turn into months, the one person responsible for maintaining up-to-date content often turns to other tasks or responsibilities. Before anyone realizes, the site has become woefully outdated in a matter of months.

Some sites have developed a sensible and well-conceived publishing policy ahead of time. The American Psychological Association's *Monitor* (`http://www.apa.org/monitor/`), CME's *Psychiatric Times* (`http://www.mhsource.com/psychiatrictimes.html`), and the American Psychiatric Association's *Psychiatric News* (`http://www.psych.org/pnews/`) have all developed online publication procedures that make them reliable and useful to readers. Sometimes, the online version appears before the print publication is available! A Web site does not have to offer its entire real-world print offerings online to be successful; they simply need to let their readers know what they do offer online and how often they make new items available.

Title (or descriptor):	Cape Cod Institute
Owner:	Cape Cod Institute
URL (Web address):	`http://www.cape.org/`
Rating:	★★★

The Cape Cod Institute offers symposia every summer for keeping mental health professionals up-to-date on the latest developments in psychology, treatment, psychiatry, and mental health. Renowned professionals often speak at this institute because it is a relaxed environment and allows greater interaction between faculty and participants. The Web site gracefully outlines the available workshops and offers much information about lodging and the like to potential participants. An interactive, Web-based discussion forum is even offered to allow participants to chat with one another about past and future courses.

Title (or descriptor):	Clinical Social Work Federation
Owner:	Clinical Social Work Federation (CSWF)
URL (Web address):	http://www.cswf.org/
Rating:	★★★★

The number and degree of good social work resources online is not at all large. This site goes a long way to correct that problem, in providing a central resource for clinical social workers. Its resources include information about the federation, a conference and workshop calendar, information on how to subscribe to a number of social worker mailing lists, legislative and news updates, links to state agencies and social work societies, as well as a number of publications including *The Family Therapy Practice Academy News Notes*. The site is generally well organized and information is presented in an easy-to-read manner.

Title (or descriptor):	CyberPsych
Owner:	CyberPsych
URL (Web address):	http://www.cyberpsych.org/
Rating:	★★★

This one URL hosts the following organizations, among others:

> American Psychoanalytic Foundation
>
> American Association of Suicidology
>
> Society for the Exploration of Psychotherapy Integration (SEPI)

The sites all have a somewhat similar feel but they offer different degrees of information about each association. Each is well designed and easy to navigate through.

Title (or descriptor):	The Industrial–Organizational Psychologist
Owner:	Society for Industrial and Organizational Psychology (SIOP)

URL (Web address):   http://www.siop.org/
Rating: ★★★

Home to *The Industrial-Organizational Psychologist* newsletter, the official publication of the Society for Industrial and Organizational Psychology (SIOP), this Web site has a lot of links and resources. Back issues and complete articles of the newsletter are available on the site, dating back to 1995. The site has grown in content and professionalism over the years. In addition to the newsletter, the site hosts an e-mail directory of SIOP members, organizational, membership, conference, and contact information, and postion papers adopted by SIOP. A call for proposals for its annual conference, information on how to order audio cassettes from its last conference, and available postions and internships are also included in this continuously-updated and growing site. Links to related I-O Web sites, grant searches, and discussion forums round out this site.

Title (or descriptor):   International Society for Mental Health Online
Owner: International Society for Mental Health Online
URL (Web address):   http://www.ismho.org/
Rating: ★★★

Please see the full description of this professional association in Chapter 11.

Title (or descriptor):   National Association of Social Workers
Owner: National Association of Social Workers (NASW)
URL (Web address):   http://www.socialworkers.org/
Rating: ★★★

Having grown and added extensively to their Web site in the past year, the National Association of Social Workers now has a great resource online. While the home page offers too many and sometimes repetitive choices, the site is generally well-designed and easy to navigate. The site is divided into a number of major catagories, including organizational, contact, and membership information, a "what's new" section, a jobs listing, insurance trust, publications index, ethical code of conduct, advocacy work, social work practice, NASW credentials, latest press releases and news from NASW, and links to related Web resources. In addition to this information, the site has a Clinical Register Online. This database allows a user to search for a clinical social worker within their community. It worked as expected when I tried it and quickly located 28 clinical social workers within the Columbus, Ohio area. The site sometimes loses its lower navigation bar when browsing certain areas (such as the Clinical Register Online or the NASW Press area). A listing of related meetings and calls for papers fills out an excellent online social work resource.

Title (or descriptor):	Physicians Who Care
Owner:	Physicians Who Care, Inc.
URL (Web address):	http://www.pwc.org/
Rating:	★★

Physicians Who Care is a nonprofit organization begun in 1985 and devoted to protecting the traditional doctor–patient relationship while ensuring quality health care. Their statement of purpose is succinct:

> We affirm the right of the physician, as the provider of care, to diagnose, prescribe, test and treat patients without undue outside interference. We affirm the right of the patient, as the person most affected by care, to choose his or her own physician and help determine the type of treatment received.

The Web site covers not only Physicians Who Care, but also Patients Who Care and a "Medicare Alert" section (about Medicare reform legislation). The site hadn't been updated for a few months when I visited it, but there are a lot of well-written articles in the handful of newsletters available online. Designed with minimal graphics and not very large, the Web site is easy to navigate. More information about the organization itself would help this Web site.

Title (or descriptor):	Psycgrad Project
Owner:	University of Texas/Austin
URL (Web address):	http://www.erols.com/matthew.simpson/psycgrad.html
Rating:	★★

This organization exists for graduate students in psychology to communicate ideas, share information about conferences worldwide, and to publish scientific papers in their own journal. This sparse Web site provides information on how to subscribe to their mailing list and links to other psychology resources online.

Title (or descriptor):   Society for the Exploration of Psychotherapy Integration
                                (SEPI)
                                See *CyberPsych*, above.

Title (or descriptor):   Society for Neuronal Regulation
Owner: Society for Neuronal Regulation
URL (Web address):   `http://www.snr-jnt.org/`
Rating: ★★★

A site that will mainly interest professionals in neurofeedback, such as EEG or biofeedback. Its main offerings are full-length articles as well as abstracts reprinted with
permission from their own members, as well as some reprinted from regular professional journals. This site is updated irregularly and only a few links to other pages
may be found here.

Title (or descriptor):   Teachers of Psychology in Secondary Schools (TOPSS)
Owner: American Psychological Association
URL (Web address):
         `http://www.apa.org/ed/topsshomepage.html`
Rating: ★★★

The Teachers of Psychology in Secondary Schools organization is interested in helping promote the introduction of students to psychology in high school through cur-
riculum suggestions, essay contents, and teacher workshops. Information about the
organization may be found here, as well as specific unit plans for teachers on a variety of psychology subjects (e.g., personality, biological bases of behavior, statistics).
A well-organized site with a wealth of information for psychology teachers.

Title (or descriptor):   World Health Organization
Owner: World Health Organization
URL (Web address):   `http://www.who.org/`
Rating: ★★★

Certainly an international organization the size and scope of the World Health Organization (WHO) should offer a Web site equally large. WHO doesn't fail to de-

liver on its Web presence, offering readers a large site full of background and history of the organization, descriptions and information on its multitude of programs administered throughout the world, and a large archive of statements published by the organization on international medical and health issues and crises. Statistical information in the form of the *Weekly Epidemiological Record* (WER) and the *Statistical Information System* (WHOSIS) is available through the Web site, as is a complete list of WHO publications and database offerings. Readers may also find press releases, contact information, online newsletters (although how up-to-date they are varies widely), and the *World Health Report*, published annually. Some files are in the "portable document format" (PDF), which requires the Adobe Acrobat reader. The Web site itself is well designed and offers an internal search engine.

HOW CAN I FIND THE ADDRESS OR PHONE NUMBER OF MY STATE PROFESSIONAL ASSOCIATION?

While there is no central organizational listing online for professional associations at the state or local level, you may find them through a number of common methods. The first place to check is with the national organization's Web site. For example, a listing of contact information for state associations of psychologists is available on the American Psychological Association's Web site (http://www.apa.org/practice/state.html). Such a list will often indicate whether a state association has a Web site (and provide an appropriate link). Division information is also available. Psychologists, for instance, will find complete division information (including contacts, addresses, Web sites, and e-mail addresses) on the American Psychological Association Web site (http://www.apa.org/); psychiatrists will find similar types of information on the American Psychiatric Association's Web site (http://www.psych.org/).

You can also check one of the Web sites that specializes in this kind of information or a subject guide. For example, Myron Pulier, MD offers a listing of over 1,400 mental health organizations around the world (http://www.umdnj.edu/psyevnts/psyjumps.html#Meetings). Mental Health Net (http://mentalhelp.net) has a smaller listing of such associations (including, for some, addresses and telephone numbers) under its "Professional Resources" section.

In many cases, at this time at least, obtaining information about state and local chapters of professional associations or related organizations can only be obtained by making a telephone call. Any agency or organization directly related to the government, however, might be found on your local state government's home page. For a listing of where your local government's Web site is located, check Yahoo!'s index of U.S. states (`http://www.yahoo.com/Government/`).

HOW DO I GET INVOLVED IN COMBATING THE SOCIAL STIGMATIZATION OF MENTAL DISORDERS?

There are many national and international organizations whose sole purpose is to educate the public and reduce the stigmatization of mental disorders. Nowhere are such advocates more vocal than in the online world, where an individual can reach thousands of people with very little effort and at almost no cost. Naturally professional associations such as the American Psychological Association (`http://help.apa.org/`) and the American Psychiatric Association (`http://www.psych.org/`) have taken leadership roles in this effort. On each of their Web sites, you will find specific areas devoted to publicizing what is currently known about mental disorders to the public and media. Certainly these sites are a good place to find such information and get started in becoming more actively involved in promoting mental health issues online.

The quality and bias of the information is determined by the organization publishing it, just as it is in the real world. With that caveat in mind, I will now discuss a few other organizations, in the real world as well as online, whose sole goal is to promote the dissemination of information about mental disorders and to help educate the public about proper and effective treatment options. These organizations usually go beyond simply presenting information and allowing consumers and laypeople to form their own opinions. Often they are promoting a particular viewpoint, which may or may not be validated by current research. Many professionals are involved within these organizations, however, and their online efforts reflect their commitment to their cause.

Title (or descriptor):	NAMI New York City Metro
Owner:	Alliance for the Mentally Ill

URL (Web address):   `http://www.nami-nyc-metro.org/`

Rating: ★★★

The Web site, maintained by NAMI New York City Metro, has a great deal of useful information on mental disorders, reducing the stigmatization of them in our society today, and how you can become more active in mental health advocacy in your local community. As one of the largest chapters of the National Alliance for the Mentally Ill, NAMI/NYC adopts the same philosophical stance on mental disorders being "neurobiological disorders (NBDs)." They heavily emphasize neurochemical interventions and radical treatments such as electroconvulsive therapy (ECT). Both NAMI/NYC (as well as NAMI) were set up to help support family members and individuals who suffer from mental disorders. They also support education to the society at large about these disorders. Addressing a common misunderstanding that people with mental disorders are somehow morally weak, these organizations have become recognized authorities for their advocacy and education efforts on behalf of the mentally ill.

NAMI/NYC's Web site reflects this ambitious goal by its inclusion of dozens of articles about mental disorders. Categories of information covered within this site include information about the NAMI/NYC organizations, press information and media kits, mental disorder diagnostic and treatment information, coping issues, advocacy guides as well as a multitude of additional articles, press releases, and announcements. The organizations publish articles on medications as treatment for mental disorders, but pro-psychotherapy articles and research are noticeably absent. The site is perhaps too simply organized, as some of the categories do not appear distinct. I found the solicitation for donations on the bottom of every page a bit annoying. There are no graphics on the site, so every page loads quickly.

Title (or descriptor):   Human Rights & Psychiatry Home Page

Owner: Support Coalition

URL (Web address):   `http://www.efn.org/~dendron/`

Rating: ★

At the other end of the spectrum from AMI/FAMI/NAMI is Support Coalition. This organization is against nonconsensual psychiatric treatment, as well as certain forms of treatment, such as electroconvulsive therapy (ECT). Their Web site is poorly conceived and implemented, however. It offers only tidbits of information supporting their viewpoint and does no better job of presenting an accurate portrayal of our current state of knowledge of mental disorders. About the only useful thing this site *does* offer is information on the pitfalls of ECT, as well as additional information about how to join Support Coalition. Virtually no real-world contact information could be culled from this site, even though they claim to be an independent nonprofit federation of 45 grassroots groups in six countries (although none were listed). The information offered is sensationalized, with overuse of exclamation points and large fonts.

Title (or descriptor):	National Alliance for the Mentally Ill (NAMI)
Owner:	National Alliance for the Mentally Ill
URL (Web address):	`http://www.nami.org/`
Rating:	★★★

The National Alliance for the Mentally Ill (NAMI) follows much the same philosophical guidelines as outlined in the NAMI/NYC review. On their home page, under "Facts About Mental Illness," NAMI states, "Severe mental illnesses are biologically-based brain diseases . . . " It is precisely because of this type of misinformation that NAMI is sometimes controversial and doesn't count an abundance of nonmedical mental health professionals and psychologists among its ranks.

NAMI's Web site *is* full of generally useful information and articles on mental disorders, although biased toward a medical model and, hence, medical treatment. Readers will find membership and NAMI conference information, as well as articles on a number of disorders such as schizophrenia, bipolar disorder, major depression, obsessive–compulsive disorders, and "neurobiological brain disorders" in general. The articles are oriented toward laypeople and contain little detailed information (except when discussing medications). Updates of the articles and news occur irregularly—there was a 4-month gap between some of them. The research findings (which highlight only medical research, not social science research) are also irregularly updated.

The site itself is quick to load, but the organization of the site makes it difficult to quickly find basic information on disorders. Information appears to be arranged chronologically. An internal search engine doesn't help find information that much more quickly. The site has gradually improved in its organization and layout and will likely be of benefit to consumers and others interested in NAMI's advocacy efforts.

Title (or descriptor):	National Mental Health Association (NMHA)
Owner:	National Mental Health Association
URL (Web address):	`http://www.nmha.org/`
Rating:	★★★

Probably the best and by far the most balanced organization devoted to mental health advocacy and education efforts, the National Mental Health Association (NMHA) offers an educational site. According to the NMHA, they are "the nation's only citizen volunteer advocacy organization dedicated to addressing all aspects of mental health and mental illnesses."

Their Web site is full of useful and relevant information on mental disorders and treatment (under the "Information" category), as well as resources on public policy and legislative alerts (under "Advocacy"), news releases, and prevention information. It is updated regularly so the news and legislative alerts are usually fresh. The organization also does a good job with providing two real-world publications for reading on their Web site, the quarterly *NMHA Prevention Update* and *The Bell*. They were a quarter behind when I checked, which isn't bad for an organization their size; it is unclear whether this delay is on purpose, though, or because of staffing limitations. The site is well designed with attractive but minimal graphics.

9

Book Publishers, Bookstores, and Journals Online

Numerous book publishers, bookstores, and journals are online and can be easily found—if you know where to look. Most book publishers provide some type of searchable online database of their current offerings, as do the online bookstores. Book publishers also offer contact information for ordering a book, a catalog, or to request further print information about something they publish. Bookstores online allow you to purchase books right from your computer with a credit card or by calling a toll-free number. Some bookstores even offer a discount up to 30% for some books and 10% for most others. What is nicest about online bookstores is the ability to enter keywords or search terms into their database search engine to locate books on a certain topic or with a certain word in their title. Potentially, this can allow you to locate, on your own, even obscure books on any particular subject. Try that at your local bookstore! Typically, journal Web sites offer you the ability to catch up with a print journal's current table of contents and read subscription information. Other journals may offer the complete text of articles online. Some journals are published *only* online, allowing you to read full-text, professional articles at no charge.

WHERE CAN I GO TO FIND BOOK PUBLISHERS AND INFORMATION ABOUT THE BOOKS THEY PUBLISH?

Nearly every book publisher has joined the age of technology and moved onto the World Wide Web. The quality of the Web sites vary greatly, as does the amount of interactivity offered (e.g., the ability to buy a book from them). Most offer a basic corporate Web site, with information about the publishing company, its corporate makeup and officers, contact information, and the like. Additionally some offer access to their publishing database, so you can hunt down titles and authors, and even find out if the book is still in print. A more extensive listing of mainstream publishers is available from Yahoo! (`http://www.yahoo.com/Business_and_Economy/Companies/Publishing/`).

Title (or descriptor):	Academic Press
Owner:	Academic Press
URL (Web address):	`http://www.apcatalog.com/`
Rating:	★★★

A searchable database makes finding a book from this publisher quick and easy. Both simple keyword searches and advanced searches are available. Their database contains over 6,000 titles.

Title (or descriptor):	American Psychiatric Press
Owner:	American Psychiatric Press, Inc.
URL (Web address):	`http://www.appi.org/`
Rating:	★★

Featured titles grace the home page of the American Psychiatric Press Web site. The site includes information and some descriptions on books, journals, and multimedia products. Listings of offerings are arranged by author or subject, and descriptions were often lacking. No search engine was found, and the online ordering form does not submit credit card information securely. *Do not use a non-secure ordering form online.*

Title (or descriptor):	American Psychological Association Press
Owner:	American Psychological Association
URL (Web address):	`http://www.apa.org/books/`
URL (Web address):	`http://www.apa.org/journals/`
Rating:	★★★

Descriptions of books and journals published by the American Psychological Association (APA) may be found on this Web site under two separate categories. The search engine works but provides cryptic results. In the books area, the "Recent Releases" category is updated monthly. Books listed under subject categories (Education Books, Scientific Books, Practice Related Books, etc.) are arranged alphabetically. You can print out an order form, but can't order online. A large, complete site for information on any publication from the APA.

Title (or descriptor):	Guilford Press
Owner:	Guilford Press
URL (Web address):	`http://www.guilford.com/`
Rating:	★★★

Information on every Guilford publication is readily accessible, either by searching for an author/editor, title, or keyword using their search engine, or by browsing a list of titles, which is organized by subject area. Graphics are professional and the site is well organized, with contact information for Guilford at the bottom of every page. Guilford is the publisher of this book.

Title (or descriptor):	MIT Press
Owner:	MIT Press
URL (Web address):	`http://www-mitpress.mit.edu/`
Rating:	★★★

You may use either their search engine (which is more complicated than necessary) or browse through their indices of books categorized by topic to find a title published from 1993 to 1997.

Title (or descriptor):	W. W. Norton & Company
Owner:	W. W. Norton & Company
URL (Web address):	http://www.wwnorton.com/
Rating:	★★

A graphics-intensive home page takes a while to load and offers a confusing array of choices. You can browse their catalog and search it.

Title (or descriptor):	Oxford University Press
Owner:	Oxford University Press USA
URL (Web address):	http://www.oup-usa.org/
Rating:	★★★

You may search or browse through their book catalog. A large home page graphic will take a while to load on most people's browsers.

Title (or descriptor):	Plenum Publishing Corporation
Owner:	Plenum Publishing Corporation
URL (Web address):	http://www.plenum.com/
Rating:	★★★

Behind a rather plain home page is a straightforward search engine that allows you to search on all of this publisher's offerings, which include books, journals, and electronic journals. A complete description, table of contents (for books), and ordering information is available for each title. A browsing option is also available for the site; it is logically arranged, if you don't quite know what you're searching for. Although an online ordering form is available, it does not process credit card information securely and *should not be used.*

Title (or descriptor):	Prentice Hall Publishing
Owner:	Prentice Hall Publishing

URL (Web address):   `http://www.prenhall.com/`

Rating: ★★★

By choosing the "Humanities and Social Sciences" division on Prentice Hall's home page, you can browse by book title through the "Course Catalog" option. Choosing "Custom Catalog" gives you a search form in which to enter a query. Book information includes a description, table of contents, and ordering information. The site is large and attractively designed.

Title (or descriptor):   Princeton University Press

Owner: Princeton University Press

URL (Web address):   `http://www.pupress.princeton.edu/`

Rating: ★★★

A large home page graphic (which appears to be common among book publishers!) detracts from an otherwise excellent and solid site. Both searching and browsing of their catalog is available, as is a list of out-of-print titles (which is handy).

Title (or descriptor):   Sage Publications

Owner: Sage Publications

URL (Web address):   `http://www.sagepub.com/`

Rating: ★★

Sage has constructed a site that is too hierarchical in nature and requires too many steps to actually search for a book. Queries on their database also took an extremely long time to answer.

Title (or descriptor):   John Wiley & Sons, Inc., Publishers

Owner: John Wiley & Sons, Inc., Publishers

URL (Web address):   `http://www.wiley.com/`

Rating: ★★★

Offering a large and somewhat difficult-to-navigate Web site, John Wiley & Sons' on-line catalogs vary in quality. For instance, most of the journals listed have their own

Web pages, with lengthy descriptions, editorial board listings, notes for contributors, and subscription information. Books, on the other hand, often are lacking any descriptive information. Numerous broken links were discovered. You may browse through titles or use their search engine (which was also broken when I tried using it).

WHERE DO I GO TO BUY A BOOK ONLINE?

What's nice about the online world today is the ability to shop at your convenience and in the privacy of your home or office. And book buying is a type of shopping ideally suited to the online world. Especially useful is the ability to find and order used or out-of-print books through some online bookstores. While there is no central location online to find a listing of all the online bookstores as of this writing, there are a number of such listings for specific categories. I suggest checking out The Complete Guide to On-line Bookstores (`http://www.paperz.com/bookstores.html`). It is not comprehensive, but it is as close as you're likely to get. It includes categories of "Rare and Used Bookstores," "Special Interest Bookstores," "University and College Bookstores," among dozens more.

amazon.com

Title (or descriptor):	Amazon.com
Owner:	Amazon.com
URL (Web address):	`http://www.amazon.com/`
Rating:	★★★★

Amazon.com offers nearly every book published by anyone through their database and ordering system online. Since they don't actually have to warehouse every title, they can stack the virtual shelves as high as they'd like! They've done exactly that, listing millions of titles within their extensive database. Naturally they don't actually have *every* in-print book available for immediate shipment. But for most popular, mainstream books, they offer quick delivery times and easy online ordering. A "Special Order" notation next to many of their professional titles means the book may take 4 to 6 weeks to receive. Each book listing includes the availability of the book (most are shipped within 2 to 3 days), publisher, author(s), publication date, binding (hardcover or paperback), and number of pages. Most books are available at a discounted retail price. Ordering can be conducted through a secure online transaction server (where it is safe to enter in credit card information and transmit it over the Internet) or through a toll-free phone number.

Searching through the Amazon.com database is preferable to browsing, although a browsing option is available. Using one of their many search engines (keyword, title, author, subject, advanced), users can enter in any terms or part of a term they are searching on. The only drawback to a database so large is that it is generally geared more toward popular books, not professional titles. So some professional titles may not be available within 2 to 3 days, and they will usually not be offered at any discount. As with any search engine, you should read their "Search Tips" to get the most from your queries. Amazon.com has expanded far beyond its original bookstore model, and now offers one-stop shopping for books, videos, music, toys, electronics, auctions, and more. They don't do as good a job in these additional areas, and often their prices are higher than other Web sites that specialize in them.

Title (or descriptor):	AnyPsych Book
Owner:	Behavior OnLine
URL (Web address):	`http://www.behavior.net/AnyPsych/`
Rating:	★★

AnyPsych Book is an online bookstore catering to the psychology and mental health professional. With a database of over 50,000 titles to choose from, this "smaller" bookstore has most of them readily available and in stock. I easily located a number of the most popular MMPI (a psychological assessment measure) books, such as those written by Roger L. Greene and James N. Butcher. What this Web site lacks, though, is any type of online ordering mechanism (a toll-free phone number is provided instead), and it offers less information about each book than other databases do. This database only lists the author's last name, the title of the book, and the book's price. This would be a stronger and more useful resource if their database were more robust and additional information were provided about shipping charges, shipping time, and how new the "New Acquisitions" really are. The site itself is simple and consists of only a handful of pages with a few inoffensive graphics.

Title (or descriptor):	Barnes & Noble
Owner:	Barnes & Noble
URL (Web address):	http://www.bn.com/
Rating:	★★★

Barnes & Noble came to the game of online book selling later than Amazon.com, and so had a fair amount of catching up to do. Despite having a recognizable real-world brand name, and brick-and-mortar stores to back it up, the Barnes & Noble site doesn't leverage either very well. Barnes & Noble seems to have duplicated key aspects of the Amazon.com model of success, from low prices, a selection covering millions of books, and allowing people to enter their own review of books, right down to navigational tabs to move from section to section on the site. The resemblance and feature-match is perhaps just a bit too canny and unoriginal. Originality would be allowing a user to order a book through the site and pick it up at one of their local bookstores, a feature Amazon.com couldn't easily match. Nothing like that exists on the site today, though.

But competition is good for you, the consumer. If Amazon.com can't deliver a book you need at the time and price desired, visit Barnes & Noble's site to see if they can.

ABOUT PRINT AND ELECTRONIC JOURNALS

With all of the benefits of online technology at your fingertips, it makes sense that publishing research in a more timely manner is in the front of many professionals' minds. With traditional peer-reviewed print journals, going from submission to final publication of a research study can take years for some journals, and many months for others. Imagine what could be done by removing the lengthy print publishing step and replacing it with a streamlined online process.

There are two types of journal Web sites found online: print journals with a Web site and electronic journals that have no print counterpart. The former is far more common than the latter. Print journals will publish a Web page to offer information about the journal and how to subscribe to it. They may also publish the current table of contents as a service to online readers and potential subscribers. Some publishers take this a step further and also publish abstracts of recent or current articles. Finally, some "go all the way" and make the full text of one or two of their current articles available on their Web site. Whatever the amount of information found on a journal's Web site, that information (whether it's a table of contents or full-length articles) is accessible online without charge.

The second type of Web site is one on which the journal is published exclusively online. These journals were originally experiments in electronic publishing, such as the American Psychological Association's sponsorship of *Psycoloquy*. They have quickly caught on with online readers, though, because they are available without charge and offer refreshing content online (which is all too often lacking in print journals). If online publishing of your own work is an intriguing concept to you, you'll find more information about it at the end of this chapter.

WHERE CAN I GO TO FIND BOTH PRINT JOURNALS AND ONLINE JOURNALS (E-JOURNALS) IN MY FIELD?

The first step to finding online, refereed, professional journals devoted to the kind of topics you're interested in is to look in one of the large journal indices, referred to as "guides" below. They all include some descriptive information about the journal's Web site. This information usually includes the journal's title, and a brief description of the journal.

Some guides list how much information a print journal hosts on its Web site. It is most common to find a print journal's current (and sometimes, past) tables of contents online. This may be helpful in browsing journal titles that interest you to see whether any articles in that issue may be worth reading. It is less common to find abstracts from current and past issues, and least common is to find the actual full text of the articles themselves. All the guides listed below index both electronic journals as well as print journals. Some guides may also include links to professional papers that may not have ever appeared in regular print journals, conference proceedings, and bibliographies.

Guides to Journals and Professional Articles

Title (or descriptor):   Electronic Journals and Periodicals
Owner: Hanover College Psychology Department

URL (Web address):

   `http://psych.hanover.edu/Krantz/journal.html`

Rating: ★★

This is one of the older and smaller listings of psychology and related journals and periodicals online. It is still regularly updated and organized alphabetically. Other listings include all the journals found here, but this is a good place to stop by if you're already on the Web or can use a quicker, smaller list of journals. This site also includes listings of some general periodicals that aren't necessarily specific to psychology (e.g., *Academe This Week, Discover Magazine, Electronic Journal on Virtual Culture, Journal of Computer Mediated Communication, Computer-Mediated Communication Magazine, The Journal of NIH Research, Nature Genetics*). It offers some select conference proceedings (e.g., the Sixth and Seventh Annual Convention of the American Psychological Society, 23rd International Conference of Applied Psychology, among others) and has links to one of many MEDLINE search engines available online and a few online bibliographies (*Chinese Psychological Studies, The Drug Discrimination Bibliography, Hong Kong Psychological Studies*). There's really no rhyme or reason to the topics listed here, except that they are available online. This journal listing is compiled and maintained by John H. Krantz, PhD.

Title (or descriptor):   Links to Psychological Journals
Owner: Armin Guenther
URL (Web address):

   U.S. mirror site: `http://www.psychwww.com/resource/journals.htm`

URL (Web address):

   European site: `http://www.wiso.uni-augsburg.de/sozio/hartmann/psycho/journals.html`

Rating: ★★★★

By far one of the superior listings available online today, this is a large and nearly comprehensive listing of psychology-related journals that have Web sites. The listing includes journals that have not yet been published, though, as well as links to journals whose connection to psychology and related fields is tenuous. But with nearly

1,000 entries cataloged at this writing, it has the largest journal listing online. Because the listing is so large, you will definitely have to wait a while for it to download on slower online connections; choose the Web site closest to you to ensure the fastest download time. This listing includes links to journals, both online and real-world, as well as helpful and informative descriptions. It does offer additional listings to help narrow your search, though, such as an index of only those journals with at least one full-text article online (`http://www.wiso.uni-augsburg.de/sozio/hartmann/psycho/jtext.html`); additional sublistings are also available (`http://www.wiso.uni-augsburg.de/sozio/hartmann/psycho/jsub.html`).

Title (or descriptor):	MedWeb: Electronic Newsletters and Journals
Owner:	MedWeb–Emory University Health Sciences Center Library
URL (Web address):	`http://www.medweb.emory.edu/`
Rating:	★★

A very large index of journals and newsletters that have some type of online presence. Although large, the descriptions are less than informative, often involving nothing more than the name of the journal. While a good list to browse for a medically related journal, it is not as helpful or mental health–specific as some other online offerings.

Title (or descriptor):	Neurosciences on the Internet
Owner:	Neil A. Busis, MD
URL (Web address):	`http://www.neuroguide.com/`
Rating:	★★

This listing consists of journals oriented toward the neurosciences, divided into four categories: (1) journals that offer full-text articles online, (2) journals that offer abstracts online, (3) journals that have only their tables of contents online, and (4) other journals. Dr. Busis also provides a list of other online indices of journals. The lists of journals he provides are lengthy and complete. However, no additional information other than the journal's name is available through this site.

PsychJournalSearch

Title (or descriptor):	PsychJournalSearch
Owner:	Armin Guenther and Mental Health Net
URL (Web address):	`http://mentalhelp.net/journals/`
Rating:	★★★★

PsychJournalSearch, developed by myself in conjunction with Armin Guenther, duplicates his database of over 1,000 psychology, psychiatry, social work, and mental
health–related journals and publications online, but takes it a step further by making
the whole database searchable online. The search engine for this database allows you
to find journals by topic, language, publisher, and the amount of information available online (e.g., tables of contents, abstracts of articles, or full-text articles). Since
you can use a combination of these options to conduct your search, you could limit
it to finding only those journals, for instance, on cognition that offer the full text of
some articles online. Well designed and easy to use, this is a welcome addition to
Armin Guenther's excellent listing (see next resource). It is updated as often as Dr.
Guenther's database is, which is approximately once a month.

Online Journals and Publications

You can keep up with the treatment literature by examining a few regular
online journals or professional newspapers every month, or as often as they
publish. Just like perusing a regular print journal at home, you can browse
through an online counterpart to keep up-to-date on relevant treatment information. I would recommend placing the following journals on your regular reading list.

Title (or descriptor):	*The Monitor*
Owner:	American Psychological Association

URL (Web address):   `http://www.apa.org/monitor/`

Rating: ★★★★

The American Psychological Association publishes its professional newspaper, *The Monitor*, once every month and provides a wide range of selected news stories, articles, editorials, classifieds, and other useful items on its Web site. Articles date back to March, 1995, and more recent editions include the majority of articles listed in the print version of the newspaper. The site's multiple search engines either didn't work or didn't work very well when I finally tracked one down (it didn't return articles in the current issue of *The Monitor* online, for instance). The articles are often relevant and useful to clinicians in general though, and are very good mirrors of their print counterparts.

Title (or descriptor):   *Perspectives: A Mental Health Magazine*

Owner: Mental Health Net

URL (Web address):   `http://mentalhelp.net/perspectives/`

Rating: ★★★

This is an eclectic, refereed journal with a wide-ranging audience including laypeople and professionals. It features a broad selection of articles, which may be on any topic related to mental health. It is not your typical professional journal (as evidenced by the "magazine" in its name), but it does offer the occasional article on new treatment approaches for mental disorders, as well as on cutting-edge therapies and modalities (e.g., online psychoanalysis). Graphically pleasing, it is full of interesting items in every quarterly issue.

Title (or descriptor):   *PSYCHE: A Journal on Consciousness*

Owner: Association for the Scientific Study of Consciousness

URL (Web address):   `http://psyche.cs.monash.edu.au/`

Newsgroup: `sci.psychology.journals.psyche`

Rating: ★★★

PSYCHE is a refereed, electronic journal dedicated to the interdisciplinary exploration of the nature of consciousness and its relationship to the brain. Publishing material from a wide variety of fields including cognitive science, philosophy, psychology, physics, neuroscience, and artificial intelligence. It is available via the Web, a mailing list, or the newsgroup, `sci.psychology.journals.psyche`. Updated regularly.

Title (or descriptor):	*Psychiatric News*
Owner:	American Psychiatric Association
URL (Web address):	`http://www.psych.org/pnews/`
Rating:	★★★★

Featuring full text of back issues since March, 1996, this is the official newspaper of the American Psychiatric Association. As such, it is full of informative articles on the latest treatment approaches for practicing psychiatrists. Other mental health professionals can get important treatment information here as well. It is published every other week in print and online. The Web site is full of large, bulky graphics, but the articles are easy to find (although the site would benefit from its own internal search engine).

Title (or descriptor):	*Psychiatric Times*
Owner:	CME, Inc.
URL (Web address):	
`http://www.mhsource.com/psychiatrictimes.html`	
Rating:	★★★

Another excellent offering in psychiatry, their archive is a little less complete–although it goes back to early 1994. Only select articles are published online from the *Psychiatric Times*, which is published once a month. But that still usually includes anywhere from five to a dozen articles, on a number of topics relevant to all mental health professionals. Arranged by date, author, title, or topic, the online version of this newspaper is easier to search than the APA's *Psychiatric News* and is also less graphics-intensive.

Title (or descriptor):	*PsychNews International: An Online Publication*
Owner:	Various
URL (Web address):	`http://mentalhelp.net/pni/`
Rating:	★★

A newsletter devoted to keeping readers up-to-date about psychology, psychiatry and the social sciences online, it is published somewhat erratically. A continuation of an older newsletter *(InterPsych Newsletter)*, *PsychNews International (PNI)* often presents thought-provoking editorials, as well as a roundup of employment announcements, resource updates, and a host of additional offerings. Published irregularly, primarily through its mailing list, it is also available for free via the Web site. Hosted by Mental Health Net, the Web site's articles are searchable through an internal search engine.

Title (or descriptor):	*Psychiatry Online*
Owner:	Ben Green, MB, ChB, MRCPsych
URL (Web address):	`http://www.priory.co.uk/psych.htm`
Rating:	★★★

This site is one of the older online psychiatry sites. It has always been somewhat slow to access for North American users because of its location in the U.K. It is chock full of psychiatric and medically oriented professional articles on a wide range of medication and psychopharmacology topics, as well as electroconvulsive therapy (ECT). Some of its articles can be lengthy and sometimes obscure but many are interesting and informative. The site's graphical layout and navigation have always left a lot to be desired, sporting a home page filled with way too many graphics and choices. It is unclear what type of publishing schedule this online journal adheres to, and new articles and updates are sometimes difficult to locate.

Title (or descriptor):	*Psycoloquy*
Owner:	American Psychological Association & various
URL (Web address):	
	`http://www.princeton.edu/~harnad/psyc.html`
Newsgroup:	`sci.psychology.journals.psycoloquy`
Rating:	★★

Psycoloquy started off as a simple psychology newsletter in 1985 and is currently sponsored in part by the American Psychological Association. It does not mirror print journals' traditional publication standards. Each peer-reviewed "issue" is one article, and each volume is largely based on a select number of topic areas. It is rather confusing to read on the Web at the present time, so I recommend that you subscribe to the journal in its mailing list form. It is published sporadically; some months you may receive multiple issues, and other months you will receive nothing. It can also be read via the newsgroup, `sci.psychology.journals.psycoloquy`. Although claiming a large readership, this established and unique journal is still unknown to many professionals online.

Title (or descriptor):	*Self-Help and Psychology Magazine*
Owner:	Pioneer Development Resources, Inc.
URL (Web address):	`http://www.shpm.com/`
Rating:	★★★

This general self-help magazine offers online articles on a great deal of topics, ranging from relationships, dreaming, and sex, to posttraumatic strees disorder, eating disorders, and spirituality. Articles tend to be oriented toward consumers and laypeople, so will be of limited value to most professionals. Not every article is dated, which makes it difficult to discern how up-to-date some information may be. Articles are written by a volunteer staff of professionals and published on the Web site as they are written. This group effort shines in the breadth of topics covered and in the Web site's general layout and design. More recently, this online magazine has been struggling to create more of a community for itself, and in doing so, dilutes its identity and purpose. Quirks abound, ranging a lack of a disclaimer about the magazine's income derived from books it recommends for purchase through Amazon.com to the Web site's privacy statement, which discusses anonymity more than what the company does with the information it collects on its members.

Title (or descriptor):	*Wounded Healer Journal*
Owner:	Linda Chapman
URL (Web address):	`http://idealist.com/wounded_healer/`
Rating:	★★

This "journal," published daily, is for therapists, healers, and victims of abuse. Written and published by a clinical social worker, this is a stylish and eclectic offering that may be of interest to some readers. The Web site is updated sporadically and covers a wide range of recovery and abuse topics.

HOW DO I SUBMIT AN ARTICLE TO AN ONLINE JOURNAL?

When NOT to Publish Online

There are some caveats to seeking online publication that you should be aware of. Publication in a peer-reviewed, print journal is the apex of professional accomplishment. Publication on a mailing list is equal to scribbling your study on a piece of paper and tacking it onto the department's bulletin board. Yet many print journals and their editors consider the online publication of an article or study as equivalent to any kind of previous publication. In other words, they won't accept a piece for consideration if it has already been published online in one form or another. Even if you "publish" your article in a mailing list or newsgroup, it may be considered "already published" and will be rejected on those grounds. This becomes of great concern to professionals when they need to list publications on their vitae or justify research expenditures to a department head or grant agency.

There are places online, however, which have the form and function of a print journal transplanted into an electronic version. Some of these online or electronic journals are peer-reviewed and have excellent and respected editorial boards. No matter what the form, an online publication will still garner fewer accolades than its print counterpart. For the most part, professionals tend to recognize by name which print journals have high or low quality. In the online world, though, it is more difficult to evaluate quality and respectability because everything and everyone is new. So authors need to be careful and aware of these issues before deciding to publish online.

What Is Appropriate for Online Publishing?

Sometimes the decision to publish online is an easy one. Studies or articles that have little to no chance of getting published in a print journal are ideal for online publication. These might include well-designed studies with negative results, studies with nonsignificant results but interesting trends, theoretical treatises that span professional disciplines, pilot studies with pilot data, and ideas for studies that cannot be conducted personally. Individuals who have typically been closed off from publishing results in regular print journals (usually anyone who isn't associated with a university) may also turn to an electronic journal for less academic bias.

What Are the Submission Guidelines for Online Publishing?

If you do decide your article or study is appropriate for an online publication, the next step is tailoring it for an online audience. While nearly any article *can* be published, will people actually *read* it? They probably will if you make it readable and keep it short. Every electronic journal will have their own specific publishing and submission guidelines for authors. But I believe the following are good, general points to keep in mind.

- Most people online have short attention spans. Anything over 1,500 words is likely to lose all but the most devoted readers.
- Graphs, charts, and tables should not be too complicated or large.
- Consider breaking longer articles into separate, smaller parts. These may be better published as a series in the journal, if the editors are willing and find the article needs to retain its length to remain valid and useful.

The main point is: Be flexible! Editors of electronic journals appreciate an author's willingness to edit or format an article for better online reading.

Caveats to Readers of Work Published Online

It is important to keep in mind that anyone can put up a home page or Web site nowadays and call it a "journal" or "magazine." Peer review, therefore, is still a worthwhile process and something you should look for in online journals. Another distinguishing feature of serious, professional online journals is that it has been issued an International Standard Serial Number (ISSN) through the Library of Congress or other official agency. This number means that the publication has been registered and suggests it intends to publish indefinitely online. Last, serious online professional journals will note on their masthead real-world contact information, an editorial board of professionals within the journal's field of interest, and have detailed submission guidelines for publication. While these won't guarantee that the journal's actual content will be of high quality, they *are* indicators of professionalism and stability for the online publication.

CHAPTER

10

Finding and Downloading Software Online

Software applications (also referred to as "programs") are what allows your computer to do specific tasks. Want to compile statistics for a research study? You'll need a statistical program such as SPPS or SAS. Want to write a letter to a colleague? You'll need a word processing program such as Word or WordPerfect. Want to create your own Web site? You'll need an authoring program such as Netscape Gold, HTML Assistant Pro, or HotDog Professional. Want to write clinical or assessment reports in half the time? You'll need to get a clinical report writer or assessment software, which can help you score and even interpret results. As you can probably guess, there are a wide range of reasons you may want or need additional software. People often do much more work than they need to on their computer when others have written software that can help automate repetitive or boring tasks. Just as you can purchase a book online, you can obtain useful, professional software online.

It seems logical that computer software should be available on the Internet, and it is. There are not only a wide range of computer applications in psychology freely available online, but also many general applications as well. Statistical software and applications, which help you score psychological tests (such as the Rorschach or MMPI), are examples of software available for "downloading" (transferring a program to your computer from the Internet). Futhermore, software doesn't have to be about psychology or clinically oriented to be of use to mental health clinicians or researchers. Using the Internet as a telephone is one example where general software can be of invaluable help, reviewed later in this chapter. There are four major types of software available online: shareware (the most common), crippleware, freeware, and demonstration programs.

TYPES OF SOFTWARE AVAILABLE ONLINE

Shareware

Most of the programs discussed below are "shareware" (from the terms "share" and "software"). Its authors allow you to download it to your computer and try it out for free. But if you continue to use it, you are obligated to purchase it for the asking price (often under $50.00). Many full-fledged software applications for your computer can be tried out and purchased in this manner.

Crippleware

Commercial software is also available online. Sometimes referred to as "crippleware" (from the terms "crippled" and "software"), it is software that does not contain all of its usual functionality. For example, you may able to open a file in one of these programs, but you may not be able to save any changes to the file. This allows you to try out the features of the software, but requires you to pay for it if you like it and want to continue using it. After paying for it, you will be given a registration number, which you enter into the program you already have on your computer. This special number then enables those previously crippled functions. Most major applications, such as Microsoft's word processing program, however, are still only available for purchase through a reseller or computer store.

Freeware

Another type of software is "freeware": The authors provide it at no cost to the user. But because it is free, it often does not come with support or in-depth documentation to help you out if you have questions. Sometimes you can e-mail the author directly with your questions, but if it is a popular piece of software, you may not receive a reply. (It usually doesn't hurt to try, especially if you have already looked in the "Help" file included with the software, or on the Web site from which you downloaded the software originally.)

When first published, software programs don't always work quite the way the developer intended. They may contain glitches or errors that cause your computer to do unexpected and unintended things. Software developers can fix or update programs, however, quite easily, and these fixes and updates are available online for nearly any piece of software you may have. The fixes are also referred to as "patches," "updates," or "bug fixes." Software that is still in its testing stages (referred to as "beta" software) is also often available for free online. Once it is finished its beta testing, however, the software may expire (stop working) or may become unsupported from the software developer.

Demonstration Programs

The last common type of online software is a demonstration program. Demonstration programs allow you to take a guided tour through a software application that may be too large, complex, or expensive for the software publisher to just give to you to try out on your own. After you are done taking the tour through the software, you may contact the developer for further information or to purchase the complete software package.

I'M LOOKING FOR A PIECE OF PSYCHOLOGY-RELATED SOFTWARE. CAN I FIND IT ONLINE?

Software is not only available online to download directly, but as mentioned above, you can usually try it out and use it for a period of time before deciding whether to purchase it. This is true both for shareware programs and commercial versions of many pieces of software. The software developers

DOWNLOADING SOFTWARE ONLINE

Downloading software online is almost as simple as installing software from a CD-ROM or diskette. In most cases, you simply click on the appropriate link on the software's Web site to start the process. At that point, most Web browsers will then ask you where on your computer you would like to save the program. Choose a directory and then the download begins. Download times depend on the speed of your link to the online world; slower modems result in longer download times. Most useful software can be downloaded in as little as 5 or 10 minutes, but some larger applications may take up to an hour or two. Most Web browsers can usually give you a somewhat accurate estimate of the time it will take to get the software. I cannot give more step-by-step download information for the simple reason that how one does this varies greatly by computer and operating system.

Software is compressed for downloading to decrease the overall size of the downloaded file, therefore decreasing overall downloading time in the process. Software comes compressed in two main varieties for most personal computers (PC, IBM-compatible) and one variety for a Macintosh. For a PC, the program will either be an "executable" compression (the last three characters of the filename will be ".exe") or a "zipped" file (the last three characters will be ".zip"). To uncompress an executable file, all you need to do is run the program after you've downloaded and it will take you through additional installation step by step. A "zipped" file needs an "unzip" program in order to decompress the program. (A common DOS-based utility is called "pkunzip.exe" while the Windows equivalent is "WinZip." Both utilities are available from one of the general software archives listed in the section below.) Macintosh programs most often use a compression program called "StuffIt" with the "UnStuffIt" program, available at no cost.

When downloading software from the Internet, you should be aware of software viruses. Viruses are most commonly small programs that have been inserted surreptitiously into a regular piece of software. Such viruses can be playful or harmful when they run on your computer, resulting in something as simple as a clever message being displayed on your screen to your entire hard drive being erased. Care should always be taken, therefore, when downloading software. It is always safest to check all programs obtained in this manner by running a virus-checking program on the software *before* running it (but after downloading it). Such programs are available from your local computer store or for free from one of the general software catalogs listed below.

often build into the software an expiration mechanism, so that it will expire or cease to function properly after a certain number of uses or a fixed period of time, if you do not purchase it. This gives you plenty of time to evaluate the software for your needs, and it protects the software authors from piracy and illegal use.

I've divided the following software listings into two categories. The first is mental health–related software, including psychological assessment, clinical practice, statistical, and billing software. The second category is general software. The first category I consider to be pretty comprehensive and complete as of this writing; the second category is potentially very large, so I chose a few sites, which are the largest and most popular. Some software sites offer reviews and descriptions of the programs they contain; others do not. These reviews and descriptions vary a great deal in quality and comprehensiveness. Most, however, will give you a general description of the program, its purpose, and what kind of operating systems and computers it runs on.

Because software reflects the quick changes made throughout the computer industry, any online resource which attempts to keep abreast of software programs for professionals needs to also be constantly updated. Since most Web resources available today, however, are labors of love and volunteerism for the professionals who maintain them, no site listed below for mental health-related software is comprehensive nor kept up-to-date with the latest versions of all mental health-related software available.

In addition to the sites listed bedow, Ziff-Davis has an excellent general software site which was not included in earlier printings of the book. That site may be found at `http://www.hotfiles.com/`.

Mental Health–related Software: Psychological Assessment, Clinical Practice, Statistical, and Billing Software

Title (or descriptor):	Computer Billing and Office Management Programs
Owner:	Ed Zuckerman and Mental Health Net
URL (Web address):	`http://mentalhelp.net/guide/pro24.htm`
Rating:	★★★

Want to find out more about a billing or office management software package? This Web page, a part of Mental Health Net, lists them all in one very large file. The only drawback to this page is that it takes a long time to load. The page has nine categories and covers topics such as

- a comprehensive and detailed review of computer billing and office management programs
- when to buy or use electronic claims submission
- other computer programs of interest to clinicians
- resources, references, and readings
- local resources
- computer programs for tracking citations
- computer programs for writing assistance
- "neat" computer tools
- other noncomputer resources

It is a fairly comprehensive listing, and the author updates it once or twice a year. The index covers all brands and makes of computer software. An additional listing of computer software on Mental Health Net may also be found at `http://mentalhelp.net/guide/prosale.htm`.

Title (or descriptor):	Computer Use in Social Services Network
Owner:	Computer Use in Social Services Network (CUSSN)
URL (Web address):	`http://www.uta.edu/cussn/cussn.html`
Rating:	★★

The Computer Use in Social Services Network provides a well-designed and attractive Web site to house, among other items, their "Software Connection." The Software Connection provides users with descriptions of human service freeware, shareware, and demonstration programs. The software listed on their site can be directly downloaded, or links are provided to the software's own Web site (from which it can be downloaded or purchased). Categories covered in their list include:

- clinical and therapeutic (provides or assists in treatment or intervention)
- welfare and child protection
- aging
- developmental disabilities
- education and training

■ management

■ accounting, billing, and fund raising

■ data analysis

■ miscellaneous packages and utilities

It's a good list of programs, although it is unclear how current it is.

Title (or descriptor):   Computers in Mental Health (CIMH)–Software
                              Information & Reviews

URL (Web address):   `http://www.ex.ac.uk/cimh/`

Rating: ★★★

The Computers in Mental Health (CIMH) Web site is similar to COMPSYCH in scope but does a much better job of updating. It offers current reviews and contact information for software relevant to mental health professionals. Although not nearly as large a database as some other sites reviewed, CIMH lists reviews according to categories such as anxiety, behavior analysis, billing, call schedules, child psychiatry, clinical education, depression, diagnosis, disabilities, families, informatics, medical records, neuroscience, patient assessment, patient education and treatment, patient monitoring, personality, psychological testing, psychotherapy, and reference. While reviews–available for some of the software entries–are dated, the entries themselves are not. This makes it difficult to determine how accurate and up-to-date the database really is. The reviews, however, do suggest it is far more current than some other Web offerings. Both Web sites are simple and quick to load with minimal graphics. The main Web site, however, offers an internal search engine, which makes finding relevant software programs easier.

Title (or descriptor):   CTI Directory of Psychology Software

URL (Web address):

`http://www.york.ac.uk/inst/ctipsych/dir/contents.html`

Rating: ★★★

One of the largest and most useful Web sites devoted to publishing information about psychological software, the CTI Directory of Psychology Software offers a listing of over 450 software programs for all types of computers. The resource is divided into broad category listings of general psychology, practicals and methodology (e.g., experiment generators, research tools, statistical analysis), mainstream courses (e.g., abnormal and clinical psychology, cognition, personality), specialized courses (e.g., education psychology, health psychology), assessment and treatment, studying and teaching tools, and administration. Most of the entries do not include dates of the entry or review, which is unfortunate. Online links to resources are included when they are available from the software developer. Entries also include contact information as well as pricing (sometimes in British pounds, since this is a site based in the United Kingdom).

The site is easy to navigate and offer minimal, unobtrusive graphics.

Title (or descriptor):	Kovach Computing Services (KCS)
Owner:	Kovach Computing Services
URL (Web address):	`http://www.kovcomp.co.uk/`
Rating:	★★

This Web site provides customer support and information for the KCS line of inexpensive and easy-to-use statistical software. You can get the latest shareware versions through the links and order the full versions online. There are also links to other sites related to statistics and data analysis, particularly those with shareware and public domain software. The software products found on this site include: SIMSTAT for Windows, a general purpose statistical program; xlSTAT, a statistical add-in for Excel spreadsheets; MVSP, a multivariate statistical package; SIMSTAT for DOS, a general purpose statistical program for DOS; Oriana, for circular statistics; and Wa-Tor, a population dynamics simulation, among other products and services.

Title (or descriptor):	Psyc Site: Software Sites
Owner:	Department of Psychology, Nipissing University
URL (Web address):	
	`http://www.stange.simplenet.com/psycsite/html/` `software.html`
Rating:	★★★

Psyc Site: Software Sites is intended to point to psychology-related software available on the Internet. These links are to both shareware and commercial software. Readers may find this site helpful in locating other software archives and listings online.

Title (or descriptor):	SAS Institute
Owner:	SAS Institute, Inc.
URL (Web address):	`http://www.sas.com/`
Rating:	★★★

One of the largest statistical software developers, the SAS Institute has a thorough Web site. Although their product line is complex, they do a fairly good job in describing the individual components of the SAS software system. What they (and their competitor, SPSS) do not do is provide a simple navigational path to users who have a diverse set of needs and skillsets. A first-time user has virtually no idea which product to choose or which products offer the best solution to their needs.

Their technical support area is filled with information on how to compute various statistics with their software, as well as a comprehensive set of FAQs. Their search engine works as expected with simple keyword searches leading to a listing of results ordered in confidence level.

Title (or descriptor):	Shrinktank
Owner:	Robert Bischoff, PhD
URL (Web address):	`http://www.shrinktank.com/`
Rating:	★★

This site has a lot of important and useful content but its design suffers from overuse of animated graphics. These take the reader's attention away from the useful content. In this case, the content consists of over a hundred different software programs (a subset of which reside on the GlobalPsych site, reviewed above). Suffering from the same lack of information about the programs, though—with terse and sometimes cryptic descriptions—this site only gets a better rating because it has more programs to offer (over 130 at this writing). Most of these programs are shareware or freeware, and some of the files are nothing more than text files, such as an FAQ file and NIMH informational brochures taken off the Internet and other Web sites. So be careful to ensure you are downloading a software program and not simply a file available on the Web elsewhere. This site could improve greatly if the author would drop the use of so many animated graphics and add more descriptive information, including the program's *name* and when it was placed online or the copyright date of the program itself. In the meantime, it may prove to be a useful site when you want to download an interesting psychology-related program to try out.

Title (or descriptor):	Software Information Bank (SIByl)
Owner:	iec ProGAMMA
URL (Web address):	http://www.gamma.rug.nl/sibhome.html
Rating:	★★★★

SIByl, the Software Information Bank, contains comprehensive information on computer applications for the social and behavioral sciences. Its purpose is to prevent the duplication of programming efforts by providing scientists with a library of existing (special-purpose) software. Both submitting a program description to and retrieving information from SIByl are free of charge. Each entry includes a functional description, technical and data requirements, prices, availability of manual and interface, literature references, and purchase addresses. Some entries include a review by iec Pro-GAMMA, a multisite university foundation. This is easily the best database of information for research scientists and clinicians seeking general use applications ranging from statistical programs to MMPI and Rorschach scoring and interpretation. The quickest way in which to find resources is by using their search interface and typing in a keyword. The site is easy to navigate, but may be slow for some North American users because it is based in The Netherlands. It also allows readers to submit their own software descriptions for programs not yet included within this large database.

Title (or descriptor):	SPSS
Owner:	SPSS, Inc.
URL (Web address):	http://www.spss.com/
Rating:	★★★

Compared to the SAS Institute's home page, the SPSS home page looks cluttered and unorganized. The user is given a choice of dozens of links to choose from, with very little organization to its site index layout. The home page is also graphics-intensive and sports some graphics that look confusingly similar to banner advertisements (but are not). Like the SAS Web site, SPSS provides no clear navigational path for first-time users. A listing of all of their products on the home page gives no indication if a product matches a user's specific needs without having to walk through each product's description. This is a common corporate Web site design blunder—designing around the company's business groups or divisions, not the customer's needs or expectations.

The SPSS site is somewhat less comprehensive than the SAS site, and somewhat more difficult to navigate and use. For example, the search engine in the "SPSS AnswerNet" doesn't support a simple keyword search without first associating the search with a specific product. Their search engine interface to this database of knowledge is unnecessarily complex. Like the SAS site, SPSS supports extensive FAQs on all of their products, and provides a wealth of information and support options. Scripting resources, white papers, and real-life examples of how the software can be best utilized in different scientific disciplines.

General Software Directories

Title (or descriptor):	Jumbo
Owner:	Jumbo, Inc.
URL (Web address):	http://www.jumbo.com/
Rating:	★★

With over 300,000 shareware and freeware programs available from one location, you can't go wrong by looking at Jumbo for any application or utility you may need for your computer. Its search engine leaves a lot to be desired, however, leaving you to rely on browsing through the site's hierarchy of categories. The categories available, however, don't always lend themselves to easy browsing. For example, e-mail applications are under "Internet/Windows 95" (Macintosh users are apparently out of luck) whereas Web browsers have their own category under "Internet." Users rate software listed in the directory on a 10-point Likert scale. Short descriptions are provided for each listing, as is the date it was added, the version number, and file size.

Title (or descriptor):	Shareware.Com
Owner:	C-Net
URL (Web address):	http://www.shareware.com/
Rating:	★★★

With over 250,000 titles to choose from, a less-annoying interface than Jumbo, fewer advertisements, more descriptions, and a more powerful search engine, Shareware.Com is a much better choice. Although offering a design that is still busy (and potentially confusing to new users), it is simple and easy to navigate. I could browse the most popular downloads arranged by operating system (or not—my choice!).

One of the nicest and most useful features of this site, beyond its comprehensive database and powerful search tools, is its download options. When you click on a file to download, it takes you to another screen that provides a list of download sites for the program. You choose the site that is geographically closest to you to ensure the fastest downloading time. Alternatively, you can use their own reliability ratings for the listed sites and choose the most reliable sites from which to download the software. It is key usability features such as this that make Shareware.Com a standout in a crowd.

Title (or descriptor):	ZDNet Software Library
Owner:	ZDNet
URL (Web address):	`http://www.hotfiles.com/`
Rating:	★★★★

Unlike Shareware.com and Jumbo, the ZDNet Software Library provides in-depth reviews of most of the software listed in its catalog. These reviews let you know what to expect of the freeware and shareware listed before spending the time to download it. The reviews are an invaluable addition, as it potentially can save a lot of time in evaluating new software or trying to find the right tool for your needs. In addition to the review, each software listing provides a star-review based upon the reviewer's comments, the file size, date it was added, version number, price of software (if any), and the ability to view related software titles.

The search engine was the most robust of the software directories listed here, quickly finding relevant results to search queries. Unlike the other directories, ZDNet's library doesn't attempt to be the largest. The library relies instead on choosing some of the best and most popular software titles. Its organizational scheme for categorizing software also makes the most sense. Macintosh and other computer operating system platforms, as on Shareware.com, are well supported.

CAN I USE THE INTERNET TO CHAT WITH MY COLLEAGUES ONLINE?

There are two ways you can use the Internet to chat with your colleagues, friends, or family online. One is through the use of a somewhat unreliable technology called "Internet telephony" (more commonly known as "Net-Phones"). This technology allows you to use the Internet and your computer as your telephone line and telephone, saving long distance charges.

The second way to chat with people online is via "Instant Messaging" (IM) software. More about IM in a minute.

When using a NetPhone, users at either end of a connection must use the same software, and there is a fair amount of different pieces of software to choose from. Two formats are available today: audio only and audio with video. Audio only is more popular because it is less expensive, less difficult to setup, and more reliable to use, especially on slower Internet connections. Adding video with audio is a goal, but much of the technology simply isn't available or in wide enough use. If you're a technology person who has all the latest and greatest computer hardware and online connection, you may want to look into a video software package. But you must keep in mind that for it to be of real use and value to you, the person on the other end must also be able to run the same software on her machine. I won't review the available video software packages, as they are still in their infancy. But look for updates in this area on the book's Web site as more professionals get on-line with technology that can support video transmission.

The descriptions below of Internet telephone audio products were gleaned not only from my personal experiences with the software, but also from independent, third-party reviewers, such as C-Net (http://www.cnet.com/). All such telephony applications require that your computer have sound capabilities (e.g., a sound card in your PC) and at least a 14.4-Kbps modem connection to the Internet. There are no additional costs associated with the use of these applications, outside of the normal Internet connection costs you already pay. That's why these pieces of software are especially popular for people to communicate with one another across continents. Some of the products listed below may begin to approach telephone transmission quality, but most do not except under rare conditions. This is just a sample of products available; a full comparison listing of NetPhones may be found at C-Net, or at http://www.nfe.com/owl/strouds/32phone.html.

Using the Internet for voice communications just hasn't taken off as many people had predicted, largely because of problems of interoperability (different brands of NetPhones don't know how to communicate with one another) and poor quality. In fact, as noted below, Netscape has dropped support for a client NetPhone in its latest release of its Web browser. Instead,

Netscape and other companies have seen that simple text chat is more powerful, easier to use, and more compatible with most people's computers than NetPhones have been. This movement back to basic but more widely-used communication tools online is unlikely to change in the near future.

What has taken on a life of its own are Instant Messaging (IM) applications, such as AOL's AIM and ICQ services. Instant messaging is simply being able to chat via text with others who are online the same time you are. This is typically done in a small window on your screen, through instant messaging software. The biggest drawback to these services is the same as it is for NetPhones—interoperability. It is hoped this issue will be worked out in the future, but in the meantime, ensure you are using the same software as those you want to chat with are. You may already have instant messaging software on your computer—it comes with versions of Netscape and Microsoft's Web browsers, and is a built-in feature of America OnLine.

Title (or descriptor):	AOL Instant Messenger Service (superceded CoolTalk)
Owner:	Netscape Communications (InSoft)
URL (Web address):	`http://www.netscape.com/`
Price:	Bundled free with Netscape Navigator
System:	Windows 3.x, 95/98, NT; Mac; Unix

Netscape continues to explore what users want in real-time communication tools. The company dropped support for its previous NetPhone client, CoolTalk, bundled with 3.x versions of Netscape's Navigator software. In 1998, with the release of the 4.5 version of its Web browser, Netscape dropped the successor to CoolTalk, Conference. Netscape has instead decided to bundle a free copy of America OnLine's Instant Messenger Service (AIM), which is a simple real-time text chatting tool (it is not a NetPhone). Since many millions of America OnLine's users already use AIM, this software has become a popular and widely used alternative to NetPhones.

Title (or descriptor):	Digiphone
Owner:	Third Planet Publishing
URL (Web address):	`http://www.digiphone.com/`
Price:	$19.95 (regular), $34.95 (deluxe)
System:	Windows 3.1, 95/98, Mac

An Internet phone product (which has been around a long time) with an attractive interface. Unfortunately, it suffers from poor sound quality across the spectrum of connections. It also had difficulty making connections from time to time.

Title (or descriptor):	FreeTel
Owner:	FreeTel Communications
URL (Web address):	`http://www.freetel.com/`
Price:	Free; $29.95
System:	Windows 3.x, 95

FreeTel, an advertising-based telephone solution, suffers from poor audio quality over a 14.4-Kbps modem line but does somewhat better on a 28.8-Kbps modem or higher. The user interface is poorly designed. The free version of the software includes small advertisements, which occupy an area on your screen, changing from time to time. The advertisements disappear in the $29.95 version of the product.

Title (or descriptor):	ICQ
Owner:	ICQ, Inc.
URL (Web address):	`http://www.icq.com/`
Price:	Free
System:	Any version of Windows or Mac

Since being acquired by America OnLine, ICQ remains one of the top two most popular instant messaging applications (AOL's AIM being the other). Preferred by experienced Internet users, ICQ has many of the same features of AIM, including the ability to set up a mini chat room. ICQ relies on arbitrary numbers to identify people, which isn't as user friendly as AIM's nicknames. But the search utilities found on the ICQ Web site make it relatively easy to hunt down a person's ICQ number.

Title (or descriptor):	Internet Phone
Owner:	VocalTec
URL (Web address):	`http://www.vocaltec.com/`
Price:	$49.95
System:	Windows 95/98, NT

One of the best overall performers in sound quality, it is also one of the costlier telephone solutions listed here. But with availability on multiple platforms, it may be
worth a look if you're serious about telephone applications online and have found
the other free software products to be unacceptable. This was the only product that
produced consistently reliable high-quality audio on varying modem speeds. A one-
week free trial period for the software is available from their Web site.

Title (or descriptor):	Iris Phone
Owner:	Iris Systems
URL (Web address):	`http://irisphone.com/`
Price:	$19.95 and up
System:	Windows 3.x, 95/98, NT

Offering nothing spectacular in terms of program features or sound quality, Iris
Phone is a middle-of-the-pack performer. Their software works at even the slowest
Internet connections, but I found that the sound quality also deteriorated substantially at these speeds. It offers a number of features not found in other NetPhone
products (see Iris Phone's Web site for a side-by-side comparison). Whether those
features are worth anything to you depends on whether you need them and would
use them.

Title (or descriptor):	NetMeeting
Owner:	Microsoft Corp.
URL (Web address):	`http://www.microsoft.com/netmeeting`
Price:	Free
System:	Windows 95/98, NT

NetMeeting is the only product listed here that allows users to share Microsoft-based
documents and spreadsheets with one another in a "whiteboard" area. Its sound
quality is adequate on ISDN or faster connections, but slower connection speeds
(14.4-Kbps and even some 28.8-Kbps modems) will notice especially poor quality. It
is limited to users of Windows at this writing. User configuration is simple and connecting to other users is a relatively painless experience.

11

Online Therapy (E-Therapy) and Behavior

Conducting therapy online, or e-therapy, is a new experience fraught with difficulties and some lingering concerns. As of this writing, some of these concerns have been resolved through professional association guidelines, state legislatures, or other governing bodies. You would still pretty much be a virtual pioneer if you choose to pursue this modality, and, as in the real world, you may run into very real ethical and legal problems. I would caution you that this is still an emerging field, so you must be both serious and devoted to it as a viable and useful modality. You should not look at conducting online therapy just as a way to supplement your income.

While many of the particular issues—ethical and practical—of online therapy have yet to be addressed by the mental health field, one issue has been, somewhat, addressed by the field of computer-mediated communication. Some professionals argue that since a great majority of people's interactions and communication are nonverbal, any medium that is not also nonverbal will miss important body language. Others argue that since people have been utilizing the Internet for a great deal of emotional discussion on online support groups, it is already a benefit to many individuals online. Both viewpoints are valid.

Some forms of professional helping are readily conducted online. It is not psychotherapy in the traditional sense, nor is it simply therapy transported to an online modality. Instead, it is apparent that it is an entirely new modality of helping people with life problems. Just as there are benefits when people with similar disorders "talk" to one another in online support groups (sometimes referred to as "virtual support groups" in research), it follows that some type of benefit could arise from an individual "talking" to a professional online. I leave it up to you to decide whether it is a good idea to try out this type of online service. But if you do, keep in mind that you are bound to the same ethical principles you hold in the real world. This includes such requirements as stating up front the type of service you are offering, the limits of such a service, your availability (24 hours a day, 7 days a week? by telephone or other contact?), to what extent your service replaces a regular therapist in the real world, and similar concerns.

Nonetheless, online therapy is still a somewhat risky venture, not only from an ethical point of view but also from a legal one. If an individual under your care online decides to commit suicide, can the individual's family sue you? If their heirs or family wanted to complain to a licensure board, which board would they complain to? Would you be guilty of malpractice for operating where you are not licensed? Who is legally empowered to look out for and protect the patient's rights in such an instance? Can you be brought to court for practicing in another state without a license (since your current license probably only allows you to practice within your state of residence)? What are the effects of offering your services to people in other countries whose first language may not be English and who therefore may not fully understand some of the points you are making or the terms under which you are offering your services? What are the repercussions of offering services to someone who claims he is an adult, yet later you discover he is a minor and you don't have parental consent to treat? As you can see, there are many legal issues to consider, some of which may seriously affect your professional reputation and ability to practice in the real world. New state laws, lawyers, and the courts will eventually decide these issues, as will the separate professional associations, who will set ethical guidelines on their profession's acceptable behaviors. Consider such ethical points carefully and check with your state licensing board, your professional liability insurance provider, as well as your national professional association to determine the current status of such laws and guidelines before offering any professional service online.

Emerging research is providing empirical support for using the Internet to conduct electronic therapy, or "e-therapy." There are now numerous case studies, of individuals and groups, benefiting from online interventions. Larger-scale studies using control groups and dozens of participants are already in the planning stages. So far, the results look promising that this new type of therapeutic modality is potentially safe and effective. It still requires a significant commitment on the part of the practitioner who wants to enter this field, because the legal and many of the ethical issues remain largely unaddressed.

I'M THINKING OF DOING SOME KIND OF THERAPY ONLINE. WHERE DO I FIND MORE INFORMATION ABOUT THE ECONOMICS, LEGALITIES, AND ETHICS OF THIS MODALITY?

Perhaps you have thought about this long and hard and have decided that online therapy is nonetheless the wave of the future. You would like to be on the cutting edge, not only of technology, but of the clinical profession as well. Where do you find information and resources about how to set up a useful online practice? There are some people who have beat you to this idea and have tried paving the way for others—you will find two such pioneers in this field below, who have been around long enough that I trust that they offer stable and reliable Web sites and, perhaps, services.

Title (or descriptor):	International Society for Mental Health Online
Owner:	International Society for Mental Health Online
URL (Web address):	`http://www.ismho.org/`
Rating:	★★★

Since its inception at the end of 1997, the International Society for Mental Health Online (ISMHO) has taken the lead in establishing an open forum to discuss issues relating to the provision of online mental health services. In late 1999, it released suggested guidelines for online service providers to follow in their online practice. Growing rapidly from a small group of founding members, its membership today includes many of the pioneers in the field and representatives from national and international professional associations and companies.

Title (or descriptor):	NetPsychology
Owner:	Leonard Holmes, PhD
URL (Web address):	`http://www.netpsych.com/`
Rating:	★★★

This site explores the uses of the Internet to deliver mental health services and is an excellent jumping off point for professionals looking to learn more about this topic. Netpsych's owner, Leonard Holmes, is a psychologist who is careful to describe the services he offers elsewhere online ("Shareware Psychological Consultation") as *not* being therapy. He is very much aware of the legal, professional, and ethical issues involved in doing therapy online and should be considered a good resource to contact for further information. The one drawback to this site is its reliance on heavy graphics and graphical special effects, including a multitude of ads and other services, which may annoy and slow down some Web readers.

Both of these sites, along with many others, are cataloged in the "ABCs of Internet Therapy," maintained by Martha Ainsworth at `http://www.metanoia.org/imhs/`. I have also written articles regarding online counseling, which I call "e-therapy," that can be found on my Web site, Psych Central (`http://psychcentral.com/`). These kinds of resources, because they are relatively new, are not easily discovered. New resources generally don't show up in Web search engines immediately, even if a Web site author submits the information by hand to the search engines. The savvy professional, therefore, needs to know where to go to find out about new and up-and-coming resources online. I'll discuss one such option in the next section.

IS "INTERNET ADDICTION DISORDER" REAL? WHERE CAN I FIND ADDITIONAL INFORMATION ON THIS AND OTHER PSYCHOLOGICAL DISCUSSIONS ABOUT ONLINE BEHAVIOR?

This is an interesting and ongoing topic of debate. There is neither a single nor easy answer to this question. There exists, however, many forums that have been created to discuss this question, trade opinions and barbs among professionals, and to disseminate information. Professionals around the world are conducting research into this phenomenon, led by Kimberly Young at the University of Pittsburgh. Her Web site is listed below.

While Web sites will offer you some basic background information or point you to other online resources on the issue of the psychology of online behavior, it is in resources such as mailing lists where you will find the most lively ongoing discussions. These forums are where the majority of professionals gather to discuss this issue in-depth. A few of the most active mailing lists are listed later in this section.

Internet Addiction Web Sites

Title (or descriptor):	Center for Online Addiction
Owner:	Kimberly Young, PsyD
URL (Web address):	`http://www.netaddiction.com/`
Rating:	★★★

Kimberly Young's Center for Online Addiction has been greatly revamped and improved over time. It now offers a great deal of information about addiction and compulsive behaviors toward online use, cybersex, relationship issues, and related online issues. It also acts as a marketing tool to advertise and sell her seminars, workshops, and books related to this problem. Full-length articles about "Internet addiction" and links to other related online resources are also available.

Title (or descriptor):	Psychology of Cyberspace
Owner:	John Suler, PhD
URL (Web address):	`http://www.rider.edu/~suler/psycyber/`

URL (Web address):

`http://www.rider.edu/~suler/psycyber/resources.html`

Rating: ★★★

John Suler has put together an excellent Web site devoted to disseminating information about professionals doing research online. While discussing his own research into interactive chat and role-playing environments online, he has also collected a comprehensive listing of resources for researchers, listed in the "Other Resources" category. Here you will find a number of mailing lists and other online resources offering additional information and compelling discussion on these topics. Minimal graphics make for an easy Web site to access.

Title (or descriptor):	The Psychology of Virtual Communities
Owner:	Storm A. King
URL (Web address):	`http://www.concentric.net/~Astorm/`
Rating:	★★★

An extensive archive of Storm King's articles, papers, and presentations about the psychology behind online communities. Although many of the resources are related to self-help support groups online, there is additional material about "Internet addiction," support for the effectiveness of online therapy, and the nature of online relationships.

Mailing List Discussions of Online Behavior

Title (or descriptor):	NetDynam–The Network Group Dynamics Mailing List
Commands to:	`listserv@maelstrom.stjohns.edu`
Subscribe:	`subscribe netdynam Your-name`
Unsubscribe:	`unsubscribe netdynam`
List:	`netdynam@maelstrom.stjohns.edu`
List owners:	Orrin Simon Onken (E-mail: oro@teleport.com)

NetDynam is a small yet sometimes interesting forum which "examines and reports upon the psychological, social, philosophical and aesthetic aspects of being part of the Internet community," according to the list's welcome message. It is very much a list devoted to list dynamics, and subscribers' own reactions to other people's messages on the list. It is recommended you read the list for a while to become familiarized with the dynamics of the forum before participating in it. This is good advice to follow for any online community.

Title (or descriptor):	Philosophy and Psychology of Cyberspace
Commands to:	`listserv@listserv.aol.com`
Subscribe:	`subscribe cybermind Your-name`
Unsubscribe:	`unsubscribe cybermind`
List:	`cybermind@listserv.aol.com`
List owners:	Alan Sondheim (E-mail: sondheim@panix.com) and Caitlin Martin (E-mail: caitlinm@seanet.com)

A strange, eclectic mailing list devoted to more philosophical issues surrounding uses of and in the online world. Just about any topic you can imagine is up for discussion and commentary. While the list's own welcome message suggests that the forum "is devoted to an examination of the new subjectivities that have emerged and might yet emerge in this [online] arena [. . .] in particular in the philosophical, psychological/psychoanalytic and social issues engendered, particularly as they concern the user and the social." If you're looking for a more philosophical discussion of the online world and its related technologies, this may be a forum to check out.

Title (or descriptor):	Psychology of the Internet: Research and Theory
Commands to:	`listproc@cmhc.com`
Subscribe:	`subscribe research your-name`
Unsubscribe:	`unsubscribe research`
List:	`research@cmhc.com`
List owner:	John M. Grohol (E-mail: `grohol@netscape.net`)

This mailing list, which I started and continue to host, tends to have a larger subscription base than other lists on this subject. This translates into more interesting and diverse discussions about the psychology of online behaviors. Unlike many other mailing lists, the complete archives of the mailing list's previous discussions are also available on the Web. This allows new subscribers to the mailing list to "catch-up" on the discussion and review what topics the list may have already addressed or covered. Sometimes mailing lists have the unfortunate tendency toward repeating the same topics. While this occurs as well on this mailing list, it seems to happen less frequently. The topic of "Internet Addiction Disorder" has been brought up multiple times on this list and some interesting theories have been discussed.

This mailing list, open to all interested professionals, discusses research and theory on the psychology of the Internet. The topics that are appropriate to this list are broadly defined, but can include such issues as how to conduct psychological research via the Internet; theory behind virtual support groups; online psychotherapy; "Internet Addiction Disorder"; the psychology of various online phenomenon, such as "flame wars," relationships, etc.

So how did I know to look at NetPsychology and other Web sites or online resources devoted to this topic? I found out about the site through a mailing list. If you're interested in this topic, you definitely should subscribe to one, or all, of them. They not only include timely and relevant discussions about research and theory online, but also announcements of new research, Web sites, and other online resources as they become available. Electronic mailing lists are still one of the best and most underrated resources available online today for finding information relevant to specific professional areas and topics.

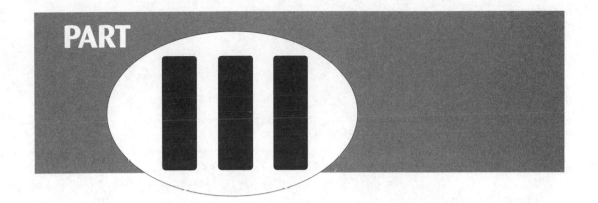

PART III

PATIENT EDUCATION RESOURCES

12

General Consumer-oriented Resources on the Web

Clients and patients come to professionals for help with their disorders, and an important part of any clinical practice is the education of patients in the causes and treatments of their disorders. But clients also often want more information than the professional can readily provide. The online world has responded to this need by creating many information resources about disorders, online resources, treatment options, and much more. But because this information is often put together by people who suffer from these disorders and reflects their own individual experiences within the mental health system, it may not always be as accurate as professionals would like.

AN OVERVIEW OF PATIENT EDUCATION RESOURCES

I cannot vouch for the accuracy or integrity of all of the information that appears on all of the Web sites and online resources in this section, since they are dynamic and everchanging. I can vouch for the fact that these resources have been some of the most enduring and the most popular online, which suggests that the marketplace of online consumers and Web visitors are finding something useful to them or their problems. The usefulness may be found in the information presented; or it may be discovered in another online resource to which the site is linked; still yet, it may be that the site offers an online patient support group or information about one.

Self-help support groups have been shown to be a useful adjunctive modality in most cases, no matter what form they take. It is easy to forget that the online world offers not only the ability to "browse" but also to take part in an interactive, supportive community. The amount and degree to which self-help support resources have taken hold in the online world suggests that it is a powerful and useful modality for many, many people around the world. Online resources in the form of education and community have taken the place of self-help books for many people. They also act as an adjunct for those people already "Net savvy." Practitioners should therefore treat such resources just as they would any outside information the patient reads or learns about their disorder. Clients and laypeople can discover a wide variety of help online through the resources below. They are listed here to allow you to direct your clients and patients, who may have online access, to useful and popular Web sites on their disorder.

So why do people turn to online self-help support resources in the first place? Individuals who live in remote or rural areas, for instance, may not have access to good-quality or affordable mental health care. There may also simply not be enough people in their local community to create a real-world support group. Getting online offers such individuals the opportunity to ask questions of professionals and participate in online support groups. Others may have difficulty in social relationships in the real world and find that starting out such friendships online may help them progress in their own real-life relationships. It is also the reward of discovering that one is not alone with one's thoughts and feelings, and the feeling of community that the online world can support and nurture in these individuals. This process of seeking community and like-minded individuals with which to discuss specific topics is mirrored in the reasons professionals, too, get online. Last, many people still feel the stigma attached to mental illness. Online, there is much less stigmatization of such problems.

MAKING THE MOST OF OUTSIDE MATERIALS

Patients have always brought outside materials to therapy sessions to share them with the practitioner. These range from a newspaper clipping about their disorder, to a book they have read and found valuable, to brochures or pamphlets published on their problem. Clinicians should take an objective and unbiased position on such materials, helping the patient understand the information in the context of the patient's presentation of the disorder and what the scientific research currently tells us about the disorder. Such a discussion is often beneficial on a number of different levels: It allows the patient to become a better-educated consumer of mental health problems and therapies; and such a discussion can open up avenues of exploration within therapy, or correct common misconceptions about what is currently known about the causes and treatment of mental disorders.

As it becomes more common for people to get online, some of your patients will want to share with you material they have come across in their online travels. This may include offerings on new treatments for their disorder, but unique additions as well. For instance, it may not be uncommon to have a patient come into a therapy session with a transcript of an online interactive chat they had with another person or professional. The patient may want to share what was learned in this interaction, or ask questions that the interaction raised in the patient's mind. A clinician can effectively incorporate this type of material into their therapy with the client by examining the meaning of the interaction. There is an endless array of possibilities such material may help uncover in therapy. The material, therefore, should be treated with all the seriousness and objectivity that any written material brought into therapy would be. Some skepticism, however, may not be inappropriate, given the anonymity of online interactions, especially if the patient is not familiar with or does not know the other online person very well. Examining the quality of the interaction, the type of content discussed, and the manner in which the people in the interaction related to one another will help you make the most of the material presented.

Naturally such material should never become the sole focus of therapy. Clinicians should be wary of clients focusing extensively or exclusively on their online interactions, especially if doing so is at the expense of real-world interactions with family members, coworkers, and friends. As with the discussion of any material brought into therapy to be shared with the practitioner, it should be done in a manner that is conducive to elaborating existing therapeutic issues and goals. It should not be used as an excuse by the patient—or the therapist—to keep from focusing on the issues of relevance within therapy.

Education, community, togetherness, and acceptance. Excellent reasons that your patients may want to utilize the online world to their advantage and take an active role in their treatment. This section will help you help your clients, by describing and reviewing resources likely to be most relevant to your clients' problems. As with all sections in this book, look for updates to the information listed here (such as new Web sites or other online resources which I believe may be important to visit) at the book's Web site (`http://www.insidemh.com/`).

There are thousands of consumer-oriented Web sites that disseminate information about mental disorders online. Many of these include not only general information about the disorder itself (such as common symptoms), but may host a frequently asked questions (FAQ) file about the disorder as well. Poems, personal stories of coping with the disorder in their lives, Web-based discussion forums, real-world resources, and contact information and links to other online resources round out many of these sites.

Because of the multitude of these resources online, I felt it would be nearly impossible to list them all here and unfair to select which disorders should be represented. Instead, I will list some of the larger, more general mental health sites on the Web. Since the Web is very easy to get around on, you can point a patient to one of these general resources, and he will be able to quickly find more specific information and additional links to his disorder. Some of the following are guides that act as indices to other online resources. Other listings below are sites that contain information about disorders themselves. The type of site (listed in alphabetical order below) is listed in the description.

Title (or descriptor):	American Psychiatric Association
Owner:	American Psychiatric Association
URL (Web address):	`http://www.psych.org/`

Rating:	★★★★
Type:	Informational site

A great deal of information about mental disorders may be found directly on this site, especially in their "Let's Talk Facts" brochure series. These brochures address most major mental disorders in depth, in an easy-to-read style and without a lot of "psychobabble." The information presented is relatively balanced and shouldn't offend most mental health professionals in the conclusions drawn or recommendations of treatment modalities. The site is attractive and easy to navigate.

Title (or descriptor):	APA HelpCenter
Owner:	American Psychological Association
URL (Web address):	http://helping.apa.org/
Rating:	★★★
Type:	Informational site

The consumer information provided on the HelpCenter is neither as comprehensive nor as helpful as that found on the American Psychiatric Association's Web site. Divided into three main categories, "Psychology at Work," "Mind/Body Connection," and "Family and Relationships," few of the articles listed discuss specific mental disorders or concerns. Subcategories, such as "How to Find Help for Life's Problems" and "Get the Facts," are nothing more than thinly veiled advertisements for the benefits of psychotherapy. Filled with a healthy dose of truisms, the site's design is mediocre. For example, it took four clicks from the home page to find a relevant article on relationships; their idea of a guestbook is really nothing more than a feedback form.

Title (or descriptor):	Go Ask Alice
Owner:	Healthwise, Columbia University
URL (Web address):	http://www.goaskalice.columbia.edu/
Rating:	★★★★
Type:	Informational site

A service of the Columbia University Healthwise program, this site is mainly oriented toward students. However, the sensible information on sexuality, sexual health, general health, alcohol and other drugs, fitness and nutrition, emotional well-being, and relationships is general enough that nearly anybody can benefit from reading through this attractive and content-rich site.

Title (or descriptor):	Health World Online
Owner:	Health World Online
URL (Web address):	http://www.healthy.net/
Rating:	★★★
Type:	Informational site

Full of mostly consumer-oriented articles on a wide range of health and mental health topics, this site can be a good starting point for patients. Nicely organized and professionally designed, its one downside is that it charges fees (ranging from $2.00 to $10.00 and up) for some informational articles and audio recordings.

Title (or descriptor):	Lifescape.com
Owner:	Lifescape.com
URL (Web address):	http://www.lifescape.com/
Rating:	★★

A new mental health resource launched in September, 1999, this site provides fairly comprehensive information on mental health topics ranging from depression, anxiety, and recovery issues, to learning new skills and understanding the transitional times in one's life. Material is written by professionals from the University of Florida's Brain Institute and seems somewhat balanced and objective in nature. The site's design, however, clearly reflects a confusing character and could use work.

Title (or descriptor):	Mental Health Net–Self-Help Resources
Owner:	Mental Health Net & CMHC Systems, Inc.
URL (Web address):	http://mentalhelp.net/selfhelp.htm
Rating:	★★★★
Type:	Guide & Informational site

This mental health subject guide offers thousands of links to online resources, which may help patients to better understand and gain support in coping with their disorder. Comprehensive and large in nature, it reviews many of the sites listed within its database to help readers discover whether a resource is worth looking at. Mental Health Net houses the American Self-Help Clearinghouse's *Self-Help Sourcebook Online* (`http://mentalhelp.net/selfhelp`), a massive database of self-help organizations throughout the world. *Psychological Self-Help*, a 1,000-page self-help book, is available here as well (`http://mentalhelp.net/psyhelp/`). This book offers hundreds of insights and tips for consumers on how to deal with many common mental disorders and, like everything else on Mental Health Net, is completely searchable. I think this is a great site, but then I'm associated with it!

Title (or descriptor):	National Alliance for the Mentally Ill
Owner:	National Alliance for the Mentally Ill (NAMI)
URL (Web address):	`http://www.nami.org/`
Rating:	★★
Type:	Informational site

Providing a great deal of information oriented toward the biological basis of severe mental disorders (e.g., schizophrenia, bipolar disorder, and depression), NAMI's Web site is large. Echoing NAMI's continuing advocacy efforts, their Web site is chock full of well-maintained news and legislative updates.

Title (or descriptor):	National Institute of Mental Health
Owner:	National Institute of Mental Health (NIMH)
URL (Web address):	`http://www.nimh.nih.gov/`
Rating:	★★★
Type:	Informational site

The National Institute of Mental Health's Web site has drastically improved over the past year. The always-useful content is now provided in a more readable and consumer-friendly (but still plain) format. An overly complex search engine allows searching for topics on its and the National Institutes of Health Web sites. Aspects of NIMH's content are becoming outdated, sorely needing updates to reflect the latest knowledge and research in mental disorders.

Title (or descriptor):	National Mental Health Association
Owner:	National Mental Health Association

URL (Web address):	http://www.nmha.org/
Rating:	★★★
Type:	Informational site

With topics covered in advocacy, outreach, prevention, and general information about mental disorders and mental health issues, this site will improve as it places more of its balanced fact sheets online.

Title (or descriptor):	Psych Central
Owner:	John M. Grohol, PsyD
URL (Web address):	http://psychcentral.com/
Rating:	★★★
Type:	Guide and informational site

A simple list of newsgroups, mailing lists, and Web sites in addition to some thought-provoking articles written for consumers. I also host three weekly mental health chats online where I answer simple questions about mental disorders and treatment; information about these chats may be found on my Web site as well.

Title (or descriptor):	Psych Web
Owner:	Russ Dewey
URL (Web address):	http://www.psychwww.com/
Rating:	★★★
Type:	Guide

A very good subject guide not only for those interested in psychology, but for anyone who is looking for additional information on psychological and mental health topics. The "Self-Help Resources on the Web" category contains a large listing of online resources for those looking for specific disorder information.

13

Consumer Mailing List Discussion and Support Groups

Mailing lists, like newsgroups listed in the next chapter, are mostly used by consumers of mental health services as mutual self-help support groups and to exchange information and opinions about their disorders. While professionals are not prohibited from subscribing to most of these lists, their participation is usually not encouraged. Subscription instructions for these lists are exactly the same as the professional mailing lists in Chapter 6. List descriptions have been summarized in their titles, arranged alphabetically. Because new support mailing lists get added every month, you might want to check the updated list found on Psych Central:

http://psychcentral.com/

or on the book's Web site,

http://www.insidemh.com/.

Title (or descriptor):   Abuse, Adult Survivors of
Web site:
    `http://www.onelist.com/community/AbusedSurvivors`
Subscribe: `AbusedSurvivors-subscribe@onelist.com`
Unsubscribe: `AbusedSurvivors-unsubscribe@onelist.com`
List: `AbusedSurvivors@onelist.com`

Title (or descriptor):   Abuse, Partners of Survivors of
Commands to: `listserv@maelstrom.stjohns.edu`
Subscribe: `subscribe abpart-L Your-name`
Unsubscribe: `unsubscribe abpart-L`
List: `abpart-L@maelstrom.stjohns.edu`

Title (or descriptor):   Abuse–Recovering Spouse Abusers
Web site: `http://blainn.cc/abuse-free/`
Commands to: `majordomo@blainn.cc`
Subscribe: `subscribe abuse-free`
Unsubscribe: `unsubscribe abuse-free`
List: `abuse-free@blainn.cc`

Title (or descriptor):   Abuse, Stop the
Web site: `http://www.zebra.net/~lfalana/stop.html`
Commands to: `stoptheabuse-request@Mailing-List.net`
Subscribe: `subscribe`
Unsubscribe: `unsubscribe`
List: `stoptheabuse@Mailing-List.net`

Title (or descriptor):   ADD/ADHD Gazette
Commands to: `gailmiller@clara.net`

Subscribe:	`subscribe ADHD`
Unsubscribe:	`unsubscribe ADHD`

Title (or descriptor):	ADD/ADHD Holistic Treatment Techniques
Commands to:	`ADD-holistic-request@mLists.net`
Subscribe:	`subscribe`
Unsubscribe:	`unsubscribe`
List:	`ADD-holistic@mLists.net`

Title (or descriptor):	ADD/ADHD Newsletter for Parents
Commands to:	`homebi@hartley.on.ca`
Subscribe:	`No message required.`

Title (or descriptor):	Parents of Attention Deficit Disorder (ADD/ADHD) Children
Commands to:	`listserver@bdtp.com`
Subscribe:	`subscribe ADD-parents`
Unsubscribe:	`unsubscribe ADD-parents`
List:	`ADD-parents@bdtp.com`

Title (or descriptor):	ADHD, Children with
Commands to:	`listserv@maelstrom.stjohns.edu`
Subscribe:	`subscribe ADDkids Your-name`
Unsubscribe:	`unsubscribe ADDkids`
List:	`ADDKids@maelstrom.stjohns.edu`

Title (or descriptor):	ADHD, Spouses/Significant Others of People with
Commands to:	`listserv@maelstrom.stjohns.edu`
Subscribe:	`subscribe ADD-mate Your-name`

Unsubscribe:	unsubscribe ADD-mates
List:	ADD-Mate@maelstrom.stjohns.edu

Title (or descriptor):	Adoptees
Web site:	http://webreflection.com/aiml/
Commands to:	listserv@maelstrom.stjohns.edu
Subscribe:	subscribe adoptees Your-name
Unsubscribe:	unsubscribe adoptees
List:	adoptees@maelstrom.stjohns.edu

Title (or descriptor):	Adults with ADHD
Commands to:	AADD-focused-request@maillist.net
Subscribe:	subscribe
Unsubscribe:	unsubscribe
List:	AADD-focused@maillist.net

Title (or descriptor):	Adults with Attention Deficit Disorder (ADD/ADHD)
Commands to:	listserv@maelstrom.stjohns.edu
Subscribe:	subscribe ADDult Your-name
Unsubscribe:	unsubscribe ADDult
List:	ADDult@maelstrom.stjohns.edu

Title (or descriptor):	Adoptive Parents
Commands to:	listserv@maelstrom.stjohns.edu
Subscribe:	subscribe APARENT Your-name
Unsubscribe:	unsubscribe APARENT
List:	aparent@maelstrom.stjohns.edu

Title (or descriptor):	Adoption
Commands to:	listserv@listserv.law.cornell.edu

Subscribe:	`subscribe adoption Your-name`
Unsubscribe:	`unsubscribe adoption`
List:	`adoption@listserv.law.cornell.edu`

Title (or descriptor):	Adult Children
Commands to:	`aca@ontosystems.com`
Subscribe:	Type `subscribe` in the "Subject:" line of your e-mail
Unsubscribe:	Type `unsubscribe` in the "Subject:" line of your e-mail
List:	`aca@ontosystems.com`

Title (or descriptor):	Adult Children, Al-Anon
Commands to:	`AlAnonAC@ontosystems.com`
Subscribe:	Type `subscribe` in the "Subject:" line of your e-mail
Unsubscribe:	Type `unsubscribe` in the "Subject:" line of your e-mail
List:	`AlAnonAC@ontosystems.com`

Title (or descriptor):	AIDS/HIV, Spirituality
Commands to:	`majordomo@hivent.org`
Subscribe:	`subscribe HIV-AIDS-spiritual`
Unsubscribe:	`unsubscribe HIV-AIDS-spiritual`
List:	`HIV-AIDS-spiritual@hivent.org`

Title (or descriptor):	AIDS/HIV Survivors
Commands to:	`green_acres-request@netcom.com`
Subscribe:	`subscribe green_acres Your-name`
Unsubscribe:	`unsubscribe green_acres`
List:	`green_acres@netcom.com`

Title (or descriptor):	Alcoholics, Family members of
Commands to:	`listproc@solar.rtd.utk.edu`

Subscribe:	`subscribe al-anon Your-name`
Unsubscribe:	`unsubscribe al-anon`
List:	`al-anon@solar.rtd.utk.edu`

Title (or descriptor):	Alopecia Areata Support
Commands to:	`listserv@np2.mcg.edu`
Subscribe:	`subscribe alopecia Your-name`
Unsubscribe:	`unsubscribe alopecia`
List:	`alopecia@np2.mcg.edu`

Title (or descriptor):	Alzheimer's Disease
Commands to:	`majordomo@wubios.wustl.edu`
Subscribe:	`subscribe Alzheimer`
Unsubscribe:	`unsubscribe Alzheimer`
List:	`Alzheimer@wubios.wustl.edu`

Title (or descriptor):	Amputees
Commands to:	`listserv@maelstrom.stjohns.edu`
Subscribe:	`subscribe amputee Your-name`
Unsubscribe:	`unsubscribe amputee`
List:	`Amputee@maelstrom.stjohns.edu`

Title (or descriptor):	Amputees, Congenital or Child
Commands to:	`MAISER@hoffman.mgen.pitt.edu`
Subscribe:	`subscribe I-CAN Your-name`
Unsubscribe:	`unsubscribe I-CAN`
List:	`I-CAN@hoffman.mgen.pitt.edu`

Title (or descriptor):	Anxiety
Commands to:	`listproc@cmhc.com`

Subscribe:	`subscribe anxiety Your-name`
Unsubscribe:	`unsubscribe anxiety`
List:	`anxiety@cmhc.com`

Title (or descriptor):	Anxiety and Panic Disorders
Web site:	`http://www.topica.com/lists/anxiety`
Commands to:	`anxiety-subscribe@topica.com`
Subscribe:	`subscribe`
Unsubscribe:	`unsubscribe`
List:	`anxiety@topica.com`

Title (or descriptor):	Autism
Commands to:	`listserv@maelstrom.stjohns.edu`
Subscribe:	`subscribe autism Your-name`
Unsubscribe:	`unsubscribe autism`
List:	`autism@maelstrom.stjohns.edu`

Title (or descriptor):	Autism, HFA, and Asperger's Forum
Commands to:	`AutiNet-request@iol.ie`
Subscribe:	Type `subscribe` in the "Subject:" line of your e-mail
Unsubscribe:	Type `unsubscribe` in the "Subject:" line of your e-mail
List:	`AutiNet@iol.ie`

Title (or descriptor):	Austistic Children
Web site:	`http://www.autistickids.org/`

Title (or descriptor):	Bereaved Mothers (Loss of Child)
Web site:	`http://members.aol.com/BrvdMomShr/`
Commands to:	`majordomo@List-Server.net`

Subscribe:	`subscribe bereavedmomsshare-digest`
Unsubscribe:	`unsubscribe bereavedmomsshare-digest`
List:	`majordomo@List-Server.net`

Title (or descriptor):	Bipolar Disorder and Depression
Web site:	
	`http://www.onelist.com/community/rosesandthorns`
Subscribe:	`rosesandthorns-subscribe@onelist.com`
Unsubscribe:	`rosesandthorns-unsubscribe@onelist.com`
List:	`rosesandthorns@onelist.com`

Title (or descriptor):	Bipolar Disorder and Manic Depression
Commands to:	`majordomo@ucar.edu`
Subscribe:	`subscribe pendulum Your-email-address`
Unsubscribe:	`unsubscribe pendulum`
List:	`pendulum@ucar.edu`

Title (or descriptor):	Bipolar Disorder and Depression
Commands to:	`majordomo@walkers.org`
Subscribe:	`subscribe walkers`
Unsubscribe:	`unsubscribe walkers`
List:	`walkers@walkers.org`

Title (or descriptor):	Birth-Parents Adoption
Commands to:	`listserv@indycms.iupui.edu`
Subscribe:	`subscribe BRTHPRNT Your-name`
Unsubscribe:	`unsubscribe BRTHPRNT`
List:	`BRTHPRNT@indycms.iupui.edu`

Title (or descriptor):	Blindtalk
Commands to:	`jmeddaug@cris.com`
Subscribe:	`subscribe blindtalk-discuss Your-name`
Unsubscribe:	`unsubscribe blindtalk-discuss`
List:	`blindtalk-discuss@cris.com`

Title (or descriptor):	Borderline Personality Disorder
Commands to:	`listserv@maelstrom.stjohns.edu`
Subscribe:	`subscribe borderPD Your-name`
Unsubscribe:	`unsubscribe borderPD`
List:	`borderPD@maelstrom.stjohns.edu`

Title (or descriptor):	Borderline Personality Disorder
Web site:	
	`http://www.onelist.com/community/welcometooz`
Subscribe:	`WelcomeToOz-subscribe@onelist.com`
Unsubscribe:	`WelcomeToOz-unsubscribe@onelist.com`
List:	`WelcomeToOz@onelist.com`

Title (or descriptor):	Brain Injuries
Commands to:	`listserv@maelstrom.stjohns.edu`
Subscribe:	`subscribe tbi-sprt Your-name`
Unsubscribe:	`unsubscribe tbi-sprt`
List:	`tbi-sprt@maelstrom.stjohns.edu`

Title (or descriptor):	Brain Tumors
Commands to:	`listserv@mitvma.mit.edu`
Subscribe:	`subscribe braintmr Your-name`
Unsubscribe:	`unsubscribe braintmr`
List:	`braintmr@mitvma.mit.edu`

Title (or descriptor): Breast Cancer
Commands to: `listserv@morgan.ucs.mun.ca`
Subscribe: `subscribe breast-cancer Your-name`
Unsubscribe: `unsubscribe breast-cancer`
List: `breast-cancer@morgan.ucs.mun.ca`

Title (or descriptor): Cancer
Commands to: `listserv@mvnvm.wvnet.edu`
Subscribe: `subscribe cancer-L Your-name`
Unsubscribe: `unsubscribe cancer-L`
List: `cancer-L@mvnvm.wvnet.edu`

Title (or descriptor): Cerebral Palsy
Commands to: `listserv@maelstrom.stjohns.edu`
Subscribe: `subscribe C-Palsy Your-name`
Unsubscribe: `unsubscribe C-Palsy`
List: `C-Palsy@maelstrom.stjohns.edu`

Title (or descriptor): Cancer, Colon
Commands to: `listserv@listserv.acor.org`
Subscribe: `subscribe colon Your-name`
Unsubscribe: `unsubscribe colon`
List: `colon@listserv.acor.org`

Title (or descriptor): Cerebral Palsy Kids
Commands to: `majordomo@tbag.osc.edu`
Subscribe: `subscribe our-kids`
Unsubscribe: `unsubscribe our-kids`
List: `our-kids@tbag.osc.edu`

Title (or descriptor):	Childfree by Choice
Commands to:	`majordomo@teleport.com`
Subscribe:	`subscribe childfree`
Unsubscribe:	`unsubscribe childfree`
List:	`childfree@teleport.com`

Title (or descriptor):	Children's Special Needs
Commands to:	`listserv@netvm.nerdc.ufl.edu`
Subscribe:	`subscribe CSHCN-L Your-name`
Unsubscribe:	`unsubscribe CSHCN-L`
List:	`CSHCN-L@netvm.nerdc.ufl.edu`

Title (or descriptor):	Children with Physical and/or Mental Disabilities and Delays
Web site:	`http://www.our-kids.org/`
Commands to:	`listserv@maelstrom.stjohns.edu`
Subscribe:	`subscribe our-kids Your-name`
Unsubscribe:	`unsubscribe our-kids`
List:	`our-kids@maelstrom.stjohns.edu`

Title (or descriptor):	Christian Individuals Who Suffer from Chronic Mental Illness
Commands to:	`hub@xc.org`
Subscribe:	`subscribe gadarene-vessel`
Unsubscribe:	`unsubscribe gadarene-vessel`
List:	`gadarene-vessel@xc.org`

Title (or descriptor):	Chronic Fatigue Syndrome—Announcements
Commands to:	`listserv@listserv.nodak.edu`
Subscribe:	`subscribe Co-CURE Your-name`

Unsubscribe:	`unsubscribe Co-CURE`
List:	`co-cure@listserv.nodak.edu`

Title (or descriptor):	Chronic Fatigue Syndrome–General
Web site:	
	`http://members.aol.com/cfslists/listhelp.htm`
Commands to:	`listserv@maelstrom.stjohns.edu`
Subscribe:	`subscribe CFS-L Your-name`
Unsubscribe:	`unsubscribe CFS-L`
List:	`CFS-L@maelstrom.stjohns.edu`

Title (or descriptor):	Chronic Fatigue Syndrome–Youth
Commands to:	`listserv@maelstrom.stjohns.edu`
Subscribe:	`subscribe CFS-Y Your-name`
Unsubscribe:	`unsubscribe CFS-Y`
List:	`CFS-Y@maelstrom.stjohns.edu`

Title (or descriptor):	Chronic Pain
Commands to:	`listserv@maelstrom.stjohns.edu`
Subscribe:	`subscribe pain-L Your-name`
Unsubscribe:	`unsubscribe pain-L`
List:	`pain-L@maelstrom.stjohns.edu`

Title (or descriptor):	Controlled Drinking
Commands to:	`listserv@maelstrom.stjohns.edu`
Subscribe:	`subscribe CD Your-name`
Unsubscribe:	`unsubscribe CD`
List:	`CD@maelstrom.stjohns.edu`

Title (or descriptor):	Crisis Situations
Web site:	
	`http://www.onelist.com/community/crisis-101`
Subscribe:	`crisis-101-subscribe@onelist.com`
Unsubscribe:	`crisis-101-unsubscribe@onelist.com`
List:	`crisis-101@onelist.com`

Title (or descriptor):	Crohn's Colitis and IBD
Commands to:	`ibdlist@menno.com`
Subscribe:	`subscribe IBD Your-name`
Unsubscribe:	`unsubscribe IBD`
List:	`IBD@menno.com`

Title (or descriptor):	Deaf Magazine
Commands to:	`listserv@listserv.deaf-magazine.org`
Subscribe:	`subscribe deaf-magazine Your-name`
Unsubscribe:	`unsubscribe deaf-magazine`
List:	`deaf-magazine@listserv.deaf-magazine.org`

Title (or descriptor):	Deafness–Children
Commands to:	`listserv@maelstrom.stjohns.edu`
Subscribe:	`subscribe Deafkids Your-name`
Unsubscribe:	`unsubscribe Deafkids`
List:	`deafkids@maelstrom.stjohns.edu`

Title (or descriptor):	Deafness and Blindness
Commands to:	`deafblnd-request@ukcc.uky.edu`
Subscribe:	`subscribe deafblnd Your-name`
Unsubscribe:	`unsubscribe deafblnd`
List:	`deafblnd@ukcc.uky.edu`

Title (or descriptor):   Deafness in Life

Commands to: `majordomo@acpub.duke.edu`

Subscribe: `subscribe beyond-hearing`

Unsubscribe: `unsubscribe beyond-hearing`

List: `beyond-hearing@acpub.duke.edu`

Title (or descriptor):   Dependency and Caretaking for Anyone Who Is Dependent on You

Commands to: `listserv@maelstrom.stjohns.edu`

Subscribe: `subscribe soc-fix Your-name`

Unsubscribe: `unsubscribe soc-fix`

List: `soc-fix@maelstrom.stjohns.edu`

Title (or descriptor):   Depression, Christian-oriented

Commands to: `hub@xc.org`

Subscribe: `subscribe xn-depression Your-name`

Unsubscribe: `unsubscribe xn-depression`

List: `xn-depression@xc.org`

Title (or descriptor):   Depression

Commands to:

   `listserv@soundprint.brandywine.american.edu`

Subscribe: `subscribe depress Your-name`

Unsubscribe: `unsubscribe depress`

List:

   `depress@soundprint.brandywine.american.edu`

Title (or descriptor):   Depression Support

Web site:

   `http://www.onelist.com/community/great-depression`

Subscribe:	great-depression-subscribe@onelist.com
Unsubscribe:	great-depression-unsubscribe@onelist.com
List:	great-depression@onelist.com

Title (or descriptor):	Depression Support
Web site:	
	http://www.onelist.com/community/melancholy
Subscribe:	melancholy-subscribe@onelist.com
Unsubscribe:	melancholy-unsubscribe@onelist.com
List:	melancholy@onelist.com

Title (or descriptor):	Partners and Family Members of Those Depressed
Commands to:	majordomo@truespectra.com
Subscribe:	subscribe guides
Unsubscribe:	unsubscribe guides
List:	guides@truespectra.com

Title (or descriptor):	Developmental Delays
Commands to:	majordomo@tbag.osc.edu
Subscribe:	subscribe our-kids
Unsubscribe:	unsubscribe our-kids
List:	our-kids@tbag.osc.edu

Title (or descriptor):	Diabetes
Commands to:	listserv@lehigh.edu
Subscribe:	subscribe diabetic Your-name
Unsubscribe:	unsubscribe diabetic
List:	diabetic@lehigh.edu

Title (or descriptor):   Diabetes—Insulin Dependent
Commands to: `listserv@netcom.com`
Subscribe: `subscribe type_one Your-email-address`
Unsubscribe: `unsubscribe type_one`
List: `type_one@netcom.com`

Title (or descriptor):   Diabetes News
Commands to: `diabetes-news-request@lists.best.com`
Subscribe: `subscribe Your-name`
Unsubscribe: `unsubscribe`
List: `diabetes-news@lists.best.com`

Title (or descriptor):   Disability—Women
Commands to: `majordomo@qiclab.scn.rain.com`
Subscribe: `subscribe living`
Unsubscribe: `unsubscribe living`
List: `living@qiclab.scn.rain.com`

Title (or descriptor):   Disabled—Families
Commands to: `listserv@maelstrom.stjohns.edu`
Subscribe: `subscribe DIS-SPRT Your-name`
Unsubscribe: `unsubscribe DIS-SPRT`
List: `DIS-SPRT@maelstrom.stjohns.edu`

Title (or descriptor):   Dissociative Disorders
Web site:
    `http://www.onelist.com/community/DissociativeDisorder`
Subscribe:
    `DissociativeDisorder-subscribe@onelist.com`

Unsubscribe:

    `DissociativeDisorder-unsubscribe@onelist.com`

List: `DissociativeDisorder@onelist.com`

Title (or descriptor):   Divorce Anonymous

Commands to: `DIVORCING-subscribe@associate.com`

Subscribe: `subscribe divorcing`

Unsubscribe: `unsubscribe divorcing`

List: `DIVORCING@associate.com`

Title (or descriptor):   Divorce Support, Spiritual

Web site:

    `http://www.egroups.com/group/divorce-support/info.html`

Title (or descriptor):   Domestic Violence, Child Abuse, Sexual Assault and Crisis/Trauma Intervention

Commands to: `majordomo@facteur.std.com`

Subscribe: `subscribe survival`

Unsubscribe: `unsubscribe survival`

List: `survival@FACTEUR.STD.COM`

Title (or descriptor):   Down Syndrome

Commands to: `listserv@listserv.nodak.edu`

Subscribe: `subscribe DOWN-SYN Your-name`

Unsubscribe: `unsubscribe DOWN-SYN`

List: `DOWN-SYN@listserv.nodak.edu`

Title (or descriptor):	Dreams
Web site:	http://www.onelist.com/community/dreams
Subscribe:	dreams-subscribe@onelist.com
Unsubscribe:	dreams-unsubscribe@onelist.com
List:	dreams@onelist.com

Title (or descriptor):	Dreams
Web site:	

    http://www.onelist.com/community/ourdreams

Subscribe:	ourdreams-subscribe@onelist.com
Unsubscribe:	ourdreams-unsubscribe@onelist.com
List:	ourdreams@onelist.com

Title (or descriptor):	Eating Disorders
Commands to:	majordomo@samurai.com
Subscribe:	subscribe ASED-LIST
Unsubscribe:	unsubscribe ASED-LIST
List:	ASED-LIST@samurai.com

Title (or descriptor):	Endometriosis
Commands to:	listserv@listserv.dartmouth.edu
Subscribe:	subscribe witsendo Your-name
Unsubscribe:	unsubscribe witsendo
List:	witsendo@listserv.dartmouth.edu

Title (or descriptor):	Enuresis
Commands to:	listserv@maelstrom.stjohns.edu
Subscribe:	subscribe enuresis Your-name
Unsubscribe:	unsubscribe enuresis
List:	enuresis@maelstrom.stjohns.edu

Title (or descriptor):	Epilepsy
Commands to:	`listserv@calvin.dgbt.doc.ca`
Subscribe:	`subscribe epilepsy-list Your-name`
Unsubscribe:	`unsubscribe epilepsy-list`
List:	`epilepsy-list@calvin.dgbt.doc.ca`

Title (or descriptor):	Existential Cafe
Commands to:	`ec-list-request@idealist.com`
Subscribe:	`subscribe ec-list Your-name`
Unsubscribe:	`unsubscribe ec-list`
List:	`ec-list@idealist.com`

Title (or descriptor):	Facial Disfigurement
Commands to:	`listserv@maelstrom.stjohns.edu`
Subscribe:	`subscribe my-face Your-name`
Unsubscribe:	`unsubscribe my-face`
List:	`my-face@maelstrom.stjohns.edu`

Title (or descriptor):	Families of Blind Individuals
Commands to:	`listserv@maelstrom.stjohns.edu`
Subscribe:	`subscribe blindfam Your-name`
Unsubscribe:	`unsubscribe blindfam`
List:	`blindfam@maelstrom.stjohns.edu`

Title (or descriptor):	Family Violence
Commands to:	`listserv@uriacc.uri.edu`
Subscribe:	`subscribe intvio-L Your-name`
Unsubscribe:	`unsubscribe intvio-L`
List:	`intvio-L@uriacc.uri.edu`

Title (or descriptor): Fat Loss
Commands to: `majordomo@list.stanford.edu`
Subscribe: `subscribe fatloss-support`
Unsubscribe: `unsubscribe fatloss-support`
List: `fatloss-support@list.stanford.edu`

Title (or descriptor): Fibromyalgia
Commands to: `listserv@vmd.cso.uiuc.edu`
Subscribe: `subscribe fibrom-L Your-name`
Unsubscribe: `unsubscribe fibrom-L`
List: `fibrom-L@vmd.cso.uiuc.edu`

Title (or descriptor): Gluten Intolerance
Commands to: `listserv@maelstrom.stjohns.edu`
Subscribe: `subscribe Celiac Your-name`
Unsubscribe: `unsubscribe Celiac`
List: `celiac@maelstrom.stjohns.edu`

Title (or descriptor): Grief, Loss, and Recovery
Commands to: `majordomo@listserv.prodigy.com`
Subscribe: `subscribe grief`
Unsubscribe: `unsubscribe grief`
List: `grief@listserv.prodigy.com`

Title (or descriptor): Grief Chat
Commands to: `majordomo@FALCON.IC.NET`
Subscribe: `subscribe grief-chat Your-email-address`
Unsubscribe: `unsubscribe grief-chat`
List: `grief-chat@FALCON.IC.NET`

Title (or descriptor):	Guilt
Commands to:	`listserv@maelstrom.stjohns.edu`
Subscribe:	`subscribe guilt Your-name`
Unsubscribe:	`unsubscribe guilt`
List:	`guilt@maelstrom.stjohns.edu`

Title (or descriptor):	Healing
Commands to:	`listserv@mb.protree.com`
Subscribe:	`subscribe heal-L Your-name`
Unsubscribe:	`unsubscribe heal-L`
List:	`healing@mb.protree.com`

Title (or descriptor):	Healing Normality Naturally
Commands to:	`majordomo@efn.org`
Subscribe:	`subscribe healnorm`
Unsubscribe:	`unsubscribe healnorm`
List:	`healnorm@efn.org`

Title (or descriptor):	Hepatitis
Commands to:	`listserv@maelstrom.stjohns.edu`
Subscribe:	`subscribe HEPV-L Your-name`
Unsubscribe:	`unsubscribe HEPV-L`
List:	`HEPV-L@maelstrom.stjohns.edu`

Title (or descriptor):	Hodgkin's, Non-Hodgkin's Lymphoma (NHL), and Multiple Myeloma
Commands to:	`listserv@maelstrom.stjohns.edu`
Subscribe:	`subscribe HEM-ONC Your-name`
Unsubscribe:	`unsubscribe HEM-ONC`
List:	`HEM-ONC@maelstrom.stjohns.edu`

Title (or descriptor):	Homelessness
Commands to:	`listproc@csf.colorado.edu`
Subscribe:	`subscribe homeless Your-name`
Unsubscribe:	`unsubscribe homeless`
List:	`homeless@csf.colorado.edu`

Title (or descriptor):	Hospice Volunteers
Commands to:	`listserv@whitman.edu`
Subscribe:	`subscribe hospice Your-name`
Unsubscribe:	`unsubscribe hospice`
List:	`hospice@whitman.edu`

Title (or descriptor):	Hospice
Commands to:	`listserv@ubvm.cc.buffalo.edu`
Subscribe:	`subscribe HOSPIC-L Your-name`
Unsubscribe:	`unsubscribe HOSPIC-L`
List:	`hospic-L@ubvm.cc.buffalo.edu`

Title (or descriptor):	Human Rights in Psychiatry
Commands to:	`majordomo@efn.org`
Subscribe:	`subscribe dendrite`
Unsubscribe:	`unsubscribe dendrite`
List:	`majordomo@efn.org`

Title (or descriptor):	Huntington's Disease
Commands to:	`listserv@maelstrom.stjohns.edu`
Subscribe:	`subscribe HUNT-DIS Your-name`
Unsubscribe:	`unsubscribe HUNT-DIS`
List:	`HUNT-DIS@maelstrom.stjohns.edu`

Title (or descriptor):   Hydrocephalus
Commands to: `listserv@vm.utcc.utoronto.ca`
Subscribe: `subscribe HYCEPH-L Your-name`
Unsubscribe: `unsubscribe HYCEPH-L`
List: `hyceph-l@vm.utcc.utoronto.ca`

Title (or descriptor):   Imagery
Commands to: `listserv@maelstrom.stjohns.edu`
Subscribe: `subscribe imagery Your-name`
Unsubscribe: `unsubscribe imagery`
List: `imagery@maelstrom.stjohns.edu`

Title (or descriptor):   Immune System Problems
Commands to: `immune-request@weber.ucsd.edu`
Subscribe: `subscribe immune Your-name`
Unsubscribe: `unsubscribe immune`
List: `immune@weber.ucsd.edu`

Title (or descriptor):   Incontinence
Commands to: `incont-L-request@maine.maine.edu`
Subscribe: `subscribe incont-L Your-name`
Unsubscribe: `unsubscribe incont-L`
List: `incont-L@maine.maine.edu`

Title (or descriptor):   Intimate Violence
Commands to: `listserv@uriacc.uri.edu`
Subscribe: `subscribe ejintvio Your-name`
Unsubscribe: `unsubscribe ejintvio`
List: `ejintvio@uriacc.uri.edu`

Title (or descriptor):   Kids Who Are Seriously Ill

Commands to: `listserv@maelstrom.stjohns.edu`

Subscribe: `subscribe sickkids Your-name`

Unsubscribe: `unsubscribe sickkids`

List: `sickkids@maelstrom.stjohns.edu`

Title (or descriptor):   Kids Who Know Someone Who Is Seriously Ill

Commands to: `listserv@maelstrom.stjohns.edu`

Subscribe: `subscribe caringkids Your-name`

Unsubscribe: `unsubscribe caringkids`

List: `caringkids@maelstrom.stjohns.edu`

Title (or descriptor):   Leaders in Self-help Support

Commands to: `listproc@cmhc.com`

Subscribe: `subscribe selfhelp Your-name`

Unsubscribe: `unsubscribe selfhelp`

List: `selfhelp@cmhc.com`

Title (or descriptor):   Learning Disabilities–Women

Commands to: `listserv@uga.cc.uga.edu`

Subscribe: `subscribe LDWOMEN Your-name`

Unsubscribe: `unsubscribe LDWOMEN`

List: `ldwomen@uga.cc.uga.edu`

Title (or descriptor):   Limited Mobility

Commands to: `listserv@maelstrom.stjohns.edu`

Subscribe: `subscribe mobility Your-name`

Unsubscribe: `unsubscribe mobility`

List: `mobility@maelstrom.stjohns.edu`

Title (or descriptor):	Mental Health NewsNetLetter
Web site:	`http://mentalhelp.net/about/newslet.htm`

Title (or descriptor):	Moderation Management (for alcoholism)
Commands to:	`listserv@maelstrom.stjohns.edu`
Subscribe:	`subscribe MM Your-name`
Unsubscribe:	`unsubscribe MM`
List:	`MM@maelstrom.stjohns.edu`

Title (or descriptor):	Moods and Madness, Voices and Visions
Commands to:	`listserv@maelstrom.stjohns.edu`
Subscribe:	`subscribe Madness Your-name`
Unsubscribe:	`unsubscribe Madness`
List:	`Madness@maelstrom.stjohns.edu`

Title (or descriptor):	Multiple Chemical Sensitivity and Other Autoimmune Diseases
Commands to:	`listserv@maelstrom.stjohns.edu`
Subscribe:	`subscribe MCS-IMMUNE-NEURO Your-name`
Unsubscribe:	`unsubscribe MCS-IMMUNE-NEURO`
List:	`MCS-IMMUNE-NEURO@maelstrom.stjohns.edu`

Title (or descriptor):	Multiple Sclerosis
Commands to:	`listserv@technion.technion.ac.il`
Subscribe:	`subscribe mslist-L Your-name`
Unsubscribe:	`unsubscribe mslist-L`
List:	`mslist-l@technion.technion.ac.il`

Title (or descriptor):	Muscular Dystrophy
Commands to:	`MD-list-request@data.basix.com`

Subscribe:	`subscribe MD-list Your-name`
Unsubscribe:	`unsubscribe MD-list`
List:	`MD-list@data.basix.com`

Title (or descriptor):	Myeloproliferative Disorders
Commands to:	`listserv@maelstrom.stjohns.edu`
Subscribe:	`subscribe MPD-NET Your-name`
Unsubscribe:	`unsubscribe MPD-NET`
List:	`MPD-NET@maelstrom.stjohns.edu`

Title (or descriptor):	Neurostimulators, People Who Use
Commands to:	`majordomo@avenza.com`
Subscribe:	

`    subscribe neuro_stim-L Your-email-address`

Unsubscribe:	`unsubscribe neuro_stim-L`
List:	`neuro_stim-L@avenza.com`

Title (or descriptor):	Obsessions and Fixations
Commands to:	`listserv@maelstrom.stjohns.edu`
Subscribe:	`subscribe fixate Your-name`
Unsubscribe:	`unsubscribe fixate`
List:	`fixate@maelstrom.stjohns.edu`

Title (or descriptor):	Obsessive-Compulsive Disorder
Commands to:	`listserv@vm.marist.edu`
Subscribe:	`subscribe OCD-L Your-name`
Unsubscribe:	`unsubscribe OCD-L`
List:	`OCD-L@vm.marist.edu`

Title (or descriptor):	Parenting
Commands to:	`majordomo@listserv.cso.uiuc.edu`
Subscribe:	`subscribe Parenting Your-email-address`
Unsubscribe:	`unsubscribe Parenting`
List:	`parenting@listserv.cso.uiuc.edu`

Title (or descriptor):	Parenting and Family Forums
Web site:	

`http://www.thefamilycorner.com/services/lists.shtml`

Title (or descriptor):	Parents of Problem Adolescents
Commands to:	`listserv@maelstrom.stjohns.edu`
Subscribe:	`subscribe tough Your-name`
Unsubscribe:	`unsubscribe tough`
List:	`tough@maelstrom.stjohns.edu`

Title (or descriptor):	Parkinson's Disease
Commands to:	`listserv@listserv.utoronto.ca`
Subscribe:	`subscribe parkinsn Your-name`
Unsubscribe:	`unsubscribe parkinsn`
List:	`parkinsn@listserv.utoronto.ca`

Title (or descriptor):	Passive Aggressiveness
Commands to:	`listserv@maelstrom.stjohns.edu`
Subscribe:	`subscribe PAL Your-name`
Unsubscribe:	`unsubscribe PAL`
List:	`PAL@maelstrom.stjohns.edu`

Title (or descriptor):	Personality Disorders
Commands to:	`listserv@maelstrom.stjohns.edu`

Subscribe:

```
    subscribe personality-disorders Your-name
```

Unsubscribe:	`unsubscribe personality-disorders`
List:	`personality-disorders@mael-strom.stjohns.edu`

Title (or descriptor):	Personality Types (as in Myers-Briggs)
Commands to:	`majordomo@sacam.oren.ortn.edu`
Subscribe:	`subscribe psych-type`
Unsubscribe:	`unsubcribe psych-type`
List:	`psych-type@sacam.oren.ortn.edu`

Title (or descriptor):	Polio
Commands to:	`listserv@maelstrom.stjohns.edu`
Subscribe:	`subscribe polio Your-name`
Unsubscribe:	`unsubscribe polio`
List:	`polio@maelstrom.stjohns.edu`

Title (or descriptor):	Psychiatric Survivors
Commands to:	`listserv@maelstrom.stjohns.edu`
Subscribe:	`subscribe WFPSU Your-name`
Unsubscribe:	`unsubscribe WFPSU`
List:	`WFPSU@maelstrom.stjohns.edu`

Title (or descriptor):	Rare Diseases
Commands to:	`listserv@maelstrom.stjohns.edu`
Subscribe:	`subscribe rare-dis Your-name`
Unsubscribe:	`unsubscribe rare-dis`
List:	`rare-dis@maelstrom.stjohns.edu`

Title (or descriptor):   Recovery from Alcoholism and Drug Abuse
Commands to: `listserv@maelstrom.stjohns.edu`
Subscribe: `subscribe JTR Your-name`
Unsubscribe: `unsubscribe JTR`
List: `JTR@maelstrom.stjohns.edu`

Title (or descriptor):   Relationships
Commands to: `majordomo@joshua.rivertown.net`
Subscribe: `subscribe relationships`
Unsubscribe: `unsubscribe relationships`
List: `relationships@joshua.rivertown.net`

Title (or descriptor):   Schizophrenia
Web site:
   `http://www.onelist.com/community/schizophrenia`
Subscribe: `schizophrenia-subscribe@onelist.com`
Unsubscribe: `schizophrenia-unsubscribe@onelist.com`
List: `schizophrenia@onelist.com`

Title (or descriptor):   Schizophrenia
Commands to: `listserv@maelstrom.stjohns.edu`
Subscribe: `subscribe schizoph Your-name`
Unsubscribe: `unsubscribe schizoph`
List: `schizoph@maelstrom.stjohns.edu`

Title (or descriptor):   Self-Esteem
Commands to: `ronald@his.com`
Subscribe: Type `subscribe` in the "Subject:" line of your e-mail

| Unsubscribe: | Type `unsubscribe` in the "Subject:" line of your e-mail |
| List: | Unknown |

Title (or descriptor):	Self-Esteem and Self-Help
Commands to:	`majordomo@majordomo.netcom.com`
Subscribe:	

`    subscribe self-esteem-self-help Your-email-address`

| Unsubscribe: | `unsubscribe self-esteem-self-help` |
| List: | |

`    self-esteem-self-help@majordomo.netcom.com`

Title (or descriptor):	Sexual Abuse
Commands to:	`recovery-request@wvnvm.wvnet.edu`
Subscribe:	`subscribe recovery Your-name`
Unsubscribe:	`unsubscribe recovery`
List:	`recovery@wvnvm.wvnet.edu`

Title (or descriptor):	Shyness
Web site:	`http://www.onelist.com/community/shyness`
Subscribe:	`shyness-subscribe@onelist.com`
Unsubscribe:	`shyness-unsubscribe@onelist.com`
List:	`shyness@onelist.com`

Title (or descriptor):	SMART Recovery (for alcoholism)
Commands to:	`listserv@maelstrom.stjohns.edu`
Subscribe:	`subscribe SMARTREC Your-name`
Unsubscribe:	`unsubscribe SMARTREC`
List:	`SMARTREC@maelstrom.stjohns.edu`

Title (or descriptor):	Social Phobia Support
Commands to:	listserv@maelstrom.stjohns.edu
Subscribe:	subscribe soc-phob Your-name
Unsubscribe:	unsubscribe soc-phob
List:	soc-phob@maelstrom.stjohns.edu

Title (or descriptor):	Spina Bifida, Parents of Children with
Commands to:	listserv@waisman.wisc.edu
Subscribe:	subscribe SB-parents Your-name
Unsubscribe:	unsubscribe SB-parents
List:	SB-parents@waisman.wisc.edu

Title (or descriptor):	Spinal Injuries
Commands to:	listserv@albnydh2.bitnet
Subscribe:	subscribe scipin-L Your-name
Unsubscribe:	unsubscribe scipin-L
List:	scipin-L@albnydh2.bitnet

Title (or descriptor):	Stop Domestic Violence
Commands to:	azhomes@netzone.com
Subscribe:	subscribe SDV Your-email-address
Unsubscribe:	unsubscribe SDV
List:	SDV@netzone.com

Title (or descriptor):	Stop Smoking
Commands to:	lindam@earthlink.net
Subscribe:	subscribe Nosmoke Your-name
Unsubscribe:	unsubscribe Nosmoke
List:	nosmoke@earthlink.net

Title (or descriptor):   Stroke
Commands to: `listserv@ukcc.uky.edu`
Subscribe: `subscribe Stroke-L Your-name`
Unsubscribe: `unsubscribe Stroke-L`
List: `Stroke-L@ukcc.uky.edu`

Title (or descriptor):   Stolen Youth–Young People with Mental Disorders
Commands to: `listserv@maelstrom.stjohns.edu`
Subscribe: `subscribe S-Youth Your-name`
Unsubscribe: `unsubscribe S-Youth`
List: `S-Youth@maelstrom.stjohns.edu`

Title (or descriptor):   Stuttering
Commands to: `listproc2@bgu.edu`
Subscribe: `subscribe stut-hlp Your-name`
Unsubscribe: `unsubscribe stut-hlp`
List: `stut-hlp@bgu.edu`

Title (or descriptor):   Subsequent Loss after a Pregnancy Support
Commands to: `SPALS-request@inforamp.net`
Subscribe: `subscribe SPALS Your-name`
Unsubscribe: `unsubscribe SPALS`
List: `SPALS@inforamp.net`

Title (or descriptor):   Suicidal Feelings and Thoughts
Send regular e-mail to: `jo@samaritans.org`

An anonymous, U.K-based charity organization that handles suicidal e-mail to this address.

Title (or descriptor):   Suicide Support
Commands to: `majordomo@research.canon.com.au`
Subscribe: `subscribe suicide-support`
Unsubscribe: `unsubscribe suicide-support`
List: `suicide-support@research.canon.com.au`

Title (or descriptor):   Suicide Survivors
Commands to: `majordomo@research.canon.com.au`
Subscribe: `subscribe suicide-survivors`
Unsubscribe: `unsubscribe suicide-survivors`
List: `suicide-survivors@research.canon.com.au`

Title (or descriptor):   Support for Creating Positive Life Changes
Commands to: `listserv@maelstrom.stjohns.edu`
Subscribe: `subscribe solution Your-name`
Unsubscribe: `unsubscribe solution`
List: `solution@maelstrom.stjohns.edu`

Title (or descriptor):   Tobacco Addiction
Commands to: `listserv@ra.msstate.edu`
Subscribe: `subscribe smoke-free Your-name`
Unsubscribe: `unsubscribe smoke-free`
List: `smoke-free@ra.msstate.edu`

Title (or descriptor):   Tourette Syndrome
Web site:
`http://www.chebucto.ns.ca/Health/Tourette/info/`
`tslists.html`

Commands to: majordomo@chebucto.ns.ca
Subscribe: subscribe tourette
Unsubscribe: unsubscribe tourette
List: tourette@chebucto.ns.ca

Title (or descriptor):   Transgendered
Commands to: listserv@brownvm.brown.edu
Subscribe: subscribe transgen Your-name
Unsubscribe: unsubscribe transgen
List: transgen@brownvm.brown.edu

Title (or descriptor):   Traumatic Brain Injury
Commands to: listserv@maelstrom.stjohns.edu
Subscribe: subscribe discuss-tbi Your-name
Unsubscribe: unsubscribe discuss-tbi
List: discuss-tbi@maelstrom.stjohns.edu

Title (or descriptor):   Trichotillomania
Commands to: majordomo@cs.columbia.edu
Subscribe: subscribe ttm
Unsubscribe: unsubscribe ttm
List: ttm@cs.columbia.edu

Title (or descriptor):   Weight-Loss
Commands to: listserv@maelstrom.stjohns.edu
Subscribe: subscribe NLC Your-name
Unsubscribe: unsubscribe NLC
List: NLC@maelstrom.stjohns.edu

Title (or descriptor):	Widowed Individuals
Web site:	`http://www.fortnet.org/WidowNet/on-line/wid_hi.htm`
Commands to:	`majordomo@fortnet.org`
Subscribe:	`subscribe widow`
Unsubscribe:	`unsubscribe widow`
List:	`majordomo@fortnet.org`

14

Consumer Newsgroup Discussion and Support Groups

Newsgroups can be an excellent forum for patients to engage in lively discussions and gain support and information. They are listed in alphabetical order in the following table. For an up-to-date listing, please consult Psych Central:

`http://psychcentral.com/`

or on the book's Web site,

`http://www.insidemh.com/.`

TABLE 14.1 Patient-oriented Newsgroups

Description	Newsgroup Name	Moder-ated?
Abortion: Support for those who have had or are going to have an abortion, and their partners	`alt.support.abortion`	No
Abuse offenders/perpetrators, recovery for	`alt.abuse.offender.recovery`	No
Abuse, alternative models of dealing with	`alt.abuse.transcendence`	No
Abuse, moderated version of `alt.sexual.abuse.recovery`	`alt.sexual.abuse.recovery.moderated`	Yes
Abuse, recovering from all types of	`alt.abuse.recovery`	No
Adoptees	`soc.adoption.adoptees`	No
Adoption information & parenting issues	`alt.adoption.agency`	No
Adoption issues, general	`alt.adoption`	No
AIDS & HIV, general discussion of	`misc.health.aids`	No
AIDS & HIV, medical discussion of	`sci.med.aids`	Yes
AIDS, partners of people with	`alt.support.aids.partners`	No
All other support topics & questions	`alt.support`	No
Allergies, causes and treatment of	`alt.med.allergy`	No
Allergies, Individuals with food	`alt.support.food-allergies`	No
Angst	`alt.angst`	No
Anxiety and panic disorders	`alt.support.anxiety-panic`	No
Anxiety and panic disorders, cognitive approaches to	`alt.recovery.panic-anxiety.self-help`	No
Attention-deficit disorders	`alt.support.attn-deficit`	No
Breastfeeding	`alt.support.breastfeeding`	No
Breast implants, people with or considering	`alt.support.breast-implant`	No
Cancer	`alt.support.cancer`	No
Cancer, medical discussion of	`sci.med.diseases.cancer`	No
Cerebral palsy	`alt.support.cerebral-palsy`	No
Childless by choice	`alt.support.childfree`	No
Children's health issues	`misc.kids.health`	No

Description	Newsgroup Name	Moderated?
Children's issues, general	misc.kids	No
Chronic Fatigue Syndrome (CFS)	alt.med.cfs	Yes
Chronic pain	alt.support.chronic-pain	No
Codependency	alt.recovery.codependency	No
Crisis situations	soc.support.depression.crisis	No
Crohn's/ulcerative colitis/Irritable bowel	alt.support.crohns-colitis	No
Cults: Former cult members & family & friends	alt.support.ex-cult	No
Dentistry, medical discussion of	sci.med.dentistry	No
Depressed people, family & friends coping with	soc.support.depression.family	No
Depression & mood disorders	alt.support.depression	No
Depression & mood disorders	soc.support.depression.misc	No
Depression, treatment of	soc.support.depression.treatment	No
Developmental delay	alt.support.dev-delays	No
Diabetes, hypoglycemia (hypoglycaemia)	misc.health.diabetes	No
Diabetes, parents & family of children with	alt.support.diabetes.kids	No
Dieting through medication	alt.support.diet.rx	No
Dieting with Weight Watchers	alt.support.diet.weight-watcher	No
Dieting/losing weight/nutrition	alt.support.diet	No
Disabled persons discussing sexuality	alt.support.disabled.sexuality	No
Disabled persons who are also artists	alt.support.disabled.artists	No
Dissociative disorders (e.g., multiple personality disorder)	alt.support.dissociation	No
Divorce/marital breakups	alt.support.divorce	No
Dwarfism	alt.support.dwarfism	Yes
Eating disorders (anorexia, bulimia, etc.)	alt.support.eating-disord	No
Effects of second-hand smoke	alt.support.non-smokers	No
Endometriosis	alt.support.endometriosis	No
Epilepsy	alt.support.epilepsy	No

TABLE 14.1   (continued)

Description	Newsgroup Name	Moderated?
Fat people, self-acceptance with no diet talk	`soc.support.fat-acceptance`	No
Fat-acceptance with no dieting talk	`alt.support.big-folks`	No
Fibromyalgia fibrosis	`alt.med.fibromyalgia`	No
Food addiction and compulsive eating	`alt.recovery.compulsive-eat`	No
Foster parents	`alt.support.foster-parents`	No
Gay youths helping each other	`soc.support.youth.gay-lesbian-bi`	Yes
Grief and loss	`alt.support.grief`	No
Headache and migraine ailments	`alt.support.headaches.migraine`	No
Hearing loss and the hearing-impaired	`alt.support.hearing-loss`	No
Height, people far from average	`alt.sigma2.height`	No
Herpes	`alt.support.herpes`	No
Hypnosis	`alt.hypnosis`	No
Infertility, causes & treatment of	`alt.infertility`	No
Learning disabilities (e.g., dyslexia)	`alt.support.learning-disab`	No
Loneliness	`alt.support.loneliness`	No
Loneliness	`soc.support.loneliness`	Yes
Looking after & taking care of another	`alt.support.disabled.caregivers`	No
Manic depression & bipolar disorder	`soc.support.depression.manic`	No
Manic depression & bipolar disorder	`alt.support.depression.manic`	No
Marfan syndrome	`alt.support.marfan`	No
Marriage	`alt.support.marriage`	No
Medicine & related products & regulations	`sci.med`	No
Menopause	`alt.support.menopause`	No
Mental health issues in society	`alt.society.mental-health`	No
Miscarriages and coping with loss in pregnancy	`soc.support.pregnancy.loss`	No
Multiple sclerosis	`alt.support.ms-recovery`	No
Multiple sclerosis	`alt.support.mult-sclerosis`	No
Muscular dystrophy	`alt.support.musc-dystrophy`	No

Description	Newsgroup Name	Moderated?
Neurological disorders	`alt.support.disorders.neurological`	No
Nicotine help	`alt.recovery.nicotine`	No
Nutrition & diet, medical discussion	`sci.med.nutrition`	No
Obesity	`alt.support.obesity`	Yes
Obsessive-compulsive disorder (OCD)	`alt.support.ocd`	No
Oppositional defiant disorder	`alt.support.opp-defiant`	No
Parenting: raising twins and other multiples	`alt.parenting.twins-triplets`	No
Parenting and adoption issues	`soc.adoption.parenting`	No
Parenting help & solutions	`alt.parenting.solutions`	No
Parenting, help being a step-parent	`alt.support.step-parents`	No
Parenting, single parenting solutions & support	`alt.support.single-parents`	No
Parenting, spanking	`alt.parenting.spanking`	No
Parenting, support and information for single fathers	`alt.dads-rights`	Yes
Personality disorders	`alt.support.personality`	No
Pet loss	`alt.support.grief.pet-loss`	No
Post polio syndrome	`alt.support.post-polio`	No
Pregnancy & childbirth issues	`misc.kids.pregnancy`	No
Procrastination help	`alt.recovery.procrastinate`	No
Prostate cancer	`alt.support.cancer.prostate`	No
Prostatitis	`alt.support.prostate.prostatitis`	No
Psychological problems, general help with	`alt.psychology.help`	No
Recovering adults from dysfunctional families	`alt.recovery.adult-children`	No
Recovering from gambling addictions	`alt.recovery.addiction.gambling`	No
Recovering from sexual abuse	`alt.sexual.abuse.recovery`	No
Recovering from sexual abuse discussion	`alt.sexual.abuse.recovery.d`	No
Recovering from sexual addictions	`alt.recovery.addiction.sexual`	No
Recovering from the effects of religion	`alt.recovery.religion`	No

TABLE 14.1 (continued)

Description	Newsgroup Name	Moder-ated?
Recovery from Catholic upbringing	`alt.recovery.catholicism`	No
Recovery issues, general	`alt.recovery`	No
Recovery through Alcoholics Anonymous	`alt.recovery.aa`	No
Recovery through Narcotics Anonymous	`alt.recovery.na`	No
Repetitive strain injuries	`misc.health.injuries.rsi.misc`	No
Repetitive strain injuries	`misc.health.injuries.rsi.moderated`	Yes
Schizophrenia support and information	`alt.support.schizophrenia`	No
Seasonal affective disorder	`soc.support.depression.seasonal`	No
Seasonal affective disorder (SAD)	`alt.support.depression.seasonal`	No
Self-improvement tips & techniques	`alt.self-improve`	No
Sex reassignment surgery or procedures, people going through	`alt.support.sexreassign`	No
Sexual abuse survivors, partners of	`alt.support.abuse-partners`	No
Short people, issues of interest to	`alt.support.short`	No
Shyness	`alt.support.shyness`	No
Sleep disorders & problems sleeping	`alt.support.sleep-disorder`	No
Smoking, stopping or quitting	`alt.support.stop-smoking`	No
Smoking like above, but moderated	`alt.support.non-smokers.moderated`	Yes
Spina bifida	`alt.support.spina-bifida`	No
Stuttering & other speaking difficulties	`alt.support.stuttering`	No
Suicide discussion	`alt.suicide.holiday`	No
Survivors of Prozac & other SSRIs	`alt.support.survivors.prozac`	No
Tall people, issues of interest to	`alt.support.tall`	No
Tinnitus/ringing ears/other head noises	`alt.support.tinnitus`	No
Tourette's syndrome	`alt.support.tourette`	No
Transgendered & intersexed persons	`soc.support.transgendered`	No
Trauma and PTSD (posttraumatic stress disorder)	`alt.support.trauma-ptsd`	No

PART

IV

APPENDICES

APPENDIX A
Glossary of Terms

This is a glossary of technical terms discussed throughout this book. It has been compiled from a wide variety of sources and reflects my current knowledge.

bookmark An option within your Web **browser** that allows you to save the name and address of a Web site for future reference and easy access. Also referred to as "favorites" or "favorite places."

Boolean See **operator**.

bps, bits per second A measurement of data transmission speed particularly over a **modem**. Most popular modems transmit at either 14.4 Kbps (14,400 bps) or 28.8 Kbps (28,800 bps). Newer modems are capable of 33.6 Kbps and 56 Kbps. Some special modems may go up to 128 Kbps (over **ISDN** telephone lines).

browser Also known as a "Web browser." Any program used to access and search the World Wide Web. For instance, Netscape Navigator or Communicator, Microsoft Explorer, Mosaic, Lynx, etc.

cable modem A piece of computer hardware which gives a user high-speed access to the Internet, through your existing T.V. cable connection.

closed Used to refer to a type of mailing list. A closed mailing list only allows members of the mailing list to send messages to it. *See also* **open** and **moderated**.

COM port Serial port for connecting a cable to an IBM PC-compatible computer, usually, but not always used for data communications. They are referred to by the operating system as COM1, COM2, COM3, etc.

conference A group of public messages on a system, usually focused on a particular topic and sometimes moderated by a conference host or moderator who guides the discussion. Also called "forums," "folders," "message boards," "boards," or

"SIGs" (for Special Interest Groups"). Very similar to the newsgroups on the Internet, conference is another term for public, topical, threaded discussion areas.

crawlers   The software used to index the World Wide Web. Also called "robots" and "spiders."

domain   An organization's name on the Internet. The last two parts of an e-mail address or an URL are referred to as a "domain." For example, "`aol.com`" refers to America OnLine, "`harvard.edu`" refers to Harvard University, and "`cape.org`" refers to the Cape Cod Institute.

download   Transfering files or software from another computer to your computer.

DSL, **digital subscriber line**   A service that provides high-speed Internet access through a person's regular telephone line. Is comparable and the direct competitor to a **cable modem** in terms of offering high-speed Internet access.

e-mail   Electronic mail—messages can be sent anywhere in the world via the Internet at the cost of a local phone call. E-mail addresses generally consist of a part of your name (or your account name), the "at" sign (@), followed by your domain name. For example, `webmaster@cmhc.com` is a valid e-mail address. For most e-mail addresses, it does not matter if the letters are upper- or lowercase (that is, e-mail addresses are not case-sensitive).

encryption   A secure method of encoding data, most often through a Web page or e-mail. This encoded data can only be decoded by the person or computer system authorized to access it. Used on the Web to protect financial information.

e-therapy   Another term for online counseling or online therapy. A new modality of providing helping services to people online through e-mail, forums, audio/video, or chat rooms.

FAQ   Frequently Asked Questions—A file established for many public discussion groups containing common questions new users often ask and answers to those questions.

favorite places   *See* **bookmark**.

flame   An angry, often abusive and denigrating message sent in response to another message in a public discussion forum online. Sending a flame, or "flaming" another, is frowned on and should be avoided.

form   A form is a Web page with areas you fill out (called "fields") with requested information. Forms are used to submit search queries, feedback, and requests for additional information on many Web sites.

forums See **conference.**

frame Also known as "framed." A framed Web site is one that divides your Web browser's screen into smaller areas. Each area is then filled in with different information, often in an attempt to help you navigate the Web site or to display advertising.

ftp, file transfer protocol The standard method for transfering files over the Internet or the software program that implements this method. Using an ftp software program, you can connect to another computer online and transfer files to your local desktop computer using a GET command. Many sites allow "anonymous" ftp. At the login prompt, enter "anonymous" as the login name (without the quotes), and at the password prompt enter your e-mail address as the password. You will have access to a limited number of public directories from which you can retrieve files.

GIF, graphical interface format A standard graphics or image file widely used on the Web. Typically works best when the graphic or image is not a photograph. *See also* **JPEG.**

gopher The precursor to the World Wide Web. A storage-and-retrieval protocol for text and software files on the Internet. It makes finding files and useful information easier than with ftp, but harder than through the Web.

guide A general or specialized index of online resources (most often Web sites) compiled by human editors. Less comprehensive than many search engines, but often more to the point. Also called a "search" or "subject guide."

hard drive Your computer's internal storage device in which you save data, files, and programs.

hit A single access of a Web page, recorded each time a Web browser displays a page. Counting the number of hits a particular Web page receives is a popularly displayed number on many people's home pages. Webmasters use hits to determine which pages are most popular and therefore should receive the most attention.

home page or **homepage** The top-level hypertext document in a hierarchical collection of linked HTML documents. The home page is often the document implied in a WWW site's URL. For instance, `http://www.behavior.net/` actually pulls up that site's home page document, `http://www.behavior.net/index.html`.

HTML, Hypertext Markup Language The publishing standard used to create WWW pages. It defines what happens when one clicks on a **hypertext link** embedded in the page. HTML is a publishing standard, not a programming language, hence its ease of use. HTML documents go to make up the core of a Web site, and usually end with a `.html` or `.htm` suffix.

HTTP, Hypertext Transport Protocol   The standard by which the World Wide Web operates.

hypertext link   Also known as a "link," it is often displayed as highlighted and underlined text on a Web page; graphics can also be links, however. By choosing a hypertext link (by clicking on it with your mouse), you are instructing the computer to go to and display a specific Web document. This allows individuals to move within a Web site, or across Web sites residing on different computers, with ease. A "bad" link is one that does not work properly. When a bad link is encountered, you will receive an error message instead of the Web page you were trying to visit. Links become bad most often because a Web page has moved (and has left no forwarding address) or because the page was simply removed from the Web.

Internet   The largest global network of business and personal computers connected through regular and high-speed telephone lines. Requires specific types of software to access it, such as a Web browser.

IP, Internet Protocol   An alternative method for accessing Web sites, based on the Web site's technical address. This takes the form of a four-part number, such as 207.87.223.39.

ISDN, Integrated Services Digital Network   An all-digital telephone system slowly gaining more use and acceptance throughout the United States, ISDN allows individuals to use higher speed modems than standard telephone lines. Requires specialized installation and equipment at the present time.

Java, Javascript   These are two separate but related, largely Web-based programming languages. They allow for increased functionality of and enhancements to a Web site. If your browser is not capable of using these languages, the enhancements or features found in the Web site will most often simply not be displayed. Netscape and Microsoft support both types of languages.

JPEG, Joint Photographic Experts Group   A standard for compressing digital photographic images. *See also* **GIF**.

Kb, Kilobyte   1,024 bytes; often generically applied to 1,000 bytes as well.

link   *See* **hypertext link**.

mailing list   A public, topical discussion group that is conducted exclusively through e-mail. Once a user subscribes to a mailing list, any messages she subsequently sends to the list are copied and re-distributed to every other user on the mailing list. A common way to carry on topic-specific discussions online; the other is via **newsgroups**. Mailing lists are also sometimes known as "listservs" or "majordomos," named after the types of software used to maintain them.

Mb, Megabyte Technically 1,024 kilobytes or 1,048,576 bytes, but often applied to the more rounded term of 1 million bytes as well.

mirror A Web site that duplicates another Web site at a different physical location. Often done to help speed access to that resource because it resides on another continent. For example, a popular Web site in Europe may be slow to access for many North American users. Hence a mirror Web site may be set up in North America, which duplicates the content of the original site.

modem A device that allows your computer to communicate with another computer over a regular telephone line. Modems are often identified by the speed (in bits per second or bps) of communication they allow. The higher the bps, the faster the modem.

moderated Used in reference to either mailing lists or newsgroups. A moderated forum is one in which every message sent to that forum is first reviewed by an individual, often referred to as the "moderator." If the message is appropriate to the forum's topic, it is then approved and published on that forum. If it is not accepted for publication, the author is notified and the message is returned to the author. *See also* **open** and **closed**.

MPEG, Motion Picture Experts Group A standard for compressing digital video images.

NetPhone Also known as "Internet telephone." Refers to the software used to allow two individuals to talk to one another using the Internet as the connection.

Netiquette Rules of etiquette for online interactions. *See* `http://www.albion.com/netiquette/` for more detailed information.

newsgroups Also known collectively as "Usenet." Public discussion groups where individuals can read and add new messages (or "articles"). Uses a hierarchical topic structure (or "threads") to ease navigation through them. Messages posted to newsgroups are sent to every computer connected to the Internet, where the article is then stored for a few days to give people an opportunity to read it. Individual users elect to subscribe or not subscribe to newsgroups. While there are currently over 18,000 newsgroups available for subscription, most users only subscribe to, read, and contribute to a handful of them. A common way to carry on topic-specific discussion on-line; the other is via **mailing lists**.

newsgroup reader   The software used to access, read, and post to newsgroups.

open   In reference to a mailing list. An open mailing list allows anyone to post a message to it, regardless of whether they are a member of that list. *See also* **closed** and **moderated**.

operating system   The underlying system software that allows a computer to oper-ate. Popular types of operating systems include DOS, Windows, and Macintosh Sys-tem 7, 8, or X.

operator   A symbol or word used to help broaden or limit a search query. A spe-cific type of operator, called a "Boolean operator," includes words such as `and`, `or`, and `not`.

PDF, Portable Document Format   Allows you to read a document and print it out using Adobe's Acrobat reader, a free piece of software. PDF files can *only* be read or printed using this software.

post   The act of adding a new message or article to a newsgroup, conference, or mailing list discussion area online.

PPP, Point to Point Protocol   A type of computer protocol used by modems for online communication.

protocol   A system of rules and procedures governing communications between two computer devices. File-transfer protocols in your communications program refer to a set of rules governing how error checking will be performed on blocks of data.

RAM, Random Access Memory   The temporary memory area on a computer that allows you to run software. Often increasing the amount of RAM in a computer can help poor computer performance.

RTF, Rich Text Format   A set of word processing instructions that can be read by most word processing programs, to retain the formatting rules of the document.

search engine   A Web site that indexes an online resource and makes that index available to others for searching. Most often in reference to a site that has indexed Web documents, but search engines also index mailing lists and other online re-sources. An "internal" search engine has only indexed the documents of that particu-lar Web site, which can allow you to find information on that site more easily and quickly.

server   A computer dedicated to providing specific services to other computers. Print servers, for example, do nothing but accept, store, and print out documents sent to them by other computers. Web servers allow users from around the world to access the Web sites and documents stored on them.

shareware   Computer software that users are encouraged to copy and distribute to others, and to evaluate for a specified or indefinite period. The author gives the user a license to "try before you buy," and requires voluntary payment of a specific sum of money if the user continues to use the software. Failure to pay the requested fee is a legal violation of the author's copyright.

site   An area or location online, usually on the Web, where an organization, individual or business stores its information.

SLIP, Serial Line Internet Protocol   A type of computer protocol used by modems for online communication.

spam   Off-topic messages (usually advertisements) sent to a wide range of discussion forums (mailing lists or newsgroups) or e-mail addresses online. "Spamming" is frowned on in the online world.

T1   A kind of telephone line service offering high-speed data or voice access.

telnet   An application program that allows users to interactively logon to any computer on the Internet. For example, a telnet program could be used to search the holdings of a library and receive results.

thread   Messages on a single, specific topic that appear in the order they were written in an online discussion forum, such as on a newsgroup. Threads allow for easier reading of a particular subject, since they are all grouped together.

upload   Transfering files or software from your computer to another computer.

URL, Uniform Resource Locator   A format for an address on the Internet. For example, `http://www.cape.org/` indicates a Hypertext Transport Protocol (http) address on the World Wide Web (www) with location "cape" and the type of owner (org). Other valid protocols may include **ftp** and **gopher**. URLs are always sensitive to whether letters are in upper- or lowercase; that is, they are case sensitive.

user interface   The visual and design elements of a Web page that instruct users on how to access the Web site's information.

V.32bis   International standard for modem data communications at speeds of up to 14,400 bits per second.

V.34   International standard for modem data communications at speeds of up to 28,800 bits per second. Look for this designation when purchasing a new modem.

V.FC, V.Fast Class   A pre-V.34 proprietary modem modulation for 28.8 Kbps connections, which is no longer a supported standard.

Web browser   *See* **browser.**

Webmaster   The person responsible for the ongoing maintenance of a Web site.

wildcard   Most often an asterisk (*), a wildcard symbol allows you to tell the computer that you're uncertain what you're searching for. It can be used to ensure a search turns up all forms or variants of a word (e.g., `chil*` will turn up both `child` and `children`).

World Wide Web   Also known as "the Web" or "WWW." A network of graphical hypertext servers linked by the Internet offering graphics, sound, text, and in some cases video clips providing information. This is the newest (since 1993) and fastest growing aspect of the Internet because of its ability to offer more than just plain text online.

XML, eXtensible markup language   A higher-level language, similar to **HTML,** XML describes the content or data in a document, rather than how it is to be formatted. When companies in a single field, such as health care, all agree upon a single set of data definitions, they can then more easily exchange and find relevant information.

.zip   An extension for a file name indicating the file is catalogued and compressed using Phil Katz's PKZIP compression utilities. You need a program called "pkunzip.exe" to decompress and extract the programs within this file.

APPENDIX B
Further Reading

Ferguson, T. (1996). *Health online*. Reading, MA: Addison-Wesley.

Grohol, J. M., Kimball, C., Ungerleider, S., Meyer, G., Kramer, S., Zevnik, B., & Sheerer, L. (Eds.). (1997). *Health resources online: A guide for mental health and addiction specialists*. Providence, RI: Behavioral Health Resources Press.

Hahn, H., & Stout, R. (1994). *The Internet complete reference*. Berkeley, CA: Osborne McGraw-Hill.

Honeycutt, J., & Pike, M. A. (1996). *Using the Internet: The most complete reference* (3rd ed.). Indianapolis, IN: Que Corporation.

Kent P. (1996). *The complete idiot's guide to the Internet* (3rd ed.). Indianapolis, IN: Que Corporation.

Linden, T., & Kienholz, M. L. (1995). *Dr. Tom Linden's guide to online medicine*. New York: McGraw-Hill.

Maloy, T. K. (1996). *The Internet research guide*. New York: Allworth Press.

McFedries, P. (1996). *The complete idiot's guide to creating an HTML web page*. Indianapolis, IN: Que Corporation.

Rosen, L. D., & Weil, M. M. (1997). *The mental health technology bible*. New York: John Wiley and Sons.

Scharf, D. (1996). *HTML visual quick reference* (2nd ed.). Indianapolis, IN: Que Corporation.

Sctoo, R., Reber, S., Poulsen, T., & Sandler, G. (1996). *HTML 3.2 Quickstart*. Emeryville, CA: Ziff-Davis Press.

Wallace, P. M. (1997). *Psych online 97*. Madison, WI: Brown and Benchmark.

White, B. J., & Madara, E. J. (Eds.). (1995). *The self-help sourcebook*. Denville, NJ: Northwest Covenant Medical Center.

APPENDIX C
How to Get Online

Getting online—if you aren't already—is an easier task than you might imagine. You will need three things: a computer, a modem, and some type of online service provider.

THE COMPUTER

Virtually any computer can be turned into a connected online computer. You probably already have a computer or are thinking of getting one soon. Nearly any computer manufactured or purchased within the past 3 years will suffice. It can be something as old as an Intel-based "486" machine. "486" refers to the type of the main computer processor found inside the computer. The microprocessor chip is the main brains of a computer. At one time, most personal computers (PCs) had Intel-brand microprocessor chips that carried numbers. A computer with a "386" microprocessor is slower than a "486." The Pentium class of processors are newer and faster yet.

Each microprocessor found in a computer runs at a set "speed" (megaherz [Mhz]). This speed determines how fast the computer is. While nearly every Pentium chip is faster than most 486 chips, there are also different speeds of Pentium chips. A Pentium 600 Mhz is faster than a Pentium 300 Mhz. When deciding to purchase a new computer, always get the fastest and newest microprocessor you can afford. It will quickly be surpassed by the next generation. And while microprocessors can be upgraded in today's machines, it is cheaper to upgrade memory or hard drive space. In older machines, a microprocessor upgrade to something faster usually isn't economically sensible. For the cost of such an upgrade (as well as the usual upgrade

301

in memory), you would have half the cost of buying a newer and much faster computer.

Minimum Computer Requirements

You should have at least a Pentium-class computer running at 133 Mhz to surf online. Memory is also an important factor, but it is somewhat dependent on your operating system. For older Windows-based machines, 16 megabytes is usually sufficient; for Windows 95 or 98, 32 megabytes is the minimum, and Windows NT/2000 likes 64 megabytes or more. A Macintosh II, Quadra, Performa, PowerPC, G3, G4, or iMac of any kind will work best in the Apple Macintosh world, with at least 16 Mb of RAM for Macintosh System 7.x or 8.x (although 32 Mb is recommended). On any computer you use, you generally should have about 100 Mb of hard drive space available or free.

THE MODEM

A modem allows your computer to communicate with another computer over a regular telephone line. Most computers nowadays come with modems, but you can easily add one if necessary. Modem speed is usually the slowest link between you and the online world, so keeping up with the faster speeds within a year or two after they come out is usually a good idea. Modem speeds are measured in bits per second (bps); higher bps means a faster modem. You should get the fastest modem speed available at the time you buy. The newest, fastest modems are usually expensive in the first few months they're available, and then the price drops drastically.

If you're planning to spend a lot of time online or do daily business through an online connection, there is another option besides using your modem over your regular home telephone line. You can purchase and have installed something called "ISDN." ISDN allows potential speeds of up to 128k, although 64k is often the case. For most clinicians, the costs and hassles involved in obtaining and maintaining this service outweigh the speed benefits. A third option coming down the road is "cable modems." Using your local cable company's coaxial cable, these modems can transmit data at speeds up to 800 to 900k and higher to your computer. A fourth option is a service that uses your existing telephone line to offer high-speed Internet access. This service is called digital subscriber line, or DSL. DSL is typically available in areas where cable modems are offered, providing some competition and choice in those markets. At this writing, DSL has many fewer subscribers and is typically more expensive than the faster cable modem. A minimum of a 14.4 Kbps modem or better is needed for getting online, but a 28.8 Kbps or a 56 Kbps modem is highly recommended.

THE ONLINE SERVICE PROVIDER

There are dozens of ways to get online and access any of the resources discussed within this book. These include big commercial services, national or local Internet Service Providers (ISPs), your company or academic institution, or a "free-net."

Commercial Services

A common and popular method is to use one of the big commercial services, such as America OnLine (AOL) or CompuServe. The benefits to using one of these services include easy software installation and setup of your computer and modem. You not only will get good customer service around the clock, but also additional online areas and content you could not access through the Internet alone. These areas often include content (*Oprah*, for instance, is on America OnLine, as is *Car & Driver* magazine), discussion areas, interactive real-time chat with other members (all services), and interactive real-time game playing. The user interface tends to be well designed in these services, where "ease of use" is the underlying concept. You also get access to the Internet, although this access may not be as complete as that from an Internet Service Provider.

Naturally, all of this additional content, customer service, and ease of use comes at a price. In the past, the price of commercial providers has traditionally been higher than that of other commercial service providers offering only access to the Internet. But that has changed as more people have gotten online. Now these commercial services offer pricing that is usually competitive with Internet Service Providers (ISPs, see below). The other big drawback to using one of the commercial services is that their Internet access tends to be slower than if you were to access the Internet directly. This is due to the fact that you are accessing the Internet through the same computers as the commercial service's other 10 or 15 million subscribers. The providers try to reduce this traffic problem by using some software tricks (such as making copies of the most popular Web pages and serving them directly off of their machines instead of allowing the user to access the Web page directly), but it often isn't enough. The other common complaint I hear about accessing the Internet through these services is the number of times they *can't* be accessed due to busy signals. No matter how great an online service provider is, if you can't reach the online world through them, you won't remain a customer of them for long.

Internet Service Providers

Alternatives to the big three services come in the form of Internet Service Providers (ISP). ISPs may be nationally recognized companies providing Internet access or they may be a local company providing the same access. Typically this access includes not only the usual e-mail address and access to the Web and Internet newsgroups, but also the ability to set up your own Web page without any additional charge. Average charges for most areas of the country for these services range from $16.95 to $29.95 per month (at this writing), for unlimited access time while online. There usually is little difference in terms of the quality of services offered, busy signals, and other similar measurements between a national and a local ISP. However, national ISPs may not have a local phone number in your city or geographical location. You may have to select a local ISP to save on any long distance charges. Local ISPs can give more personalized service, but if something goes wrong on Saturday, they may not get around to fixing the problem until Monday; national ISPs often offer 24-hour customer service.

The other advantage to national over local Internet Service Providers is that—like commercial services—they will often provide you with all the necessary software to get started. This often comes on one or two diskettes, which you simply load into your computer and follow their instructions. Compare this with many local ISPs. You may be given a diskette (if you're lucky!) with a number of different programs on it and minimal, photocopied instructions (or worse yet, a "readme.txt" file on the diskette itself!). If you are knowledgable and comfortable with configuring your computer to use the programs, this software is usually enough to get you started; but because this can sometimes be a bit complicated, it is not recommended for the computer novice.

Workplace and Institutional Access

A third common way for people to access the online world is through their workplace or academic institution. However, unless it is a part of their job, I would caution clinicians accessing online resources from their workplace. Inappropriate or overuse of online surfing at work has been the cause of many supervisory meetings with employees. Check with your employer to see if they have a policy in place about online use. Universities and colleges have traditionally offered unlimited online access to faculty, staff, and students at no cost, not only from their offices and dorm rooms, but also from your home. With either of these means of access, you'll be able to get to all of the traditional online resources, including the Web, e-mail, and Internet newsgroups. What you may not get is any type of customer service or help in answering your technical questions. Online access speed may also be slower at some universities, because their connection to the Internet can't adequately support the number of simultaneous users at the institution. This is especially true when all of the students decide to go online at the same time!

Free-nets

Free-nets are the last typical method for accessing online resources. A free-net is exactly what it sounds like—a free way of accessing the Web, e-mail, and newsgroups. Often sponsored by local governments and administered through the public library, they grant an account to anybody who asks for one. Terminals are usually available on a first-come, first-served basis. Many of these types of services offer only rudimentary access, for instance, e-mail, newsgroups, and gopher access. As their budgets increase, many offer expanded services that rival a local ISP's, including Web access and your own Web page.

Which Provider Is Best for You?

I encourage people to start out with the easiest method for getting online—a commercial service—and see how they like it. Many times, staying with such a service is appropriate. For people who just want to access e-mail and the occasional Web site, such a commercial service is probably adequate. For others who do more serious Web surfing and make use of online Web technologies (such as Java, RealAudio, Web chat systems and the like), a direct Internet connection through an Internet Service Provider is a better long-term choice. Academic and work accounts are fine (and usually free), but you will often lose access to such accounts when you leave the university or employer. This loss of service may also come with little warning and with no guarantee of giving you time to transfer or copy personal files or e-mail you may have been saving. It's always a good idea to learn of your institution's policy on such matters before the time comes. In the meantime, enjoy the free account and make use of the unlimited access that comes with it. Whatever method you choose, don't become emotionally attached to it. Since the online world changes so quickly—and sometimes, drastically—be prepared to go with a better deal if one comes around.

APPENDIX D
Creating Your Own Web Resource

Creating your own World Wide Web site may seem like an enormous, expensive, and difficult undertaking. In fact, your own Web site can be online and functioning in less than a half hour once you master the basics of Web creation. Those basics are not as complicated as you may think.

Many programs exist to help you create your own Web presence. You can then choose to publish your Web page (or pages) on your Internet Service Provider's machine, or through one of the handful of free sites online, such as GeoCities (`http://www.geocities.com/`). Once your site is online and you can access it through the Web, so can the millions of other individuals throughout the world connected to the Internet.

People choose to set up Web sites for a multitude of reasons. Clinicians often like to publish an advertisement for their practice or place of business, detailing their philosophical orientation for psychotherapy treatment, insurance accepted, business hours, other services offered, etc. Academicians or researchers may want to share their research interests with others, using their Web site as a publishing platform for their articles and theories. Other professionals simply would like a place to publish links to some of their favorite places online, or start a site that will act as a clearinghouse for online information in their particular specialty area in mental health.

There are two common ways to create a Web site. The simplest method is to choose what is called a "visual editor." The second method is to edit the language behind a Web page manually. Choosing the latter method means learning Hypertext Markup Language (HTML). HTML is *not* a programming language, such as BASIC or perl. Instead, it is similar to the insertion of formatting codes, such as that seen when a person chooses to "Reveal Codes" in the popular WordPerfect word processor. It specifies only how to display text in a Web browser. You tell it that a headline is a headline and it enlarges the font used, centers, and bolds the text on a person's Web browser. You tell it a paragraph ends here, and it places a blank line between two paragraphs. It is really that simple, regardless of whether you learn HTML or use the simpler visual editor.

There are dozens of software applications available on the market today to help you author Web pages in HTML. Some of these are free to download from select Web sites and many others are shareware, where you pay a fee only if you continue to use the program. You can, however, create a basic Web page in Netscape Navigator Gold, a software program that is not only popular Web browser, but it also includes a built-in HTML visual editor. This is certainly one of the easiest methods to use for creating a new Web page. Some popular word processors also allow you to publish a word processing document as an HTML document. My experience with leaving it to the word processor to make the translation has suggested that this is a good start to publishing a Web site. But you may need to go back and manually edit the HTML document anyway, because of problems in the translation. To supplement this wealth of programs available, I would also suggest buying a good book on the subject. See the bibliography for some of my suggestions.

Manual editors such as *HomeSite* (`http://www.allaire.com/products/homesite`) and *HTML Assistant* (`http://www.brooknorth.com/`, also available as a visual editor) exist for the Windows environment, as well as the popular *HotDog* (`http://www.sausage.com/`) and Microsoft's FrontPage (`http://www.microsoft.com/frontpage/`). You don't even to need to use a specialized editor such as these; any text editor (such as Notepad in Windows) will work just as easily. That's because HTML is nothing but plain text. For instance, this is a Web page that will print the words "Hello World!":

```
<html>
<head>
     <title>Type in your Document Title Here</title>
</head>
```

```
<body>

        <h1 align="center">Hello World!</h1>

<center>
        <a href="http://www.grohol.com/">This is a link
                                    to my home page</a>

</center>

</body>
</html>
```

You'll notice that each HTML code (also referred to as HTML "tags") has a start and an end. Look at the "title" tag, for example. The ending tag for a particular HTML tag always begins with a regular slash (/). Not all HTML tags require an end tag, but most do. The specifics of what each tag means and what it does is more detailed than what I can go into here. I suggest either going to a good online reference for further explanation (see Yahoo! below) or purchasing a beginner's guide to HTML authoring (see the bibliography). Save your file with a "HTM" (Windows) or "HTML" (Macintosh) extension (e.g., "myfile.htm" or "myfile.html").

A Web page typically is made up of graphics and links to other Web sites as well. You can obtain graphics, as well as a great deal of additional authoring tips and tutorials, from dozens of online resources that have been developed to help new Web authors. Check a general subject guide, such as Yahoo! (http://www.yahoo.com/) for the links to these resources. You may link to any page online today *without* asking that page's owner for permission to do so. This allows you to create a Web page full of useful links to you on nearly any topic you'd like. It is also what makes the World Wide Web much like the spider's web, in that every Web page is linked to dozens or hundreds of others.

The most common question I receive after someone authors a Web page is, "What do I do with it now?" Well, one of the things you can do with it is open it up in your Web browser to see how it looks (if you haven't done so already). You can do this in Windows-based browsers by choosing the "File" menu, then the "Open File . . ." option. Specify the location of the HTML file and the name of it, and it will appear in your browser.

But how do you put it somewhere where others can access it? In order to do this, you will need to upload the file to a *Web server*. A Web server is a computer that serves Web pages. GeoCities (mentioned above) makes this easy for you, in that you just go to a specific place on their Web site and they walk you through this process, step by step. Others servers and Internet Service Providers have different procedures which vary. One common method is to use a piece of software called "ftp." ftp allows you to transfer a file between your computer and the Web server. You can get ftp through Shareware.Com (`http://www.shareware.com/`), which has further instructions on how to use it.

APPENDIX E
Grant Searches Online

Since I wrote this book, a new category of information has appeared online that may be of interest, especially to researchers. Grant searching can now largely be conducted online. While a search at your local university library will still likely yield researchers more results, online grant searchers can be a helpful place to start. Many Web sites, especially federal government resources, allow you to download the grant applications online. Most such applications, to retain their original formatting, are available in *PDF* format. A PDF viewer, which allow you to view and print out PDF documents, is available for free from Adobe's Web site (`http://www.adobe.com/`).

Title:	Office of Research, Health Sciences
Owner:	University of Pittsburgh
URL:	`http:/www.ofres-hs.upmc.edu/`
Rating:	★★

The Office of Research, Health Sciences (OORHS) "nurtures research activities in the health sciences by providing support for the specialized needs of biomedical researchers" for the University of Pittsburgh. This site provides an up-to-date listing of funding opportunities related to the university.

Title:	NIMH Grants
Owner:	National Institute of Mental Health (NIMH)

URL: `http://www.nimh.nih.gov/grants/index.cfm`

Rating: ★★★

Information related to research, research training and career development, and special program grants and funding opportunitites are available from the NIMH'a site. Updated regularly, the resources on the site are logically organized and are simple to navigate. A lengthy introductory article about NIMH grants is especially useful to first-time grant authors.

Title: The Foundation Center Online

Owner: The Foundation Center

URL: `http://fdncenter.org/`

Rating: ★★★★

Whether you're an experienced or beginner grant-seeker, the Foundation Center Online is an invaluable resource. The Foundation Center is **the** resource for grant writing, publishing *FC Search: The Foundation Center's Database on CD-ROM*. This database, while not available for searching from their Web site, is available for purchase or access at no charge within over 200 libraries throughout the United States. The database acts as a comprehensive starting point for anyone interested in grant funding for their research, program, or nonprofit organization. The Foundation Center's Web site offers users practically every piece of information related to grant writing except this database. Extensive, well-written tutorials help first-time grant authors understand the process and walks them through it, step by step. Additional resources include additional information about the Foundation, funding trends and analysis (including the U.S.'s top corporate funders), and a complete searchable archive and current issue of *Philanthropy News Digest*.

Title: GrantsNet

Owner: American Association for the Advancement of Science

URL: `http://www.grantsnet.org/`

Rating: ★★★

This Web site, updated regularly, offers funding opportunities for training in the biological and medical sciences. While not offering a whole lot of funding opportunities for the behavioral health professions, some researchers may find the grants listed useful to their research. The site sports a fullly searchable database of over 200 programs. Regularly updated funding news is a helpful aid to keep on top of emerging funding opportunities. Nearly 700 organizations' names and contact information are listed in their funding directory. This site is attractively designed and simple to navigate, although a one-time, free registration is required to access their datebase.

Title:	GrantsNet
Owner:	U.S. Department of Health and Human Services (HHS)
URL:	

`http://www.os.dhhs.gov/progorg/grantsnet/`

Rating:	★★

A basic U.S. government Web site which offers a limited amount of information and links to funding opportunities online. It is not clear how often the site is updated, and the links to actual HHS funding information were difficult to find and navigate. This was due in part to the site's reliance on the older gopher file and retrieval system (which has largely been superseced by the World Wide Web).

Title:	APA Research Awards
Owner:	American Psychiatric Association
URL:	`http://www.psych.org/res_res/awards.html`
Rating:	★★

Provides application guidelines for a handful of psychiatric and psychobiological research awards. Most of the grants listed are funded by pharmaceutical companies.

Title:	NIH Grants Information
Owner:	National Institutes of Health (NIH)
URL:	`http://grants.nih.gov/grants`
Rating:	★★★

The National Institutes of Health (NIH) offers one of the most comprehensive and useful online databases for federal funding opportunities. The NIH is also one of the few sites which actually allows you to search (via a powerful and useful search engine) for grants based upon keywords, research interests, or topics. The Guide for Grants and Contracts, as NIH calls its grants database, is also browseable by date. Users may also subscribe to a free mailing list which notifies recipients of changes made to the grants database every week. The two biggest drawbacks to the database is that out-dated grant announcements are not removed from it and that the text of the announcements is lengthy and poorly formatted (it is, therefore, best printed out). The NIH should sort out archival announcements from current announcements to aid grant seekers. As with nearly any government program, a great deal of the documentation associated with NIH grants is lengthy and complex. This includes not only NIH's introductory information to grant writing and submissions, but also its frequently asked questions article. The search help was not customized to reflect the content and queries users of the NIH site are likely to form. This made it difficult to determine how best to form a useful query. For those with experience in obtaining NIH grants, the site will be a valuable resource offering tools and aid in their funding quest. For those with lesser grant experience, the site may be confusing and difficult to navigate.

Title:	Grants Central
Owner:	Polaris Services
URL:	`http://polarisgrantscentral.net`
Rating:	★★

Generally an annotated list of real-world references and resources which may be of value to grant writers. Polaris is a company which helps train individuals through publications and workshps on the subject of grants acquisition.

Index of Web Sites

General Index